CW00530197

Weird Realism:

Lovecraft and Philosophy

Weird Realism:

Lovecraft and Philosophy

Graham Harman

Winchester, UK
Washington, USA

First published by Zero Books, 2012
Zero Books is an imprint of John Hunt Publishing Ltd., Laurel House, Station Approach,
Alresford, Hants, SO24 9JH, UK
office1@jhpbooks.net
www.johnhuntpublishing.com
www.zero-books.net

For distributor details and how to order please visit the 'Ordering' section on our website.

Text copyright: Graham Harman 2011

ISBN: 978 1 78099 252 5

A CIP catalogue record for this book is available from the British Library.

Design: Stuart Davies

Printed and bound by CPI Group (UK) Ltd, Croydon, CR0 4YY

We operate a distinctive and ethical publishing philosophy in all
areas of our business, from our global network of authors to
production and worldwide distribution.

CONTENTS

Preliminary Note

All citations of Lovecraft stories refer to the collection: H.P. Lovecraft, *Tales*. (New York: Library of America, 2005.) Each reference consists of a two-word abbreviation followed by a page number. For example, (CC 167) would refer to page 167 of "The Call of Cthulhu" in the Library of America volume. Abbreviations for the individual stories are as follows:

CC	"The Call of Cthulhu"
CS	"The Colour Out of Space"
CW	"The Case of Charles Dexter Ward"
DH	"The Dunwich Horror"
HD	"The Haunter of the Dark"
MM	"At the Mountains of Madness"
SI	"The Shadow Over Innsmouth"
ST	"The Shadow Out of Time"
WD	"The Whisperer in Darkness"
WH	"The Dreams in the Witch House"

All of these stories refer to one another to an unusual extent, giving them the flavor of a loosely assembled novel told by diverse narrators of barely differentiable personality. But for simplicity's sake, Part Two will focus only on the eight most commonly recognized "great tales," as plausibly listed by Michel Houllebecq in his wonderful book on Lovecraft.[1] Yet his list coincides only partially with my own taste. For instance, "The Shadow Out of Time" strikes me as unworthy of Lovecraft's mature talent, while I remain rather fond of "The Case of Charles Dexter Ward."

Through the writings of Heidegger, the poems of Hölderlin have become a staple of analysis in continental philosophy. The present book makes an analogous case for elevating Lovecraft to the philosophical stage. Lovecraft can be dismissed as a pulp writer only under the presupposition that *all* writing about otherworldly monsters is doomed to be nothing but pulp. But this would be merely a social judgment, no different in kind from not wanting one's daughter to marry the chimney sweep. There can be good and bad "weird" writing, just as we find both excellent and banal naturalistic fiction. Strong and weak elements sometimes co-exist in the same Lovecraft stories, but at his best, he is a major writer who also deals with philosophical themes of emerging interest.

For many readers, Lovecraft is a discovery of adolescence. I myself never read a word of his stories until reaching the age of thirty-seven. Whether this colors my interpretation with the ripeness of maturity, or with stolid bourgeois mediocrity, is a question for each reader to decide by experiment.

Part One:

Lovecraft and Philosophy

A Writer of Gaps and Horror

One of the most important decisions made by philosophers concerns the production or destruction of *gaps* in the cosmos. That is to say, the philosopher can either declare that what appears to be one is actually two, or that what seems to be two is actually one. Some examples will help make the theme more vivid. In opposition to common sense, which sees nothing around us but a world of normal everyday entities, Plato created a gap between the intelligible forms of the perfect world and the confusing shadows of opinion. The occasionalists of the medieval Arab world and seventeenth century Europe produced a gap between any two entities by denying that they exert direct influence on one another, so that God became the only causal agent in the universe. The philosophy of Kant proposes a gap between appearances and things-in-themselves, with no chance of a symmetry between the two; the things-in-themselves can be thought but never known.

But there are abundant examples of the opposite decision as well. We might think that horses are one thing and atoms are another, but hardcore materialists insist that a horse is completely reducible to physical atoms and is nothing over and above them. In this way the supposed gap between horses and atoms is destroyed, since on this view there is no such thing as a "horse" at all, just atoms arranged in a certain pattern. Instead of atoms, we might also claim that the whole world is made of water, air, fire, or a gigantic and indeterminate lump. In ancient Greece these were the various tendencies of the pre-Socratic philosophers. Alternatively, we might hold that there are individual objects on one side and the various qualities of those objects on the other. David Hume denounced this gap, reducing supposed unified objects to nothing more than bundles of qualities. There is no such thing as an apple, just many different qualities that occur together so regularly that through force of habit we begin to call them an "apple." And as for Kant's gap between appearances and things-in-themselves, the German Idealists tried to destroy this gap by calling it incoherent: to think of things-in-themselves outside thought is meaningless, for given that we do think of them, they are obviously an element of thought. The destruction and production of gaps can easily co-exist in the same philosopher, just as black and white co-exist in the same painting. For example, if Hume is a *destroyer* of gaps by holding that objects are nothing more than bundles of qualities, he is also a *producer* of gaps through his denial that we can prove causal relationships between objects (this latter point is an inheritance from the occasionalists he so admired). Nonetheless, there is generally a dominant tone in every philosopher favoring one technique or the other. Since those who destroy gaps by imploding them into a single principle are generally called *reductionists*, let's coin the word *productionists* to describe philosophers who find new gaps in the world where there were formerly none.

If we apply this distinction to imaginative writers, then H.P. Lovecraft is clearly a productionist author. No other writer is so perplexed by the gap between objects and the power of language to describe them, or between objects and the qualities they possess. Despite his apparently limited interest in philosophy, Lovecraft as a tacit philosopher is violently anti-idealist and anti-Humean. Indeed, there are times when Lovecraft echoes cubist painting in a manner amounting almost to a parody of Hume. While Hume thinks that objects are a simple amassing of familiar qualities, Lovecraft resembles Braque, Picasso, and the philosopher Edmund Husserl by slicing an object into vast cross-sections of qualities, planes, or adumbrations, which even when added up do not exhaust the reality of the object they compose. For Lovecraft, the cubists, and Husserl, objects are *anything but* bundles of qualities. In parallel with this tendency, Lovecraft is

3

anti-idealist whenever he laments the inability of mere language to depict the deep horrors his narrators confront, to the point that he is often reduced to hints and allusions at the terrors inhabiting his stories. The present book will consider numerous examples of both sorts of gaps in Lovecraft's writings. But while Lovecraft is a writer of gaps, he is also a writer of horror, and the two should not be conflated. One could imagine a very different writer who used Lovecraft's staple techniques for other purposes– perhaps a sensual fantasist who would place us in a world of strange and indescribable pleasures, in which candles, cloves, and coconut milk were of such unearthly perfection that language would declare itself nearly powerless to describe them. A literary "weird porn" might be conceivable, in which the naked bodies of the characters would display bizarre anomalies subverting all human descriptive capacity, but without being so strange that the erotic dimension would collapse into a grotesque sort of eros-killing horror. We will see that while the stylistic production of gaps augments Lovecraft's power to depict monstrous horrors, the horrors themselves must occur on the level of literal content, not of literary allusion. Lovecraft as an author of horror writes about horrific content (monstrous creatures more powerful than humans and with no regard for our welfare), while Lovecraft the author of gaps is one who could have flourished in many other genres featuring many different sorts of content.

It should be obvious to readers of my previous books why Lovecraft, when viewed as a writer of gaps between objects and their qualities, is of great relevance for my model of object-oriented ontology (OOO).[2] The major topic of object-oriented philosophy is the dual polarization that occurs in the world: one between the real and the sensual, and the other between objects and their qualities. The two will be described in greater detail below. One involves a "vertical" gap, as found in Heidegger, for whom real objects forever withdraw behind their accessible, sensual presence to us. The other is a subtler "horizontal" gap, as

4

found in Husserl, whose denial of a real world beyond all consciousness still leaves room for a powerful tension between the relatively durable objects of our perception and their swirling kaleidoscope of shifting properties. Once we note that the world contains both withdrawn real objects with both real and sensual qualities and fully accessible sensual objects that are also linked with both real and sensual qualities, we find ourselves with four basic tensions or gaps in the world. These gaps are the major subject matter of object-oriented philosophy, and Lovecraft's constant exploitation of these very gaps automatically makes him as great a hero to object-oriented thought as Hölderlin was to Heidegger.

In 2008 I published a widely read article on Lovecraft and Husserl.[3] Having recently reread this article, I find that I am mostly happy with the ideas it develops. Nonetheless, it also makes two proposals that I now see as unfortunately one-sided. First, the article holds that there is no Kantian or "noumenal" aspect of Lovecraft, and asserts that Lovecraft should be paired solely with Husserl as an author confined to the phenomenal plane even if he produces strange new gaps within that plane. Second, it strongly downplays the importance of the fact that Lovecraft is a writer of horror and Husserl (though more "weird" than most people realize) is not a philosopher of horror. My fresh reservations about these two points are in many ways the engine of the present book. First, Lovecraft must be read not as a Husserlian author, but as jointly Husserlian-Kantian (or better: Husserlian-Heideggerian). This places him closer to my own position than either Husserl or Heidegger taken singly. And second, horror as the specific content of Lovecraft's stories must be accounted for, despite the fact that he is also an author of *gaps* that might be stylistically incarnated in numerous different genres other than horror. In short, the tension between style and content now becomes very important. In our efforts to fight the overly literal reading of Lovecraft as just a portrayer of scary monsters, we must also acknowledge that those monsters are his almost exclusive subject matter in a way that is true neither of Husserl nor of the vast majority of fiction writers. In this first part of the book I will show why this presents a problem; in the concluding third part, I will try to provide a partial solution, one that goes hand in hand with the fact that Lovecraft works along *two* separate axes of gaps, not just one. In the longer second part I will examine numerous passages of Lovecraft in detail, thereby setting the stage for the concluding argument.

The Problem with Paraphrase

When one of our friends speaks ill of another, the effect is awkward and painful. The situation is different when the two friends in question are both admired authors: here, the dispute is often fascinating. One of my favorite literary critics is Edmund Wilson, but Wilson does not share my admiration for the fiction of H.P. Lovecraft. His dismissive assessment begins as follows:

> I regret that, after examining these books, I am no more enthusiastic than before. The principal feature of Lovecraft's work is an elaborate concocted myth… [that] assumes a race of outlandish gods and grotesque prehistoric peoples who are always playing tricks with time and space and breaking through into the contemporary world, usually somewhere in Massachusetts.[4]

Like a sharp college quarterback mocking the Dungeons & Dragons games of his less popular hallmates, Wilson continues:

> ["At the Mountains of Madness" concerns] semi-invisible polypous monsters that uttered a shrill whistling sound and blasted their enemies with terrific winds. Such creatures would look very well on the covers of the pulp magazines, but they do not make good adult reading. And the truth is that these stories were hackwork contributed to such publications as *Weird Tales* and *Amazing Stories*, where, in my opinion, they ought to have been left.[5]

If Wilson were alive today, he would be appalled to find his long-projected Library of America series tainted by the shared presence of Lovecraft.[6] Yet there is a problem with Wilson's approach, since any of the unchallenged classics of world literature can also be reduced to literal absurdity in the same way as Lovecraft. Consider what a severe critic might say about *Moby-Dick*:

> The hero of the book is a bipolar one-legged skipper who cruises the world from Nantucket with a team of multi-ethnic harpooners. The climax comes when a scary, evil white whale (the object of their hunt) swims around the ship so fast that everyone is sucked into a whirlpool– everyone except the narrator, that is, who somehow survives to tell the tale. When reflecting on such inanity, I marvel once more at the puerile enthusiasm of Melville's admirers.

Even Dante might be converted to the ludicrous in similar fashion:

> The plot of the work is visibly cracked. An Italian poet, age thirty-five, is lost in a forest. He is sad and confused and pursued by several ravenous African animals. At this point he happens to run into the ghost of Virgil, in whose company he enters a cave issuing into Hell. There, they meet scores of demons and observe a drooling Satan chewing the heads of three historic villains. They then descend Satan's body and climb a giant mountain in the Pacific Ocean where people are forced to push boulders as punishment for minor sins. Virgil is then suddenly replaced by the dead sweetheart of the Italian poet's childhood years. The Italian and his late muse (we are not told whether she carries a lollipop or a teddy bear) magically fly past all the planets and finally see Jesus and God. And appropriately so, I might add: for if this is the future of poetry, then only these Divine Persons can save us.

Any literature, even the greatest, is easily belittled by such a method. The mere fact that a work of art can be literalized in this manner is no evidence against its quality. Wilson gets away with it in Lovecraft's case only due to the continuing low social status of science fiction and horror compared with mainstream naturalistic fiction; by contrast, no critic would be allowed to offer such rude handling to Melville or Dante. But there are only good and bad works of art, not inherently good and bad *genres* of art. As Clement Greenberg puts it: "One cannot validly be for or against any particular body of art *in toto*. One can only be for good or superior art as against bad or inferior art. One is not for Chinese, or Western, or representational art as a whole, but only for what is good in it."[7] By the same token, one cannot be for or against all naturalistic novels, science fiction, horror, Westerns, romance novels, or even comic books, but must learn to distinguish the good from the bad in each of these genres– which is not to say that all genres are equally filled with treasure at all moments in history. Lovecraft, Chandler, and Hammett emerged from the social slums of pulp. Even Batman and Robin may find their Tolstoy in the twenty-fourth century, once their Metropolis is reduced to vine-covered ruins. Wilson cannot refute Lovecraft's value with mocking phrases such as "invisible whistling octopus,"[8] for there is no inherent reason why such a creature could not inhabit the greatest story of all time, just as the aforementioned poem about a middle-aged Italian walking through Hell and flying to see God is possibly the greatest ever written.

The present book will have much to say about the sort of literalizing attempted by Wilson. Let's use "paraphrase" as our technical term for the attempt to give literal form to any statement, artwork, or anything else. The problem with paraphrase has long been noted by literary critics: by twentieth century "New Critic" Cleanth Brooks,[9] for example, whose line of reasoning we will consider near the end of this book. What Wilson misses is that Lovecraft's major gift as a writer is his deliberate and skillful obstruction of all attempts to paraphrase him. No other writer gives us monsters and cities so difficult to describe that he can only hint at their anomalies. Not even Poe gives us such hesitant narrators, wavering so uncertainly as to whether their coming words can do justice to the unspeakable reality they confront. Against Wilson's blunt assertion that "Lovecraft was not a good writer,"[10] I would call him one of the greatest of the twentieth century. The greatness of Lovecraft even pertains to more than the literary world, since it brushes against several of the most crucial philosophical themes of our time.

The Inherent Stupidity of All Content

The problem with paraphrase is discussed with typical humor by Slavoj Žižek, when he teases the *Shakespeare Made Easy* series of editor John Durband. As Žižek informs us, "Durband tries to formulate directly, in everyday locution, (what he considers to be) the thought expressed in Shakespeare's metaphoric idiom– 'To be or not to be, that is the question' becomes something like: 'What's bothering me now is: Shall I kill myself or not?'"[11] Žižek invites us to perform a similar exercise with the poems of Hölderlin, so piously revered by Heidegger. Hölderlin's oracular lines *Wo aber Gefahr ist, wächst das Rettende auch* ("But where danger is, the saving power also grows") is transformed with grotesque wit into this: "When you're in deep trouble, don't despair too quickly, look around carefully, the solution may be just around the corner."[12] Žižek then drops the theme in favor of a long series of dirty jokes, but by then he has already made the same complaint lodged against Wilson in the previous chapter: literal paraphrase can turn absolutely anything into banality.

Žižek takes up a related topic elsewhere, in his commentary on Schelling's *Ages of the World*. The passage in question concerns "the inherent stupidity of proverbs," and is too wonderful not to quote in full:

> Let us engage in a mental experiment by way of trying to construct proverbial wisdom out of the relationship between terrestrial life, its pleasures, and its Beyond. If one says "Forget about the afterlife, about the Elsewhere, seize the day, enjoy life fully here and now, it's the only life you've got!" it sounds deep. If one says exactly the opposite ("Do not get trapped in the illusory and vain pleasures of earthly life; money, power, and passions are all destined to vanish into

thin air– think about eternity!"), it also sounds deep. If one combines the two sides ("Bring eternity into your everyday life, live your life on this earth as if it is already permeated by Eternity!"), we get another profound thought. Needless to say, the same goes for its inversion: "Do not try in vain to bring together eternity and your terrestrial life, accept humbly that you are forever split between Heaven and Earth!" If, finally, one simply gets perplexed by all these reversals and claims: "Life is an enigma, do not try to penetrate its secrets, accept the beauty of its unfathomable mystery!" the result is no less profound than its reversal: "Do not allow yourself to be distracted by false mysteries that just dissimulate the fact that, ultimately, life is very simple– it is what it is, it is simply here without reason and rhyme!" Needless to add that, by uniting mystery and simplicity, one again obtains a wisdom: "The ultimate, unfathomable mystery of life resides in its very simplicity, in the simple fact that there is life."[13]

Beyond the entertainment value of this passage, it may be one of the most important things Žižek has ever written. While the annoying reversibility of proverbs provides a convenient target for his comical analysis, the problem is not limited to proverbs, but extends across the entire field of literal statement. Indeed, we might speak of the inherent stupidity of all *content*, a more threatening result than the limited assault on proverbial wisdom. Žižek overlooks this broader problem because his remarks are overly guided by the Lacanian theme of "the Master." As Žižek puts it: "This tautological imbecility [of proverbs] points towards the fact that a Master is excluded from the economy of symbolic exchange... For the master, there is no 'tit for tat'... when we give something to the Master, we do not expect anything in return..."[14] Stated more simply, the implicit Master who utters each proverb does so in a lordly manner apparently immune to counterargument. But once we consider the actual verbal content of a proverb, devoid of the Master's tacit backing, all proverbs sound equally arbitrary and stupid.

Now, it might be assumed that we can settle the issue in each case by giving "reasons" for why one proverb is more accurate than its opposite. Unfortunately, all reasons are doomed to the same fate as the initial proverbs themselves. Consider the following argument between a miser and a spendthrift. The miser cites the proverb "a penny saved is a penny earned" while the spendthrift counters with "penny wise, pound foolish." In an effort to resolve their dispute, they both give reasons for their preference. The miser explains patiently that in the long term, cutting needless losses actually accrues more wealth than an increase in annual income; the spendthrift objects that aggressive investment opens up more profit opportunities than does penny-pinching cost savings. The intellectual deadlock remains, with neither able to gain ground on the other. In the next stage of the dispute, both speakers produce statistical evidence and cite various economists in defense of their views, but the evidence on both sides looks equally good and no progress is made. In the ensuing stage, both combatants hire vast teams of researchers to support their positions with crushing reams of data. The miser and the spendthrift are now locked into what is essentially an endless version of *Shakespeare Made Easy*– turning their initial proverbs into a series of ever more detailed statements, none of them directly and immediately convincing. Neither of them claims any longer to be the Master, as in the initial proverbial stage; both realize that they need to give evidence for their claims, yet both fail to establish those claims decisively. The point is not that the miser and the spendthrift are "equally correct." When it comes to specific questions of public policy, one of them may be far more right than the other. The point is that no *literal* unpacking of their claims can ever settle the argument, since each remains an arbitrary Master for as long as he attempts to call upon literal, explicit evidence. There may be an underlying true answer to the question, assuming that the dispute is properly formulated, but it can never become directly present in the form of explicit content that is inherently correct in the same way that a lightning flash is inherently bright.[15]

The same holds true for any dispute between philosophical theses. For example, to argue between "the ultimate reality is flux" and "the ultimate reality is the stasis beneath the apparent flux" risks stumbling into Žižek's bottomless duel of opposing proverbs. It is true that in different historical periods one of these philosophical alternatives is generally the cutting edge while the other is the epitome of academic tedium, just as three-dimensional illusionistic painting was fresh as the dawn in Renaissance Italy but crushingly banal in Cubist Paris. There is no reason to think that any philosophical statement has an inherently closer relationship with reality than its opposite, since *reality is not made of statements*. Just as Aristotle defined substance as that which can support opposite qualities at different times, there is a sense in which reality can support different truths at different times. That is to say, an absolutism of reality may be coupled with a relativism of truth. Žižek's comical translation of Hölderlin's poem turns out to be stupid *not* because the original poem is stupid, and *not* because the translation misunderstands Hölderlin's advice, but because all content is inevitably stupid. And content is stupid because *reality itself is not a content*. But this requires further explanation.

The Background of Being

The most important moment of twentieth century philosophy came in 1927, when Heidegger raised the question of the meaning of being. While this question might sound so pompously obscure as to be fruitless, Heidegger makes genuine progress in addressing it. What we learn from all of his thinking is the insufficiency of presence, or presence-at-hand (*Vorhandenheit*). From the age of twenty-nine onward, Heidegger transformed the phenomenology of his teacher Husserl, who tried to preserve philosophy from the encroachments of natural science by insisting that all theories must be grounded in evidence presented directly to the mind. Heidegger's counter-claim is that most of our interaction with things *is not* with things presented to the mind, but rather with items silently taken for granted or relied upon. Entities such as chairs, floors, streets, bodily organs, and the grammatical rules of our native language are generally ignored as long as they function smoothly. Usually it is only their malfunction that allows us to notice them at all. This is the theme of Heidegger's famous tool-analysis, found in his 1919 Freiburg lectures[16] but first published eight years later in *Being and Time*.[17] I have written about this analysis frequently,[18] and indeed, my own intellectual career has been nothing more than an attempt to radicalize its consequences.

As is often the case in intellectual history, the tool-analysis can be pushed further than Heidegger himself ever attempted. Most of his readers hold that the analysis establishes a priority of unconscious praxis over conscious theory, so that explicit theoretical awareness emerges from a shadowy background of tacit everyday "coping." What this reading misses is that coping with things distorts them no less than theorizing about them does. To sit in a chair does not exhaust its reality any more than visual observation of the chair ever does. Human theory and human praxis are both prone to surprises from sudden eruptions of unknown properties from the chair-being of the chair, which recedes into the darkness beyond all human access. Pushing things another step further, it must be seen that the same holds for inanimate entities, since the chair and floor distort one another no less than humans distort the chair.

Here we can see the reason for the inherent stupidity of all content that emerged from Žižek's attack on proverbs. No literal statement is congruent with reality itself, just as no handling of a tool is the same thing as that tool in the plenitude of its reality. Or as Alfred North Whitehead puts it: "It is merely credulous to accept verbal phrases as adequate expressions of propositions."[19] The meaning of being might even be defined as *untranslatability*. Language (and everything else) is obliged to become an art of allusion or indirect speech, a metaphorical bond with a reality that cannot possibly be made present. Realism does not mean that we are able to state correct propositions about the real world. Instead, it means that reality is too real to be translated without remainder into any sentence, perception, practical action, or anything else. To worship the content of propositions is to become a *dogmatist*. The dogmatist is someone who cannot weigh the quality of thoughts or statements except by agreeing or disagreeing with them. If someone says "materialism is true" and the dogmatist agrees, then the dogmatist salutes this person as a kindred spirit no matter how shoddy his or her reasoning, and the dogmatist equally denounces the one who says "materialism is false," no matter how fresh and insightful the basis for this statement may be. The dogmatist holds that truth is legible on the surface of the world, so that correct and incorrect statements –perhaps someday formalized and determinable by a machine– comprise the arena where truth is uncovered.

Yet this is precisely what Kant renders impossible with his split between appearances and things-in-themselves. As Kant sees it, the problem with dogmatic philosophy is not that it believes in the things-in-themselves (so does Kant himself). Instead, the problem is that the dogmatist wishes to make the things-in-themselves accessible through discursive statements. In this way Žižek's assault on proverbs should be viewed as a jesting younger version of Kant's famous antinomies, in which positive propositions about various metaphysical issues are placed side-by-side on the page and shown to be equally arbitrary. Yet the mistake made by Kant, and even more so by his German Idealist successors, is to hold that the relation of appearance to the in-itself is an all-or-nothing affair– that since the things-in-themselves can never be made present, we are either limited to discussions of the conditions of human experience (Kant) or obliged to annihilate the very notion of things-in-themselves by noting that this very notion is an accessible appearance in the mind (German Idealism). What few have noted is that both attitudes abandon the mission of *philosophia*: a love of wisdom by humans who at all times both have and do not have the truth. The inability to make the things-in-themselves directly present does not forbid us from having *indirect* access to them. The inherent stupidity of all content does not mean the inherent impossibility of all knowledge, since knowledge need not be discursive and direct. The absent thing-in-itself can have gravitational effects on the internal content of knowledge, just as Lovecraft can allude to the physical form of Cthulhu even while cancelling the literal terms of the description. Instead of representational realism, Lovecraft works in the idiom of a *weird realism* that inspired the title of this book.

Further ancient and contemporary support can be found for this approach. Despite the condemnation of rhetoric by Socrates and Plato, Aristotle saw fit to teach his students rhetoric for half of the school day. This was not a cynical concession to the regrettable corruption of our fellow humans, but stems from the fact that rhetoric is the indispensable art of the background lying behind any explicit statement. Rhetoric is dominated by the *enthymeme*, a proposition that need not be stated since it is already known to one's audience. If we say: "Obama will be in the White House two years from now," no contemporary reader of this book needs an explanation that this means that Barack Obama will be re-elected in 2012 as President of the United States, whose official residence in the city of Washington is called the White House. These further inferences can be taken for granted, just as Heidegger showed that most of the tool-beings in our vicinity are taken for granted. Rhetoric is the art of the background, and if philosophy is not the science of the background, then I do not know what it is. Aristotle pursues similar insights in the *Poetics*. Jacques Derrida is simply wrong[20] when he claims that Aristotle wishes to enslave all figurative meanings to a single literal meaning for each word. What Aristotle defends is not a single literal meaning for each word, but the rather different notion of a single univocal *being* for each thing. Aristotle is by no means a defender of literal paraphrase, as can be seen from his admiring tributes to poets and his view that metaphor is the greatest of all human gifts.

In more recent times, the Canadian media theorist Marshall McLuhan is the little acknowledged master of rhetoric and the secrets it conceals from literal visibility. This always happens through some background medium: for McLuhan, all arguments over the good and bad content of television programs miss the fact that the medium of television itself alters our behavior and lifestyle irrespective of what content it depicts. This is why for McLuhan "the medium is the message," whereas the usual assumption is that "the content is the message." This view takes on its most extreme form in McLuhan's infamous statement that "the content or message of any particular medium has about as much importance as the stenciling on the casing of an atomic bomb."[21] In important late work conducted jointly with his son Eric,[22] McLuhan frames this idea in terms of the classical Trivium, as a defense of rhetoric and grammar as opposed to the dialectic of explicit surface content. While the dogmatist is a dialectician in this classical sense, the artist and the lover of wisdom are rhetoricians. This is not from some devious desire to seduce the unwary, but from recognition that the background is where the action is.

We have already noted several instances of failed awareness of the tacit background of our actions and utterances. In perception and action we fail to exhaust the deeper reality of the things with which we are engaged. German Idealist philosophy holds that there is no more to things or thoughts than their ultimate accessibility to reason. In dogmatic assertions it is assumed (contra Whitehead) that verbal propositions can in principle exhaust whatever they describe. These phenomena are strikingly similar to *academic art* as defined and denounced by the great art critic Greenberg. In his Sydney lecture "Modern and Postmodern," he states it as follows: "Academicism consists in the tendency to take the medium of an art too much for granted."[23] McLuhan would be pleased by these words. The point is neither to take the medium for granted (like academic art), nor to believe falsely that the medium can be made explicit (like dogmatic philosophy), but rather to generate content that has an oblique or allusive relation with the background medium that is effective nonetheless.

Along with academic art, Greenberg speaks frequently of its trashy younger sister *Kitsch*,[24] the lowbrow imitation that offers a tasteless execution of high art's hard-earned technique. One obvious form of Kitsch in literature would be *pulp*. Here too the background medium is largely taken for granted. If you wish to submit a story to a pulp Western magazine, simply throw in a dozen cowboys, a few gunfights, a rodeo, a love interest, some cattle rustling, a stagecoach, a few stereotypical Mexicans and Indians, and other stock elements of the genre. Pulp detective writing will surely include a hard-boiled hero and a number of criminal villains, with occasional murders sprinkled in along the way. Pulp horror and science fiction will consist of the arbitrary postulation of new monsters and planets, each equipped with amazing qualitative features designed to stun the reader with the novelty of their *content*, while merely adopting the banality of the established framework of the genre. There is even a kind of pulp philosophy, in which the rational materialist hero (generally a first-person narrator) slays hordes of irrational alchemists, astrologers, witch doctors, vitalists, and Christians. The dogmatist is a pulp philosopher. Although I am unaware of any comments by Greenberg on the writings of Lovecraft, it is unfortunately easy to imagine him reacting in much the same way as Edmund Wilson: "And the truth is that these stories were hackwork contributed to such publications as *Weird Tales* and *Amazing Stories*, where, in my opinion, they ought to have been left."[25] But if we define pulp as fiction unaware of its medium, there is a problem with any dismissal of Lovecraft as a pulp writer: namely, Lovecraft was by no means unaware of his medium, as one of his key theoretical works makes clear.

The most frequently cited essay by Lovecraft is probably his "Supernatural Horror in Literature,"[26] a detailed survey of the genre that earned surprising praise from Edmund Wilson as "a really able piece of work."[27] But of greater interest for us here is Lovecraft's biting four-page polemic "Some Notes on Interplanetary Fiction."[28] In this essay Lovecraft speaks in almost Wilsonian tones of the horrible quality of most work in this genre: "Insincerity, conventionality, triteness, artificiality, false emotion, and puerile extravagance reign triumphant throughout this overcrowded genre, so that none but its rarest products [including the novels of H.G. Wells] can possibly claim a truly adult status."[29] Most such stories contain "hackneyed artificial characters and stupid conventional events and situations... [that are] a product of weary mass mechanics,"[30] and are filled with "stock scientists, villainous assistants, invincible heroes, and lovely scientist's-daughter heroines of the usual trash of this sort."[31] And in a final wonderful litany, Lovecraft denounces further clichés of the genre such as "worship of the travelers as deities," "participation in the affairs· of pseudo-human kingdoms," "weddings with beautiful anthropomorphic princesses," "stereotyped Armageddons with ray-guns and space-ships," "court intrigues and jealous magicians," and best of all, "peril from hairy ape-men of the polar caps."[32] All of these examples establish that Lovecraft is perhaps an even more acerbic critic of pulp literature than Wilson himself, and that as an author he is fully aware of the minefields of banality that one must scrupulously avoid.

And yet, Lovecraft pivots in a direction that Wilson never attempted, but that Greenberg would surely have approved: "The present commentator does not believe that the idea of space-travel and other worlds is inherently unsuited to literary use."[33] For there is just one essential fallacy that leads interplanetary writers into pulp banality, and "this fallacy is the notion that any account of impossible, improbable, or inconceivable phenomena can be successfully presented as a commonplace narrative of objective acts and conventional emotions in the ordinary tone and manner of popular romance."[34] As he explains two paragraphs later: "Over and above everything else should tower the stark, outrageous monstrousness of the one chosen departure from Nature."[35] There follows the most important passage in the essay:

> The characters should react to it as real people would react to such a thing if it were suddenly to confront them in daily life; displaying the almost soul-shattering amazement which anyone would naturally display instead of the mild, tame, quickly-passed-over emotions prescribed by cheap popular convention. Even when the wonder is one to which the characters are assumed to be used, the sense of awe, marvel,

and strangeness which the reader would feel in the presence of such a thing must somehow be suggested by the author.[36]

In other words, the mere deviant *content* of other worlds is not enough to be credible. If Zartran the half-alien hero slays the enemy on distant ice-planet Orthumak with an argon-based neuron degenerator, and then marries the princess inside a volcano while wearing heat-resistant triple neonoid fabrics, and if all this is stated as a matter-of-fact event, then what we have is nothing but a cheap novelty of "unprecedented content." Ten thousand rival pulp writers can then try to invent even more unprecedented species, weapons, chemicals, and incidents. The clichés cannot be eliminated by simple variation: replacing the stock mad scientist with a sane and goodhearted dog-man scientist, and dropping all weddings in favor of heroes who reproduce via gelatinous spores, would not address the deeper cliché at work. Namely, the true banality of most interplanetary fiction is the idea that simple novelty of content is enough to produce genuine innovation. What Lovecraft argues instead is surprisingly similar to Greenberg's vision for modern art: the content of an artwork should display some skillful relation with the background conditions of the genre. To innovate in science fiction, we cannot simply replace New York and Tokyo with exotically named extra-galactic capitals, which is merely trading a familiar content for a bizarre but comparable one (Greenberg's critique of surrealism is similar). Instead, we must show the everyday banality of New York and Tokyo undercut from within, by subverting the background conditions assumed by the existence of any city at all. Rather than inventing a monster with an arbitrary number of tentacles and dangerous sucker-mouths and telepathic brains, we must recognize that no such list of arbitrary weird properties is enough to do the trick. There must be some deeper and more malevolent principle at work in our monsters that escapes all such definition. That is the manner by which Lovecraft escapes all pulp, all Kitsch, and all academic art: by systematically debilitating content, all to the greater glory of the background enthymeme. In Lovecraft the medium is the message.

Not Unfaithful to the Spirit of the Thing

A dogmatic acquaintance of mine once objected to the Lovecraftian monster Cthulhu on the grounds that "a dragon with an octopus head is not scary." But that is not exactly how Cthulhu is described. Lovecraft's first description of a Cthulhu idol runs as follows: "If I say that my somewhat extravagant imagination yielded simultaneous pictures of an octopus, a dragon, and a human caricature, *I shall not be unfaithful to the spirit of the thing...* but it was the *general outline* of the whole which made it most shockingly frightful..." (CC 169; emphasis modified). The fact that the t-shirts and fantasy paintings of the world depict Cthulhu straightforwardly as a dragon with an octopus head is not Lovecraft's fault. If he had written: "I looked at the idol and saw a horrifying monster that was part dragon, part octopus, and part human caricature," we would simply be in the realm of pulp. But capitalizing on the indirect character of literature as opposed to painting or cinema, Lovecraft *hints* at an octopoidal dragon while also suspending that literal depiction in three separate ways: (1) he downplays it as merely the result of his own "extravagant imagination"; (2) he evasively terms his description "not unfaithful to the spirit of the thing" rather than as dead-on correct; (3) he asks us to ignore the surface properties of dragon and octopus mixed with human and to focus instead on the fearsome "general outline of the whole," suggesting that this outline is something over and above a literal combination of these elements. Any practiced reader of Lovecraft knows that this sort of de-literalizing gesture is not an isolated incident in his stories, but is perhaps his major stylistic trait as a writer. It is what I have called the "vertical" or allusive aspect of Lovecraft's style– the gap he produces between an ungraspable thing and the vaguely relevant descriptions that the narrator is able to attempt.

A different sort of example is found in "The Dunwich Horror" when the three professors observe the decaying corpse of Wilbur Whateley on the Miskatonic Library floor: "It would be trite and not wholly accurate to say that no human pen could describe it, but one may properly say that it could not be vividly visualized by anyone whose ideas of aspect and contour are too closely bound up with the common life-forms of this planet and the known three dimensions." (DH 389) So far, we have a "vertical" gap resembling the one found in the description of the Cthulhu idol, and this is the sort of case where I am now willing to concede a "noumenal" element in Lovecraft's style. The sentence just quoted could have been ruined if Lovecraft had adopted either of two extreme alternatives. If he had said simply that "no human pen can describe it," we would have one of the cheapest tricks of bad pulp writing and shallow thinking. If he had tried instead to shock us with monstrous detailed descriptions alone, we would also have veered toward pulp. Instead, we find a disclaimer that neutralizes the initial cliché by calling it "trite and not wholly accurate," but which then delves into a descriptive effort that is nearly impossible to visualize in literal terms anyway: "Above the waist it was semi-anthropomorphic; though its chest... had the leathery, reticulated hide of a crocodile or alligator. The back was piebald with yellow and black, and dimly suggested the squamous covering of certain snakes. Below the waist, though, it was the worst; for here all human resemblance left off and sheer fantasy began..." (DH 389) Here we have something different: a "horizontal" weirdness that I would not call allusive but rather "cubist," for lack of a better term. The power of language is no longer enfeebled by an impossibly deep and distant reality. Instead, language is overloaded by a gluttonous excess of surfaces and aspects of the thing. Again there is reason to be impressed with Lovecraft's technique. The explicitly described image is difficult enough to visualize, but becomes all the more so when this elusive description is further qualified as "dimly suggestive" of a snake and its "squamous" covering, a word that even educated readers will probably need to look up in the dictionary. And then comes the crowning transition, telling us that while all of this might have been intelligible enough, what comes next will enter the realm of sheer fantasy.

Let's take another example of the "horizontal" kind, shifting from zoology to architecture– another field where Lovecraft excels at obstructed description. In "At the Mountains of Madness," Professor Dyer and his party are flying across Antarctica towards the campsite of Professor Lake, which they will soon discover to be utterly annihilated. En route they witness what Dyer terms a "polar mirage," though it later turns out to have been a disturbing projection of an actual hidden city. Dyer describes it as follows: "The effect was that of a Cyclopean city of no architecture known to man or to human imagination, with vast aggregations of night-black masonry embodying monstrous perversions of geometrical laws and attaining the most grotesque extremes of sinister bizarrerie." (MM 508) Edmund Wilson would dismiss such descriptions as of low literary quality, but here we must disagree, for the simple reason that the passage is highly effective. "Vast aggregations of night-back masonry" is a perfectly suggestive and frightening phrase, if somewhat hard to visualize accurately. The "monstrous perversions of known geometrical law" would be impossible to film or paint, but this phrase has a powerful effect on the reader, who can sense the metaphysical darkness of any place where such perversions are permitted to exist. The final element, "the most grotesque extremes of sinister bizarrerie," might well be dubious in isolation. But here the only weight it bears is to sum up Dyer's personal anguish after the real literary work is already completed by the first two elements of the sentence. "Sinister bizarrerie" is the rhetorical cherry on the sundae, after the sundae itself was purchased through the labors of night-black masonry and perver- sions of known geometrical law.

This is the stylistic world of H.P. Lovecraft, a world in which (1) real objects are locked in impossible tension with the crippled descriptive powers of language, and (2) visible objects display unbearable seismic torsion with their own qualities. An account such as Wilson's, which immediately advances to a literalizing mockery of the *content* of the stories, overlooks Lovecraft's primary trait as a writer– a gift that Lovecraft (though Wilson misses this) shares with Edgar Allan Poe. Normally we feel no gap at all between the world and our descriptions of it. But Lovecraft unlocks a world dominated by such a gap, and this makes him the very embodiment of an *anti-pulp* writer. And this is the grain of truth in the descriptions of Lovecraft as a Kantian writer of "noumenal" horror. It is true that this description becomes dangerous if it leads us to overlook Lovecraft's materialist and utterly non-noumenal side. As Houellebecq puts it: "What is Great Cthulhu? An arrangement of electrons, like us."[37] But if Houellebecq's statement is true in the negative sense that Lovecraft's monsters are not spirits or souls, they are also not just electrons, any more than Kant's things-in-themselves are made of electrons.

The Phenomenological Gap

Lovecraft is not simply a pulp writer who tries to force our credence with mere declarations concerning the amazing properties of alternate otherworldly creatures. Instead, he is almost disturbingly alert to the background that eludes the determinacy of every utterance, to the point that he invests a great deal of energy in undercutting his own statements. In this way, Lovecraft's prose generates a gap between reality and its accessibility to us; this is the "Kantian" side of his writing. Nonetheless, as described in my 2008 article, there is something else going on in Lovecraft that involves a new gap within appearance itself. In order to understand this, we should briefly review the misunderstood greatness of Edmund Husserl, founder of phenomenology.[38]

Earlier, we discussed Heidegger's attempt to radicalize phenomenology. Whereas Husserl grounded philosophy in a description of how things appear to consciousness, Heidegger noted that we usually deal with things insofar as they *do not* appear. Essentially, Heidegger is accusing Husserl of idealism, and scientistic philosophy often makes the same accusation against him with even greater harshness. Nor is the charge unwarranted. Although Husserl speaks endlessly of how the intentionality of consciousness means that we are always already outside ourselves, aiming at objects in the world, these objects still have no reality except as the correlate of some consciousness. To speak of entities interacting without a potential conscious observer would strike Husserl as absurd. But while phenomenology is certainly an idealism, this very idealism contains the seeds of Husserl's greatness. For whereas earlier members of the Brentano School had tried to distinguish between an object outside consciousness and a content inside it, Husserl's idealism left him no alternative but to collapse *both* object *and* content into the sphere of conscious awareness. And with this step he arrived at the chief insight of his career, rarely or never acknowledged as such.

The empiricist tradition, by which Husserl's mentor Brentano remained deeply influenced, treats objects as arbitrary bundlings of qualities. To observe a banana is really just to observe such qualities as "yellow," "long," "soft," and "sweet." Since these are all that we encounter directly, there is no reason to speak of an underlying object called "banana." This word is simply a nickname for a collective assembly of directly encountered properties. Now, since this empiricist view of things apparently limits itself to what is directly accessible to consciousness, it might seem like the very height of phenomenological rigor in Husserl's eyes. But this is not the case. In the *Logical Investigations*, Husserl departs from Brentano with understated radicalism, telling us it is not true that experience is of "experienced contents." Instead of content, what we experience primarily is *objects*, such that specific perceptual content always remains subordinate to these objects. When I observe a dog named Woody, he is always seen from a specific angle and distance, either barking or calm. But what I am looking at is the dog Woody, not Woody as seen in a specific, highly determined fashion. If Woody begins to run or bark, I do not say that he is now a closely related object with mere "family resemblances" to the former Woody. Instead, I say that Woody the dog has changed some of his features while still remaining Woody.

This is what Husserl calls an "object-giving act," and it is not just an intermittent event among many others in our conscious life. He explicitly asserts that experience is made of object-giving acts rather than of specific, determinate contents. Note that this is the sort of argument one would normally expect from a philosopher of individual substances such as Aristotle, but with one crucial difference. Whereas Aristotle speaks of individual things quite apart from human contact with them, what Husserl has in mind is a rift *within* the experiential realm, one that holds good even for imaginary entities that have no reality outside my encounter with them. To hallucinate a unicorn is an object-giving act as well, even if there is no real unicorn in the outer world. The crack smoker's fantasy unicorn is always seen running at a specific speed with a greater or lesser degree of aggression, yet these qualities can shift from one moment to the next without the unicorn becoming a different thing. Now, it might be asked how one can prove that the unicorn appears as the same unicorn, or Woody as the same Woody. The answer is that since we are not dealing here with anything real, hidden, or withdrawn, but only with objects of immediate experience, then we ourselves are the judges.

For Husserl, what we have are intentional objects viewed in different specific ways at different moments, according to various adumbrations (*Abschattungen*). These shift at every moment, meaning that along with the Heideggerian tension between hidden real objects and their accessible surface features, we have a separate Husserlian tension between completely unhidden intentional objects and their swirling rainbow-like surface of qualities. It is often mistakenly claimed that Husserl's intentional objects withdraw behind their adumbrations just as Heidegger's tool-beings do, but this is incorrect. In fact, no Heideggerian withdrawal is possible at all in Husserl's philosophy. To intend a Rhode Island state flag means that I am already in direct contact with the flag as an object of experience, acknowledging its reality in the realm of experience; the specific qualities of the flag encountered at any given moment do not hide the flag as a unitary object, but exist as something extra, encrusted on its surface.

Due to the sterile flavor of the term "intentional," as well as a widespread misunderstanding that takes this term to mean "pointing outside" the sphere of consciousness,[39] it is better to rename the intentional sphere as the "sensual" realm. What we found in Heidegger was a tension between *real* objects and *sensual* qualities, with the appearance of a real hammer lurking somewhere behind the hammer-qualities that we experience. What we have just seen in the case of Husserl's adumbrations is a different tension between *sensual* objects and *sensual* qualities, with the flag of Rhode Island remaining what it is for us despite all flapping variations in the breeze of the Providence waterfront. And here we have the two major axes of Lovecraft's literary style: the "vertical" gap between unknowable objects and their tangible qualities, and the "horizontal" or "cubist" gap between an accessible object and its gratuitous amassing of numerous palpable surfaces.

But Husserl is also aware of a strange additional tension between *sensual* objects and their *real* qualities. This becomes clear from the phenomenological method itself, which works by way of "eidetic variation." For instance, if we want to discover the truly essential features of the experienced flag that make it a flag rather than a towel, and a Rhode Island flag rather than that of Iowa or Maryland, we can either observe its numerous variations over time to determine which features are truly crucial and durable, or (what is more likely) vary its features in our minds through imagination. What we are left with at the end of this process is not the adumbrations, which are merely accidental qualities of sensual objects. Instead, what we end up with are the truly pivotal qualities of the thing. But these qualities are not themselves sensual, since no specific appearance of the flag at any moment can ever fully live up to them. Husserl tells us that such qualities can only be known intellectually, not in sensual form. And while Husserl does think that they can be grasped directly in "essential intuition," we in the twenty-first century have long been to school with his rebellious pupil Heidegger, and are therefore aware that the non-sensual always withdraws into the shadows of being, untranslatable into any sort of human access.

To summarize, Heidegger gives us a tension between real object and sensual quality. Husserl gives us the normal case of tension between sensual object and sensual quality, as well as the case of theoretical comportment in which we try to discover the real qualities of a sensual object. It must now be asked if there is a parallel tension between real objects and their real qualities. The answer is yes, though because such a tension occurs entirely on the level of withdrawal, it remains inaccessible to us in any manner except allusion. Leibniz is aware that monads must be unified, but also that they must have many traits if they are not to be interchangeable with all other monads in a featureless identity of so-called bare particulars.[40] Xavier Zubíri also discusses this tension between the real thing as a unit and the same real thing as a systematic plurality of features.[41]

We now have four basic tensions in our map of the world, which could be expanded to ten if we did not confine ourselves to object/quality pairs. Yet four will suffice for the purposes of the present book. In *The Quadruple Object* I considered these tensions within the framework of what I called "ontography."[42] In that book I tried to show that Heidegger's tension RO-SQ can be termed "space," Husserl's SO-SQ can be called "time," Husserl's SO-RQ can be dubbed "eidos," and the RO-RQ tension of Leibniz and Zubíri can be named "essence." But since this book is concerned more with literature than with metaphysics per se, it is not important to remember these terms specifically. We need only take note that Lovecraft is a writer who is strangely attuned to all four of the basic tensions of ontography, and that this suffices to make him the poet laureate of object-oriented philosophy.

A Lovecraftian Ontography

As mentioned, the German poet Hölderlin has been the dominant literary hero of recent continental philosophy. This is largely Heidegger's doing, since it was he who repeatedly gave lecture courses on Hölderlin's hymns and treated him as a figure of staggering significance for philosophy. What makes Hölderlin so great in Heidegger's eyes? The philosopher addresses this question openly at the beginning of his essay "Hölderlin and the Essence of Poetry":

> Why choose *Hölderlin's* work if our purpose is to show the essence of poetry? Why not Homer or Sophocles, why not Virgil or Dante, why not Shakespeare or Goethe? Surely the essence of poetry has come to rich expression in the works of these poets, more so indeed than in Hölderlin's creation, which broke off so prematurely and so abruptly. That may be so. And yet I choose Hölderlin, and him alone... because Hölderlin's poetry is sustained by his whole poetic mission: to make poems solely about the essence of poetry. Hölderlin is for us in a preeminent sense *the poet's poet*. And for that reason he forces a decision upon us.[43]

A similar question might be asked in connection with Lovecraft. If we are looking for philosophical depth in a writer of fiction, then why not Cervantes or Tolstoy, Joyce or Melville, Mary Shelley or Dostoevsky? Why not even Poe, who is Lovecraft's canonized literary ancestor? Our answer is similar to Heidegger's response on the question of Hölderlin, but with the following twist: I am not making the Heideggerian claim that Lovecraft writes stories about the essence of writing stories, but the even more extreme claim that Lovecraft writes stories about the essence of *philosophy*. Lovecraft is the model writer of ontography, with its multiple polarizations in the heart of real and sensual objects. For this reason, as I wrote in the 2008 article: "In symbolic terms, Great Cthulhu should replace Minerva as the patron spirit of philosophers, and the Miskatonic must dwarf the Rhine and the Ister as our river of choice. Since Heidegger's treatment of Hölderlin resulted mostly in pious, dreary readings, philosophy needs a new literary hero."[44]

We have already discussed Lovecraft's tendency to undercut his own literal descriptions, a primary method by which he escapes falling into a pulp literature unaware of its own background conditions. We have also seen that he does this in more than one way. At times Lovecraft does it by splitting a thing off as a dark, brooding unit in distinction from its palpable qualities. This happens for instance when the sailor Parker is bizarrely "swallowed up by an angle of masonry... which was acute, but behaved as if it were obtuse." (CC 194) As a general rule, anytime we run across a passage in Lovecraft that is *literally* impossible to visualize, like this one, we are dealing with this first kind of tension between a real object and its sensual qualities, so reminiscent of Heidegger's tool-analysis. At other times, there is the "cubist" tension between sensual or non-hidden objects and their sensual qualities that pile up in disturbing profusion. A good example is found in "The Shadow Over Innsmouth" when the narrator first encounters the repulsive local bus driver, who is mostly likely one of Innsmouth's fish-frog-human hybrids: "This, I reflected, must be the Joe Sargent mentioned by the ticket-agent; and *even before I noticed any details* there spread over me *a wave of spontaneous aversion that could be neither checked nor explained.*" (SI 597; emphasis added) While this might initially seem like a vertical allusion to depths of reality lying far beneath all language, it is followed with a detailed list of the various problematic features of Sargent's physical appearance. While too long to quote here in full, suffice it to say that the passage resembles the labor of

Husserl or Picasso in analyzing the multi-faceted surfaces of a blackbird that is *not* withdrawn from all experience, but simply encrusted with a multitude of sensual planes.

Another good example occurs in Lovecraft's description of the witch's familiar known as Brown Jenkin: "Witnesses said it had long hair and the shape of a rat, but that its sharp-toothed bearded face was evilly human while its paws were like tiny human hands... Its voice was a kind of loathsome titter, and it could speak all languages." (WH 658) Although Brown Jenkin is not unvisualizable in the way that an acute-obtuse angle is, the little monster hardly qualifies as an empiricist "bundle of qualities," due to the unsettling range of traits it unifies. Indeed, Brown Jenkin might even be read as a parody of Hume's empiricism, in which we sense that beyond its mass of qualities, there must be some vile underlying unit holding all these grisly features together. An additional case occurs in "At the Mountains of Madness" concerning the distant city distorted via polar mirage:

> There were truncated cones, sometimes terraced or fluted, surmounted by tall cylindrical shafts here and there bulbously enlarged and often capped with tiers of thinnish scalloped discs; and strange, beetling, table-like constructions suggesting piles of multitudinous rectangular slabs or circular plates or five-pointed stars with each one overlapping the one beneath. There were composite cones and pyramids either alone or surmounting cylinders or cubes or flatter truncated cones and pyramids, and occasional needle-like spires in curious clusters of five. (MM 508-9)

No other figure in world literature is able to make such outbursts work so effectively. Here as with cubist painting, there is a clean separation between the multiple facets the thing displays to the outer world, and whatever organizing principle is able to hold together the various monstrous features.

There is also the second Husserlian case, in which a sensual object is in tension with its *real* qualities. While far rarer in Lovecraft than in Husserl, it occurs in his stories whenever scientists enter the scene and have trouble classifying the features of a given object despite all their analytic labor. We return to "The Dreams in the Witch House," where the object retrieved by Gilman from a supposed dream baffles a scientific expert:

> One of the small radiating arms was broken off and subjected to analysis, and the results are still talked about in college circles. Professor Ellery found platinum, iron, and tellurium in the strange alloy; but mixed with these were at least three other apparent elements of high atomic weight which chemistry was powerless to classify. Not only did they fail to correspond with any known element, but they did not even fit the vacant places reserved for probable elements in the periodic system. (WH 677)

The fact that we are not dealing here with any mysterious withdrawn object, but with a perfectly accessible one whose *features* are withdrawn from scrutiny, is emphasized by Lovecraft's witty touch of informing us that there is *a public museum exhibit* in Arkham devoted to the object. A similar incident already occurs in "The Colour Out of Space," when fragments of the meteorite are tested but lead science to a dead end, despite the use of state-of-the-art glass beakers, silicon, borax bead tests, anvils, and oxy-hydrogen blowpipes. (CS 344)

That leaves us with the fourth tension between a real object and its real qualities. Such moments are most evident in Lovecraft's fiction whenever there is talk of outermost regions of the cosmos ruled by deities or forces so bizarre that an empty proper name is all that can be used to designate something for which no tangible qualities are available. For instance, again in "The Dreams in the Witch House," we read that Gilman "must...

go with them all to the throne of Azathoth at the centre of ultimate chaos... to the throne of Chaos where the thin flutes pipe mindlessly... [He] had seen the name 'Azathoth' in the *Necronomicon* and knew it stood for a primal evil too horrible for description." (WH 664) Here the final phrase lets us know that we are dealing with a real or indescribable object, while the thin and mindless flutes are sufficiently inconceivable that we can interpret them as dark allusions to real properties of the throne of Chaos, rather than literal descriptions of what one would experience there in person.

On Ruination

A college classmate of mine once asked a witty faculty member to explain the philosophy of Richard Rorty. The response was as follows: "Basically, you debunk everything, and what you're left with is pragmatism and American democracy." Here we have yet another version of critique through literalizing. But even if it might be disputed whether this is a fair summary of Rorty's intellectual career, the proposed summary is so devastating that Rorty's caliber must be frankly measured by the extent to which his work is able to escape it.

We also find that *jokes* are highly vulnerable to literalizing, which almost always ruins them. Consider the following simple joke, rated as the favorite of the Belgian populace in a survey some years ago (the favorites of other nations were far worse): "There are three kinds of people– those who can count, and those who can't." This mildly humorous remark can be ruined in at least two different ways. One way is to transform it into a literal statement devoid of all paradox: "There are *two* kinds of people– those who can count and those who can't." Here we have a banal classification, not a joke. Another way of ruining the joke is to spell it out in excessive detail: "There are three kinds of people– those who can count and those who can't. And the funny thing is, the person telling the joke obviously can't even count properly himself! Did you notice that he said three kinds of people but only gave two options? The joke is on him!" This feature is one that jokes share with magic tricks: among the international fraternity of magicians we find the credo that the secrets to tricks must never be shared with outsiders. In similar fashion, scantily clad bodies are usually more tantalizing than completely naked ones– a nudist colony filled with candid sex talk would hardly be more arousing than the everyday world of clothed innuendo.

But there are other ways besides literalization to ruin statements, jokes, magic tricks, eros, or anything else. Let's consider a typically well-written passage from Nietzsche, who might be the greatest literary stylist in the history of philosophy (his chief competition would surely be Plato). Writing of Shakespeare in *Ecce Homo*, Nietzsche exclaims: "What must a man have suffered to have such need of being a buffoon!"[45] Here we have a fine sample of Nietzschean prose– crisp, concise, and delightfully paradoxical. But imagine that Nietzsche were a boring literalizer who did not know where to stop. In that case he might have written as follows: "What must a man have suffered to have such need of being a buffoon! For although we might expect the contents of Shakespeare's writing to be a direct reflection of his personality, modern psychology teaches the contrary lesson. For in fact, what people write is often the *opposite* of what they are feeling inside. In Shakespeare's case, the clowning in his comedies may actually be an effort to counterbalance painful personal experience with an outward show of good cheer." Unless this person is a schoolteacher trying to make things plain for children, he is the bane of social conversation, tediously spelling out points that are already clear to everyone. He is the equivalent of Žižek's trite reducer of Hölderlin: "the solution may be just around the corner."

But to be allusive is not the sole aim of a writer, and transforming allusion into literal statement is not the only way to ruin a brilliant remark. Along with the bore just described, we can add other personae capable of leading Nietzsche's remark into ruin.

- The Simpleton: "How happy Shakespeare must have been that he played the buffoon so often!" (Here the twist of paradox is destroyed in favor of a facile correspondence between an author's life and work.)
- The Judgmental Resenter: "What must a man have suffered to have such need of being a buffoon! And I must

say I find it a bit pathetic that Shakespeare is so needy and always clowns around to try to make us like him." (Nietzsche's cool distance and non-judgmental appreciation of human pathos is extinguished in a cesspool of private bitterness.)

- The Waffler: "What must a man have suffered to have such need of being a buffoon! At least I'm pretty sure about that. The other possibility is that he was actually happy. I could go either way on this one." (Here we lose Nietzsche's gallant decisiveness.)

- The Self-Absorbed: "What must a man have suffered to have such need of being a buffoon! But I'm not like that at all. Personally, I take a balanced approach to life and don't feel the need to overcompensate." (Nietzsche's vigorous interest in the outer world gives way to a petty Main Street narcissism.)

- The Down-Home Cornball: "Whenever he has those comical scenes, I ain't fooled. I know Ole Billy's got somethin' stickin' in his craw!" (Here we completely lose the aristocratic elegance of Nietzsche's style.)

- The Clutterer: "What people like Shakespeare, Molière, Aristophanes, Plautus, Menander, Juvenal, Rabelais, and Brecht must have suffered to have such need of being buffoons!" (No longer is Shakespeare addressed as one solitary figure by another. Instead, we have a confusing general proposition about a long list of comic authors.)

- The Pedant: "Shakespeare's plays exhibit instantiations of a ludic affect that, as it were, bespeak an inversion of his 'true' state of mind. Much work has been done in this area, but a full consideration lies beyond the scope of this essay. See Johnson 1994a, Miner & Shaltgrover et al. 1997." (This character combines aspects of both the Waffler and the original Literalizing Bore.)

By Karl Popper's famous principle, a theory is scientific only if it can be falsified. I would go further and say not only that a statement is effective only when it can be ruined, but that the statement is of higher quality the more ways it can be ruined. After all, the fact that a statement *can* be ruined means that this has not already occurred. It also means that we can use possible ruinations, and sometimes possible *improvements*, as a method of analyzing the effects of a literary statement. Part Two of the present book will often make use of this method.

A Lonely and Curious Country

Fissures between objects and their qualities are not always as explicit as in those cases where Lovecraft deliberately paralyzes his own power of language. Simple metaphorical effects can also do this without taking on truly Lovecraftian proportions. As I argued in *Guerrilla Metaphysics*[46] when discussing the closely related theories of Max Black and José Ortega y Gasset, metaphor succeeds by transferring sensual qualities from a sensual object to a real one: in Black's rather bland example "man is a wolf," wolf-qualities are stripped from their usual alliance with a sensual wolf and placed in servitude to a vague and withdrawn human-object, which both attracts and repels its new wolf-qualities. Choosing an especially metaphorical passage from Lovecraft, there is the case when Cthulhu temporarily explodes after collision with a ship: "There was a bursting as of an exploding bladder, a slushy nastiness as of a cloven sunfish, a stench as of a thousand opened graves, and a sound that the chronicler would not put on paper." (CC 195) The final clause is the crowning horror. It falsely implies that putting the sound on paper would be of help in the first place, and thereby ascribes to the chronicler an impossible capacity to explain the sound if only he so chose. The dual attraction and repulsion between object and quality also occurs in the figure known as catachresis. Consider Lovecraft's phrase "great Cthulhu slid greasily into the water," (CC 195) in which it is not immediately clear how a sliding movement into water could have a "greasy" consistency. Yet the reasonable liquid similarity between water and grease makes the combi-nation disturbingly feasible, much like the two minutely different shades of brown found in the jacket and tie of a chic young architect.

But we should also consider cases of good writing that are not actually metaphorical. Since I have referred already to Clement

Greenberg, one of the finest prose stylists of the twentieth century, let's consider a sample from his 1941 memorial essay on Paul Klee: "In spite of Klee's own aspirations [his art] pretends to no statements in the grand style; it concentrates itself within a relatively small area, which it refines and elaborates. It moves in an intimate atmosphere, among friends and acquaintances. It belongs to Berne, Basel, Zurich, old-fashioned Munich, a region of bright, alert small cities..."[47] Here there are no Lovecraftian self-erasures in the face of indescribable withdrawn entities, and no toying with masses of unmanageable qualities to create a flickering spirit or "general outline" of Switzerland imperfectly manifest in its individual cities. Instead, the writing is good simply because Greenberg says something relevant and fresh about Klee's milieu, evokes the warmth of limited circles of friendship (in contrast with Picasso's frenzied cosmopolitan circles), and mentally pinpoints a region on the map by citing four well-known cities where the spirit in question is embodied–provincial, yet bright and alert. Without creating any explicit fissures in the heart of objects, Greenberg retrieves relevant objects from the shadows of indifference, and makes them the target of our awareness in a plausible way.

This point is worth raising because Lovecraft is fully capable of such writing as well. I know of few better passages of English prose than the opening two pages of "The Dunwich Horror," which begins as follows: "When a traveller in north central Massachusetts takes the wrong fork at the junction of the Aylesbury pike just beyond Dean's Corners he comes upon a lonely and curious country." (DH 370) In stylistic terms this is hardly Lovecraft *shtick*, since it lacks any indescribable substrata or vast agglomerations of contradictory qualities, or even favorite adjectives along the lines of "eldritch" or "abominable" or "monstrous" (words of the sort that Wilson is so quick to condemn). Instead, Lovecraft begins with a subtly menacing tone that succeeds in stirring up a serious and slightly worried mood in the reader. The traveler has taken the wrong fork in the road; the terrain is lonely and curious; Dean's Corners and Aylesbury are invoked with a note of geographic authority, though both places seem to be inventions of Lovecraft himself. The passage goes on to offer more of the same: "The ground gets higher, and the brier-bordered stone walls press closer and closer against the ruts of the dusty, curving road. The trees of the frequent forest belts seem too large..." (DH 370)

Not all art explicitly produces gaps in the heart of objects in the way that Lovecraft so often does. But it must produce something like *sincerity* or *involvement*; we must be truly fascinated by whatever is placed before us. Lovecraft's abominable crevices between objects and qualities can do this, but so can a joke, a simple story well told, or the quiet rhythm of a passage that brings objects before us as somehow relevant to our concerns. By "sincerity" I do not mean that artworks need be prudish or morally upright, simply that they must be engrossing. The brother Jason in Faulkner's *The Sound and the Fury* is one of the most repugnant cynics in world literature, yet he fascinates us for precisely this reason. The same holds for Sade's criminal libertine friends in the *120 Days of Sodom* and Sartre's joyless Roquentin in *Nausea*. Sincerity means that a character or object is truly wrapped up in being what it is, and it becomes of interest to us for precisely this reason. If in our normal dealings with the world we use things hazily as bland instruments of our will, a thing is marked by sincerity when it seems to exhibit a genuine inner life of its own. Yet in this way a certain gap is still created between the thing and its accessibility, and hence Lovecraft's unease before indescribable objects display the aesthetic rift in its most explicit form.

Comic and Tragic Intentionality

The medieval term "intentionality" was revived by Franz Brentano in his 1874 philosophical classic, *Psychology from an Empirical Standpoint*.[48] It quickly became a pillar of the writings of his students, Husserl among them. Readers from outside professional philosophy should not think that the word has anything to do with "intentions" in the sense of what someone hopes to accomplish with their actions. Instead, intentionality in the philosophical sense means that mental acts (unlike physical acts, says Brentano) are always aimed at some object. To wish is to wish for something; to love or hate is to love or hate something or someone; to make a judgment is to judge about some particular thing. Contrary to the mistaken view of many who footnote Brentano and Husserl, these intentional objects are not something that we point at *outside* the mind, but exist *inside* the mind as purely immanent features of experience. We can hate or doubt imaginary objects, for instance. But even though the intentionality of consciousness is not enough to escape idealism,[49] there is no experience from which intentional objects are missing.

In this way intentionality works as an "adhesive" term, gluing together subject and object as permanent correlates of one another. But in addition to its adhesive function, intentionality also has a "selective" one. For my intentions not only show that I am bonded to the world rather than being a free-floating disembodied consciousness; instead, they also show what is specifically "at issue" in my life in contrast with others. To some extent we are what we intend, and the same holds true for authors. In Hemingway's world we find that bullfights, military actions, hunting, and the seduction of nurses fall within the range of likely and frequent events; in Lovecraft, of course, all such incidents are unthinkable. When reading Lovecraft we often encounter apparently human voices with disturbing undertones of buzzing, vibration, or slopping noises, while nothing of the sort could ever happen in Jane Austen. Austen's provincial English courtships and inheritance battles are absent in turn from the literary world of Kafka, whose dithering obscurities of legal process would be unthinkable in a novel written by Sade. In similar fashion, we might allow for a flexible range of possible surprising things to occur in a book of philosophy, but would be truly startled if a treatise of metaphysics also contained the report of a horse race or a pornographic centerfold. In this sense, along with speaking of intentionality as a general feature of all conscious experience, we can also speak of *specific* intentionalities as defining the world of any individual or any literary work.

Strictly speaking, there are two distinct kinds of intentionality. One is the first-hand sort that we ourselves have at any given moment. The other is the second-hand intentionality that we observe at work in some other person or animal or inanimate object (Bergson showed the latter to be possible in his treatise on laughter[50]), or in ourselves when we reflect on our status as conscious agents or as characters cutting a figure in the world. For example, the stories of Lovecraft often ask us to consider certain ominous landscapes that barely lie within the realms of the describable, certain monstrous creatures that half-emerge into tangible form, various respectable universities and their faculty members, and so forth. Yet we also encounter the *reactions* to all these things by the narrators of his stories, who in his great tales are usually first-person participants in the events described.[51] The reason for making this point is that even as great a critic as Wilson conflates the two levels, when he disdains Lovecraft's stylistic talents in the following way:

> One of Lovecraft's worst faults is his incessant effort to work up the expectation of the reader by sprinkling his stories with such adjectives as 'horrible,' 'terrible,' 'frightful,' 'awesome,'

'eerie,' 'weird,' 'forbidden,' 'unhallowed,' 'unholy,' 'blasphemous,' 'hellish,' and 'infernal.' Surely one of the primary rules for writing an effective tale of horror is never to use any of these words...[52]

True enough, it is generally a good rule of writing and of thinking not to let our adjectives do the work for us. But in this case Wilson is off the mark. In Lovecraft such adjectives rarely serve as feeble primary instruments for bullying a reader into terror, as Wilson implies. Instead, Lovecraft sprinkles them onto an already completed description, as an enhancing spice that reflects the mental turmoil of the narrator rather than our own direct grasp of the scene. Consider the following description of the strange written characters on the base of the Cthulhu idol found in Louisiana: "They, like the subject and material, belonged to something horribly remote and distinct from mankind as we know it; something frightfully suggestive of old and unhallowed cycles of life in which our world and our concepts have no part." (cc 176) Contra Wilson this is not bad writing, despite the occurrence of "horribly," "frightfully," and "unhallowed." For the heavy lifting is done not by these adjectives themselves, but by the previous description of the idol and the troubled puzzlement of the archaeologists who provide only minimal help to Inspector Legrasse. The adjectives condemned by Wilson are merely ratifications and amplifications of things we have already been led to believe by Lovecraft's skilled artisanship.

That is a first division of intentionality, then: the difference between the primary interest we take in whatever we experience at the moment, and a secondary interest that we observe in other intentional agents. But we should also recognize a second division between "comic" and "tragic" intentionality, which Aristotle defines in terms to be taken in all seriousness: "Comedy aims at representing men as worse, Tragedy as better than in actual life."[53] This definition can be adopted without reserve, as long as we are clear about what "better" and "worse" mean in this context. People can be better or worse than we are in any number of respects: social rank, wealth, intelligence, ethical probity, athletic skill, or beauty. But high status in any of these areas cannot protect those who hold it from becoming comical at times, nor does low status exclude the occurrence of tragedy. Often enough we can mock the foibles of the Kennedy Family or Miss Universe, however superior to us they may be in wealth, public position, or physical attractiveness. Conversely we find that slaves, fools, and the poor can rank among the greatest heroes of a tragic literature fit to make dictators and millionaires weep. Ultimately, the only thing that can be meant here by "better" and "worse" people is whether they are better or worse in terms of the things they invest their energy in taking seriously. The tragic figure is involved with objects and incidents that command our respect or interest, while the comic figure has invested attention in things we regard as ridiculous, from red rubber clown noses to social pomposity to absurd addictions and compulsions.

This brings us to another famous classical remark about comedy and tragedy. At the end of Plato's *Symposium* (223D), Socrates is overheard making an argument about the two genres: "Socrates was trying to prove to [Agathon and Aristophanes] that authors should be able to write both comedy and tragedy: the skillful tragic dramatist should also be a comic poet."[54] Quite aside from the evidence of figures such as Shakespeare who clearly mastered both, it is easy to see that the comic and the tragic exist in such close proximity as to flip easily into one another. If Mombo the Clown falls dead with cardiac arrest while making balloon animals for children at the mall, we have a sudden reversal from the comic into the tragic. Likewise, if the victim of marital infidelity is merely Harlequin in a *commedia dell'arte* skit, or if the destroyer of Tokyo is an unconvincing reptilian monster rather than a genuine atomic bomb, then even cuckolding and mass death can become objects of wholesome laughter.

More interesting than these examples, however, would be a deliberate and controlled combination of the comic and the tragic *simultaneously*. And this is something that Lovecraft does quite well, with the tragic element usually coming directly from the horrors he depicts for us, and the comic side stemming from the laughably genteel or prudish response of the Lovecraftian hero to incidents we know to be worse than he suspects. For instance, as the narrator winds down his conversation with the drunkard Zadok at the docks of Innsmouth, we read as follows: *"Iä! Iä! Cthulhu fhtagn! Ph'nglui mglw'nafh Cthulhu R'lyeh wgah-nagl fhtagn–* Old Zadok was fast lapsing into stark raving..." (SI 622). But this is no mere alcoholic outburst, and we the readers know it so well that the narrator thereby becomes a comical figure despite the impending danger of which he is so deeply unaware. A few pages later, with Zadok's terrible story now complete, the narrator's fright does not prevent him from saying "later I might sift the tale and extract some nucleus of historic allegory" (SI 625), a ridiculously effete and academic response to a cosmic horror that we the readers know to be unfolding. The effect is both comic and tragic simultaneously. This is a regular feature of Lovecraft as a writer that should not be forgotten in what follows.

Style and Content

Any significant writer or artist will be characterized by a *style*. This style cannot be exhausted in "empiricist" fashion by summing up all the works this person factually produced. Instead, we must defend a *realist* concept of style as something never fully embodied in any finite catalog of works. If Picasso had done a series of paintings of Mont Sainte-Victoire, they would presumably have been recognizable as Picassos, just as a series of guitar paintings by Cézanne would obviously have been Cézannes rather than Picassos. When we describe certain actions by a friend as "out of character," we do not mean solely that the actions seem inconsistent with their factual past actions, but that the actions somehow do not fit the *style* of our friend. Certain behaviors might be social *tours de force* in Boston but out of place in Los Angeles, and vice versa. Objects themselves might also be said to have style, given that an orange or a horseshoe is more than any specific visual profile of it at any given moment.

But as already suggested early in this book, it is too simplistic to present style as the source of all intellectual depth, and content as a plane of mere superficiality and banality. Lovecraft's world consists not only in his manner of holding objects at a withdrawn distance or breaking them up into a dozen or more feverish planes. For it is also characteristic of Lovecraft that his narrators tend to be taciturn academics passively observing the horrors that unfold, rather than men of action attending bullfights and being wounded in battle, as with Hemingway. In similar fashion, philosophy is not just a resistance to dogma in favor of a wisdom that can be loved but never obtained. Instead, every philosophy eventually comes to rest in some sincerity that also counts as a sort of dogma. After all, we know Leibniz best not through the hesitant uncertainties of his undogmatic love of wisdom, but through a specific set of doctrines associated with his name.

In a sense, the interaction between style and content is the central theme of this book. The title *Weird Realism* suggests that our plan is to work through Lovecraft towards a deeper conception of realism than is usual. Most philosophical realism is "representational" in character. Such theories hold not only that there is a real world outside all human contact with it, but also that this reality can be mirrored adequately by the findings of the natural sciences or some other method of knowledge. The remarks in this book against paraphrase and the stupidity of all content strongly suggest that this is impossible. No reality can be immediately translated into representations of any sort. Reality itself is weird because reality itself is incommensurable with any attempt to represent or measure it. Lovecraft is aware of this difficulty to an exemplary degree, and through his assistance we may be able to learn about how to say something without saying it– or in philosophical terms, how to love wisdom without having it. When it comes to grasping reality, illusion and innuendo are the best we can do.

In Part Two we will take a break from these general philosophical reflections and look in detail at the style of numerous passages from Lovecraft. One hundred is a good round number suggesting an immense effort, and that is why I have selected one hundred interesting Lovecraftian passages, taking a dozen or so from each of his eight most celebrated stories. Though I will cover the stories in chronological order, I will not focus on plot summaries. Instead, the technique will be to examine individual passages and discover what makes them effective. One method of determining this is that of *ruination*. By discovering how a given passage might be made *worse*, we find an indirect method of appreciating its virtues. In a few cases one might suggest *improvements* even to a writer as skilled as Lovecraft. For example, I would love to delete the opening paragraph of "The Whisperer in Darkness," with its awkward gimmick of the *in medias res*, and begin instead with the matter-of-fact second paragraph: "The whole matter began, so far as I am concerned, with the historic and unprecedented Vermont floods of November 3, 1927..." (WD 415) At the end of this lengthy exercise, we will be in a stronger position to offer some more general reflections on realism and on the oblique mode of access to reality found throughout Lovecraft's fiction.

Part Two:

Lovecraft's Style at Work

The Call of Cthulhu

This story was written in Providence in 1926, and is filled with numerous locations and institutions from Lovecraft's home city: Brown University, Williams Street, Thayer Street, the colorful Fleur-de-Lys Building, and the nearby Providence Art Club. The tale concerns several idols of a winged octopoid creature found independently in different parts of the globe – at a hideous Louisiana voodoo ritual, amidst a tribe of degenerate nineteenth-century Eskimoes, and in Providence as the recent work of a decadent sculptor. A widespread cult is apparently devoted to Cthulhu, the horrific creature after whom the story is named. Numerous deaths occur in the story as a result of attempts to protect the cult and counter-attempts by police and scholars to suppress it.

Nonetheless, this plot summary tells us little about the story qua literature. Edmund Wilson's remarks notwithstanding, particular plot lines may either be favored or mocked by the intellectual fashion of the day, yet there is nothing to exclude *a priori* the possibility that the story of a giant sleeping monster might prove to be a literary masterpiece. "The Call of Cthulhu" is best savored not by summarizing its plot, but by examining a dozen or so passages of the work directly, without paraphrasing Lovecraft's words in pulp-literal terms. And beyond this, one of Lovecraft special gifts as a writer is a keen awareness that even his own original words are already just the paraphrase of a reality that eludes all literal speech.

1. Masked by Bland Optimism

"Theosophists have guessed at the awesome grandeur of the cosmic cycle wherein our world and the human race form transient incidents. They have hinted at strange survivals in terms which would freeze the blood if not masked by a bland optimism." (CC 167)

Lovecraft's series of loosely interrelated "great tales" begins with the opening paragraph of "The Call of Cthulhu" and its dark cosmological suggestions. The passage above is a brief sample from that opening paragraph. To ruin the passage, it is enough to state it in literal form: "Some people think the human race is just one small part of a larger history in which strange extraterrestrial species are far more dominant. They try to make it sound positive, but it's actually pretty frightening when you think about it." In this comically literal version we encounter speculation of the sort usually carried out by adolescents and cranks: precisely the sort of readership Wilson ascribes to the pulp magazine *Weird Tales*, for which Lovecraft often wrote. Yet Lovecraft's original passage is chilling rather than banal, and shows masterful literary skill. We can zero in on three of the points that make it so effective: "theosophists," "transient incidents," and "if not masked by a bland optimism." Let's begin with the second.

The human lifespan is grounded in an interlocking series of traditions. As small children we meet elderly family members and eavesdrop on anecdotes of still older generations. These extend backwards in time towards primeval national and racial histories, which form a deeper background for our ultimately trivial current state. Often enough I have wondered about my distant forebears roaming the forests of Germania and Bohemia while vandalizing the more cultivated outposts of Caesar. Still further backwards in time, various shared ancestors invented cuneiform writing and the wheel, and at some distant point all human branches converge in the temperate savannah of East Africa. Evolution tells us of an even more distant series of ancestors, and at some remote point even vegetables and fungi become our immediate family members. These reflections show that all the twisted intricacies of human literary, cultural, and political history are cruelly outstripped by an engulfing background of long temporal darkness. It faintly reminds us that we in turn will be swallowed in darkness for our far-off descendants, who would probably strike us as utterly grotesque, or even worthy of genocide if it lay within our power to erase them. But Lovecraft goes further than this. We are transient not just compared with long hominid history and the geological and atmospheric genesis of the earth, but even worse, with the "awesome grandeur of cosmic cycle" that make our ancient vegetable cousins seem like yesterday's news. This trivialization of both human and planetary history is one of Lovecraft's trademarks, and provides a cosmological finitude more frightening than Kant's metaphysical kind. What evades comprehension for Lovecraft is not the ungraspable thing-in-itself, but horrible creatures from other times and places who are capable of intervening in our own.

"Theosophy" often refers to the industrial-age mysticism of Madame Blavatsky, and evokes images of the séance and the Ouija board. Yet the tradition has intellectually respectable roots among Cornelius Agrippa, Paracelsus, and Jakob Boehme, ultimately extending all the way to ancient Platonic and Indian schools. Lovecraft often expands this list of genuine figures to include the names of fictional thinkers invented by himself or his circle: names such as F.W. von Junzt and the mad Arab Abdul al-Ahazred. Since the postulation of otherworldly monsters automatically strikes many critics as mere teenager's work, Lovecraft makes sure to intertwine his fictions with the accumulated classical wisdom of the centuries. It is common for Lovecraft to mix the names of his fabricated sages with those of genuine Renaissance alchemists and medieval Arab and Jewish thinkers. In this way his writing acquires a sense of historical bulk– as though not Lovecraft himself, but all of human history, were quietly involved in struggles with the hidden beings who now erupt into Massachusetts, Vermont, and the Antarctic. By denouncing the "bland optimism" of more recent theosophists, Lovecraft seizes their purported access to other worlds for his own use while also taking a distance from their facile reassuring humanism. And here we have a second major feature of Lovecraft's writing: human history is portrayed as a cheerful façade covering a nightmarish truth apprehended by only a handful of scholars, mystics, and half-breed sailors.

It will be noticed that the effectiveness of this passage has nothing to do with any explicit fracturing of the bonds between objects and their qualities. It serves only to place humans in a context that trivializes their sum total of political, intellectual, and technical achievements, and reduces their long history to the blink of an eye. But whether this is really unrelated to the object/quality tension that is the philosophical center of this book is a question left for Part Three.

2. The General Outline of the Whole

"If I say that my somewhat extravagant imagination yielded simultaneous pictures of an octopus, a dragon, and a human caricature, I shall not be unfaithful to the spirit of the thing... but it was the *general outline* of the whole which made it most shockingly frightful." (CC 169)

The literalizer can (and often does) ruin this passage by glossing it roughly as follows: "It looked like an octopus, a dragon, and a human, all rolled into one." But this version is mere pulp fiction.

No philosopher is more Un-Lovecraftian than David Hume, a stimulating thinker and outstanding stylist whose philosophical stock is nonetheless always a bit too high. Hume is the patron saint of the philosophical debunker, and though debunking has its uses, the clearing away of rubbish is a secondary chore best done once per week. Hume famously tells us in his 1748 *Enquiry*: "When we think of a golden mountain, we only join two consistent ideas, *gold*, and *mountain*, with which we were formerly acquainted. A virtuous horse we can conceive; because, from our own feeling, we can conceive virtue; and this we may unite to the figure and shape of a horse, which is an animal familiar to us."[55] Like Edmund Husserl in the twentieth century, Lovecraft is radically anti-Hume in his views on how a thing relates to its qualities. Notice how absurd a Humean reading of the passage would be: "When we think of Cthulhu, we only join three consistent ideas, *octopus*, *dragon*, and *human*, with which we were formerly acquainted." Equally absurd would be a Lovecraftian rewriting of the passage from Hume: "If I say that my somewhat extravagant imagination yielded a picture of a golden mountain, I would not be entirely unfaithful to the spirit of the thing... but the *general outline* of the whole is what made it most shockingly frightful."

For Hume what is most accessible to the mind are qualities, and the notions we have of "things" or "objects" can be replaced by the bundle of qualities through which they are known. While there is a grain of truth in talk of "Lovecraft's materialism," it is not the confident scientistic materialism whose goal is the dissolution of mystery. Instead, it is a materialism that joins modern science to a long history of baffled alchemists and mystics. Much like Husserl, Lovecraft sees the object as a whole as primary, with any cluster of palpable qualities fully dependent on that prior whole. But whereas Husserl is concerned with everyday examples such as blackbirds and mailboxes unexhausted by their series of qualities, Lovecraft makes us *feel* the difference by using objects that threaten human well-being. For every object, including Cthulhu, there is "a spirit of the thing" and "a general outline of the whole" irreducible to cheerful bundles of octopus, dragon, and human. Those who deny that such bundles are scary are correct. They are simply wrong to think that Cthulhu consists in such a bundle.

3. Mobbed by Hysterical Levantines

"...items from India speak guardedly of serious native unrest toward the end of March. Voodoo orgies multiply in Haiti, and African outposts report ominous mutterings. American officers in the Philippines find certain tribes bothersome about this time, and New York policemen are mobbed by hysterical Levantines on the night of March 22-23." (CC 174)

Racism can only make a philosopher worse (see Heidegger's condescending reference to the "Senegal Negro" in his otherwise masterful 1919 tool-analysis[56]). But in certain rare cases, reactionary views might improve the power of an imaginative writer. Houellebecq has already noted that Lovecraft's racism may be such a case: "This is no longer the WASP's well-bred racism; it is the brutal hatred of a trapped animal who is forced to share his cage with other different and frightening creatures."[57] What Houellebecq is referring to here is the following incredible outburst in a letter from Lovecraft to Frank Belknap Long concerning the population of New York's Lower East Side:

> The organic things –Italo-Semitico-Mongoloid– inhabiting that awful cesspool could not by any stretch of the imagination be call'd human. They were monstrous and nebulous adumbrations of the pithecanthropoid and amoebal; vaguely moulded from some stinking viscous slime of earth's corruption, and slithering and oozing in and on the filthy streets or in and out of windows and doorways in a fashion suggestive of nothing but infesting worms or deep-sea unnameabilities.[58]

If found in a letter by Heidegger, this would be a final reputation-destroying sensation; if found in Hitler's *Mein Kampf* it would be quoted as one of the showcase exhibits. But while the passage reflects poorly on Lovecraft as a person, our primary reaction to it is a literary one. Note that the preposterous hyphenated form "Italico-Semitico-Mongoloid" pushes us well beyond any specific foreign race. As Houellebecq rightly asks: "what race could possibly have provoked this outburst?... The ethnic realities at play had long been wiped out... His descriptions of the nightmare entities that populate the Cthulhu cycle spring directly from this hallucinatory vision."[59]

While abominable in ethical and political terms, Lovecraft's racism is undeniably effective in purely literary ones. Previously we saw him reduce known human and planetary history to dust in comparison with the vast cycles of time and evolution guessed vaguely by theosophical tradition. But along with the flashes of truth Lovecraft finds in the works of Paracelsus, Boehme, and the fictional von Junzt, the vast cosmic cycles seem to be perceived with especially keen sensitivity by non-white races. The white imperialist nations of Lovecraft's era seem vastly overpowered by a secret conspiracy between monstrous elder beings and their colonized emissaries on earth. There are vague hints of unrest in India, apparently too disturbing to report in anything other than "guarded" fashion. There are "ominous mutterings" in Africa, detected by Western "outposts." There are problems in the Philippines. And in a crowning incident, the horror comes close to home: for even in New York itself, the police are mobbed by "hysterical Levantines." Here the dubious cluster concept of "Levantine" is treated as a unified causal agent and given the uniform quality of "hysterical," in a manner that would be quite hilarious if not that residents of the Levant are likely to feel insulted by the passage. While one can easily imagine a bitter critique of this passage by the late Edward Said, in a certain sense Said's critique would miss the point. However blameworthy as a sample of Orientalism, Lovecraft's reference to a mob of hysterical Levantines is genuinely frightening, presumably even for readers from present-day Lebanon and Syria. Nor are whites completely exempt from this contact with the elder races in Lovecraft's story, as seen from the nightmares of the decadent sculptor Wilcox.

In fact, the best way to *ruin* the passage at the head of this section would be to cleanse it of all unpalatable Orientalist content as follows: "Providence wasn't the only place where strange things were happening at that time. There were also problems in diverse cultural environments such as India, Haiti, Africa, and the Philippines." The tolerant liberal author of this passage is certainly a better twenty-first century world citizen than Lovecraft, but is nowhere near as effective at generating horror.

4. The Blackest of the African Voodoo Circles

"...the police could not but realize that they had stumbled on a dark cult totally unknown to them, and infinitely more diabolic than even the blackest of the African voodoo circles." (CC 175)

Here we see further traces of Lovecraft's aversion to Africa, as also reflected in the proliferation of dark-skinned people among the various evil sailors and cult members of his stories. In passing, it is interesting to note that in these stories *women* are not generally found to be in league with the Elder Races. The one glaring exception is Lavinia Whateley in "The Dunwich Horror," a genetically decayed and shapeless albino woman impregnated by some elder-world creature. Otherwise, the few overtly negative references we find to women in Lovecraft's stories can often be explained by an overarching component of ethnic or racial horror. A bereaved mother is dismissed as "a clod-like laundry worker named Anastasia Wolejko" (WH 680), while the abhorrent fish-frog waitress in Innsmouth is described by the unknowing narrator as "a flat-nosed wench with unbelievably thick, clumsy hands" (SI 627). But other than Lavinia Whateley, the only woman with a central role in cosmic Lovecraftian horror is the presumably Caucasian witch Keziah Mason (WH 654), though even here there is a racial echo stemming from Keziah's partial incarnation in her rat-like familiar Brown Jenkin. Given the uneasiness of Lovecraft's personal relations with women, it is easy to imagine an alternate Lovecraft with a misogynistic rather than racist bent, his stories filled with sinister leagues of females in voluntary carnal union with the elder races. But other than Lavinia's strange pregnancy, the only sexual incident in the great tales of Lovecraft is found in Old Zadok's hints at the forced interbreeding of humans with fish-frogs in "The Shadow Over Innsmouth." A less prudish or more misogynistic Lovecraft might easily have explored this theme at much greater length.

Returning to the passage at the head of this section, I propose that it could be ruined as follows: "If you think the African voodoo circles are bad, let me tell you this: the cult that the police found in the swamp was infinitely worse." It is interesting to consider why this ruination fails. In the first place, it begins on the wrong foot. Most of us do not live in fear of African voodoo circles, or think of them in anything more than anthropological terms. To begin by asking us to cringe before something that never bothers us in the least, then attempting to trump that fear by claiming to have found something even worse, is a rhetorical misfire that fails to carry the reader along.

What Lovecraft does is something subtler and more effective. "The police could not but realize that they had stumbled on a dark cult totally unknown to them." This is already a good beginning: a dark and totally unknown cult has been discovered. Better yet, it was found *by the police*, suggesting that the cult is engaged in activity both dangerous and illegal, which means that our interest is immediately ensured. But the real key to the passage is the portion after the comma: "and infinitely more diabolic than even the blackest of the African voodoo circles." Here Lovecraft is not relying on anyone's pre-existent horror of African voodoo, which as already mentioned does not horrify most of us at all. Lovecraft's technique is more clever than this. Rather than just positing the cult as something lying beyond the terrible bounds of voodoo, he triangulates. Namely, Lovecraft borrows horror from the ill-defined mysterious cult, lends it to voodoo, and then takes it back again to increase the force of the ill-defined cult. We can give a different sort of example. If someone were to say: "The young Ingrid Bergman struck Swedish viewers as even more graceful than Anja Söderblom," the comparison sounds impressive even if you have never heard of Söderblom, who in fact does not exist. The form of the sentence lures us into believing that Söderblom must indeed have been very graceful, and Bergman even more so. The same thing happens with the Lovecraft passage. If he were simply to tell us: "African voodoo circles are horrific and dangerous," we would hardly be convinced. But to use those circles as the foil of an extreme comparison subtly convinces us *not only* that the cult must really be bad if it is worse than African voodoo, but *also* that African voodoo must be really bad if it is being used as the springboard to describe something else as even worse. If someone says "George W. Bush is the worst American President since Millard Fillmore," you will not only sense an explicit negative opinion about Bush, but will also feel yourself silently *assenting* to a negative judgment about Fillmore, even if you know nothing about him at all. Or take this example: "The food offered us by the natives was a ghastly paste or oil infinitely worse than the greasiest and most pungent consistencies of peanut butter." This conveys some idea of horribleness even for those of us who like peanut butter. By analogy with the famous "straw man," we might call this figure the Straw Devil. In the passage cited at the head of this section, Lovecraft excels at making the unnameable seem horrible by telling us it is even worse than something we already know without fearing in the least.

5. Descendants of Lafitte's Men

"The squatters, mostly primitive but good-natured descendants of Lafitte's men, were in the grip of stark terror from a thing that had stolen upon them in the night." (CC 178)

The pirate Jean Lafitte worked in the vicinity of New Orleans in the early 1800's, sometimes furthering American interests against the British, at other times engaged in actions both for and against Spain. By rooting his story of the swamp-based Cthulhu Cult in a population descended from Lafitte's crew, Lovecraft follows his usual policy of lending plausibility and bulk to his weird tales by grounding them in either real or fabricated history. There are two different ways that this aspect of the passage could be ruined. The first would be to say: "The people who lived in the swamp had pirate ancestors." This sounds like a vague and possibly irrelevant assertion. But to specify them instead as the descendants of Lafitte serves to provide the color of detail to the claim, and also to lend historical credence to the tale, since Lafitte's association with Louisiana is generally known to those who are even loosely familiar with American history. A second ruination could be produced by overly detailed description: "The squatters were mostly descendants of the crewmen of Jean Lafitte, a famous pirate and privateer who lived from approximately 1776 to 1823." The tone now shifts towards that of the museum or the public library, and is too democratically informative to yield good literary effect in the present context. Instead of these possible missteps, Lovecraft's narrator simply assumes that Lafitte is a known commodity to readers, and pays him a certain respect by assuming that there is no need to explain further, giving the narrator's words a mildly comical effect. In Aristotle's terms he is momentarily "worse" than we are, since he lets himself be mesmerized by a historical personage who may be important, but who is sufficiently minor that he might enter the mind of the typical American citizen once every decade or so. For the flash of an instant, the Lovecraftian narrator is obsessed with Jean Lafitte as a historical force to be reckoned with, and this amuses us vaguely.

Two other things need to be said about this passage. First, saying that the squatters are "mostly" descendants of Lafitte's men is a way of earning our esteem for the narrator's prudent caution. He does not rashly generalize that "all" are descended from that crew, and thereby gains credibility at the rather low price of tacitly conceding that a few of the squatters might have no genetic relation to Lafitte's crew. But paradoxically enough, this does even more to crystallize the "Lafitteness" of the majority of the squatters. For if all of them could be described as such, then the Lafitte factoid would be relevant as pertaining to a collective sum of humans, nothing more. But when intermixed with others who lack such ancestry, the Lafitte squatters seem to embody a special force over and above any bulk assembly of humans. An analogy may be useful. To say that "all lizards are harmless" is clearly an exaggeration. But to say that "most lizards are harmless," vaguely separates a benevolent lizard-essence from the great horde of individual lizards, a few of which may be quite dangerous. This gesture turns that lizard-essence into an effective causal agent that must be something different from all individual lizards as a sum.

Second, "primitive but good-natured" is an amusing phrase implying that primitivity usually entails aggression or spite. It is a shorthand way of saying something like: "The squatters are primitive, but surprisingly enough, they are not ill-natured." A concealed inference is made of the sort that can be funny even when distinctly insulting: "American but subtle and insightful"; "German but not pedantic or authoritarian"; "French but not amoral or vain."

6. The Merest Fringe

"The region now entered by police was one of traditionally evil repute... The present voodoo orgy was, indeed, on the merest fringe of this abhorred area, but that location was bad enough..." (CC 179)

This passage could easily be ruined by the Literalizer with something along the following lines: "The whole area had a bad reputation, and the part where they were now was one of the least bad parts." By contrast, there are three points that make the Lovecraft passage more effective.

The first is calling the region one of "traditionally evil repute," thereby transforming what might have been regarded as an unlikely one-off incident into something woven into a long unspecified history of dismal incidents. Louisiana squatter folklore now joins the works of Paracelsus, Boehme, and Abdul al-Ahazred as testimony that malign forces are abroad in the world. This portion of the passage could also be ruined by supplying excessive detail. For instance: "The region now entered by the police was one of traditionally evil repute, due to a series of 154 kidnappings, 73 murders, and several thousand burglaries over the span of a few decades." At best, such a passage could yield comic effects through its very excess.

The second is the phrase "the present voodoo orgy," obviously somewhat comical in its genteel tone, reminiscent of "the present topic of discussion" or "the present book." It implicitly treats this horrifying incident as a manageable new instance of a recurring class of voodoo orgies. To ruin this wonderfully comic effect, it is enough to refer simply to "the voodoo orgy."

The crowning moment of the passage is the fact that the orgy is located "on the merest fringe of [the] abhorred area." Although the word "merest" is recognized by dictionaries in a way that "merer" is not, it is extremely rare in everyday speech. Indeed it is rare enough that we can probably assume that Lovecraft took it from Poe's line in "The Black Cat": "the terror and horror with which the animal inspired me, had been heightened by one of the merest chimaeras it would be possible to conceive."[60] By linking a murderous voodoo orgy with the traditional bad reputation of these swamplands, and by then telling us that the orgy now underway lies on "the merest fringe" of the accursed zone, Lovecraft obviously does much to heighten our fear of what lies even deeper within the region. This is especially the case given the further hints in the story as to even more sinister things afoot further back in the trees: a white polypous form, and possible antiphonal responses to the orgy's chants.

7. An Excitable Spaniard

"It may have been only imagination and it may have been only echoes which induced one of the men, an excitable Spaniard, to fancy he heard antiphonal responses to the ritual from some far and unillumined spot deeper in the woods." (CC 180)

This passage can be ruined by the Literalizer as follows: "Not only were there terrible chants around the fire, but one of the men claims he heard someone or something in the woods answering the chants. But the man was Spanish, and as everyone knows, Spanish people often become overly excited and emotional about things."

In the first instance, the Lovecraft passage above amplifies his previous comment about the voodoo orgy being placed at "the merest fringe" of the ill-reputed region. The ceremony as described by Lovecraft, with bizarre dances amidst flame around corpses hung upside-down from gallows, already sounds like the core of hell itself. To outbid such insanity by treating it as the "fringe" of a deeper menace leads us by analogy from known horrors to deeper unknown ones. What horrible force would need to remain even more concealed than the barbaric voodoo murderers already described? Whatever it might be, it seems to respond to the ritual chants and screams of its suppliants.

That brings us to the "excitable Spaniard." This is another case where Lovecraft uses ethnic stereotyping (possibly feigned in this instance) to achieve a literary effect, and I hope Spanish readers laugh as much at this phrase as I myself would laugh at the phrase "a loud and greedy American" if used in a parallel context. Once again we must trace the technique to Poe. In the Preface to *Arthur Gordon Pym* (Poe's vastly underrated novel) we are told that only one eyewitness can verify Pym's account, "and he a half-breed Indian."[61] In "The Cask of Amontillado," the doomed Fortunato is also described as a perfect fit for national stereotypes: "Few Italians have the true virtuoso spirit. For the most part their enthusiasm is adopted to suit the time and opportunity– to practice imposture upon the British and Austrian *millionaires*. In painting and gemmery Fortunato, like his countrymen, was a quack– but in the matter of old wines he was sincere."[62]

Yet Lovecraft's appeal to stereotype achieves a novel effect not attempted by Poe. First he introduces the specter of a sinister power deeper in the woods that answers the already devastating chants of the visible ritual. Next, Lovecraft invites us to disregard the notion he himself has just introduced. After all, the sounds may only have been echoes, or the product of someone's imagination. And beyond that, the report came from an excitable Spaniard, and we all know how Spaniards are. Yet these latter claims, *including* the stereotype, are so obviously unconvincing that we are all bound to conclude that the Spaniard is in the right. In short, Lovecraft maneuvers us into siding with the character whom he has just belittled as a witness due to innate ethnic weakness. The narrator deliberately places himself in a position inferior to the reader, since he is naïve enough to trust banal ethnic prejudice against Spaniards over the truly vivid concealed horrors that the narrator himself suggests. Houellebecq notices a related point: "Often when reading [Lovecraft's] stories, one wonders why the protagonists are taking so long to understand the nature of the horror menacing them. They appear, frankly, obtuse."[63] This is undeniably true. One of the major features of Lovecraft's narrators is their tendency to explain away all of the most bizarre incidents they encounter. But while this may seem implausible on the side of the characters, it is a deeply effective technique for luring his readers into believing more than he explicitly asks them to believe. His characters always appear as more hardboiled rationalists than we are, and at the same time as more gullible. There are few greater proofs of Lovecraft's talent as a writer.

8. A Hideous Victorian Imitation

"Wilcox still lived alone in the Fleur-de-Lys Building in Thomas Street, a hideous Victorian imitation of seventeenth-century Breton architecture which flaunts its stuccoed front amidst the lovely colonial houses on the ancient hill, and under the very shadow of the finest Georgian steeple in America." (CC 184)

The effect of this passage is comical in at least two ways. The first concerns Lovecraft's private joke of incorporating the everyday scenes of hometown Providence into a tale of cosmic horror. This is true of "The Call of Cthulhu," though perhaps equally true of "The Case of Charles Dexter Ward" and "The Haunter of Darkness." In the passage above we are asked to regard the quotidian features of Providence geography, such as Thomas Street, as the stage of serious literary events. A few doors up the hill from the Fleur-de-Lys Building, the Providence Art Club is still in operation as of 2011. It is a staid, somewhat dull and bourgeois-looking edifice, but that does not prevent Lovecraft from asking us to treat it as a force to be reckoned with: "Wilcox was a precocious youth of known genius but great eccentricity... Even the Providence Art Club, anxious to preserve its conservatism, had found him quite hopeless." (CC 170) While it is a genuine pleasure to visit Providence and tour these scenes from Lovecraft's stories, there is the inevitable comical effect of seeing how utterly non-ominous most of these places look in person.

But even more interesting here is the more explicit joke of Lovecraft's narrator interrupting a tale of earth-shaking horror to rant about the architectural flaws of Wilcox's residence. True enough, the Fleur-de-Lys Building would be regarded by many critics as rather tasteless. It does clash badly with the towering Baptist Church across the street ("the finest Georgian steeple in America"), yet somehow the scene hardly seems to warrant the angry dismissal of the narrator. Moreover, the narrator does not simply provide us with anger. He does not just say: "Wilcox lived in the Fleur-de-Lys Building. In my opinion, the building is crap in stylistic terms and ruins the whole street." Instead, he assumes the tone of a seasoned if impassioned architectural critic, even as the world faces unprecedented peril from an emerging cosmic monstrosity in the South Pacific. The clash of Victorian, Breton, and Georgian styles is thereby thrown into relief, and the use of stucco is berated as an insult to the colonial houses on the hill.

9. The Geometry Was All Wrong

"[Wilcox] talked of his dreams in a strangely poetic fashion; making me see with terrible vividness the damp Cyclopean city of slimy green stone –whose *geometry*, he oddly said, was *all wrong*..." (CC 185)

The passage can be ruined by the Literalizer as follows: "Wilcox had dreams of giant non-Euclidean cities made of slimy green stone." What ruins this alternate passage is the single word "non-Euclidean." However strange non-Euclidean geometry might seem in comparison with the everyday world, it has long since become a known quantity. University courses are offered on the subject, and classic Dover paperbacks are available that can be mastered by the intelligent layperson with a few weekends of effort. Lobachevski and Riemann may not be quite household names among the wider public, yet they are sufficiently well-known that their revolutionary impact can be assumed to belong to the past, given that far stranger geometries are now of interest to avant garde mathematicians.

We cannot say that Lovecraft's cities are non-Euclidean, any more than we can hold that Cthulhu is a bundle made up of the familiar ideas of octopus, dragon, and human. The Cthulhu idol is characterized not by an unforeseen mixture of three real and imaginary life forms, but by a deeper "spirit of the thing" and "general outline of the whole." In similar fashion, the architecture found in Lovecraft's stories cannot strictly be described as non-Euclidean, but only as "all wrong." The work of philosophy is to unearth the hidden background conditions of all visibly accessible entities, just as the function of rhetoric is to make use of this background to persuade its listeners in a way that literal argument cannot. Nothing is more Lovecraftian than his repeated vague assaults on the assumptions of normal three-dimensional space and its interrelations, as learned by students since ancient Greece. For this reason, nothing could be more threatening than the notion that something is "all wrong" in the presumed spatial contours on which all human thought and action is based.

But the passage above does more than assert the degenerate nature of Lovecraftian geometry. It cajoles us into accepting such geometry with three additional flourishes. First, it tells us that there was something "strangely poetic" about Wilcox's manner of describing the city, as if letting us know that the narrator shares our hesitation at endorsing its reality, thereby increasing its plausibility. We saw how important this is for Lovecraft in his essay "Some Notes on Interplanetary Fiction." Most science fiction fails by simply *positing* an unprecedented reality, without conveying any sense of shock or disbelief on the part of those engaged with it. Second, the narrator tells us that Wilcox described the vision of strange geometry with "terrible vividness"– an empty signifier that Edmund Wilson might disdain as a hijacking of good prose, but one that functions more effectively than any concrete list of terribly vivid things could ever do. And third, Lovecraft maintains the strangeness of Wilcox's description with the phrase "he oddly said," thereby indicating that the net result remains problematic for the narrator. In this way the narrator preserves a tangible rift between the city of Wilcox's nightmares and anything identifiable from normal human experience.

10. A Mineralogist of Note

"… [I] was visiting a learned friend in Paterson, New Jersey; the curator of a local museum and a mineralogist of note." (CC 187)

This passage is almost entirely comical in flavor, and presents the narrator as "worse" than we are. Clearly he is not worse in intellectual terms, since he spends his free time consulting with scientific colleagues, a more serious use of leisure time than most people are able to find. Yet he is worse than we are in the sense that the stock figure of the absentminded professor is worse. We may admire the narrator's scholarly achievements and bow before his intellect, which is perhaps superior to our own. Yet we somehow feel more human than he is– more flexible, more capable of taking intellectual matters in stride and assigning them to their proper subordinate place in the general economy of things. By contrast, the narrator is utterly absorbed in his intellectual sincerities, and expends his entire being in pursuing them. The category of "a mineralogist of note" is not inherently laughable, since such people do exist. Yet normally we do not mention them matter-of-factly as belonging to our circle of friends. Nor do we usually think of such a person as curating a local museum in a place such as Paterson, New Jersey, a fairly arbitrary choice of location that must have made Lovecraft chuckle while first writing it on paper.

Furthermore, the learned friend makes no additional appearance in the story, and neither do mineralogy or the city of Paterson. The setting is a purely gratuitous opportunity for the narrator to enter the museum's back room and accidentally discover a page of the *Sydney Bulletin* containing the report of a ship's encounter and battle at sea with what later turns out to be a repugnant crew of Cthulhu devotees. The narrator travels immediately to Australia, and Paterson and its mineralogist are never heard from again. The passage at the head of this section plays the role of a sincerity *en passant* that furthers the action in a tenuous, accidental way, while nonetheless giving us a laugh at the expense of the narrator himself. Just as Socrates proposed in the *Symposium*, Lovecraft is writing comedy and tragedy simultaneously.

11. Rock Chasm

"...and six of the men somehow died ashore, though Johansen is queerly reticent about this part of the story, and speaks only of their falling into a rock chasm." (CC 188)

The effect of this passage is similar to describing the voodoo orgy as lying at the "merest fringe" of the ill-reputed swamp region. There, a brutal scene of occult murder was described to us, and it was hinted further that the woods beyond contained even ghastlier entities. But here, the method works in reverse: Lovecraft begins with vagueness, and makes that vagueness even more horrifying by telling us of something obviously terrible that it is able to surpass. Moreover, the palpable horror of falling into a rock chasm distinguishes this passage from the trumped-up pseudo-horror of the passage about the African voodoo circles mentioned in Section 4 above.

Six of the men "somehow" died ashore. This death toll is bad enough, and the lack of information as to how the deaths occurred is something far worse than any possible explanation as to what happened. In everyday life, the fact that Johansen is "queerly reticent" about the deaths of his shipmates would normally give rise to suspicions that he murdered them himself, but there is no hint that anyone takes this option seriously, and certainly the reader has no reason to consider it. Instead, Johansen's reticence suggests a manner of death so horrible that he has no wish to communicate or even remember it. At this point, one would expect sheer silence on Johansen's part instead of reference to something as tangible as a rock chasm, and the passage might easily have ended after the second comma as follows: "...and six of the men somehow died ashore, though Johansen is queerly reticent about this part of the story."

But the brilliance of this passage lies in the manner in which it does continue: namely, with the news that Johansen "speaks only of their falling into a rock chasm." As if this were merely an evasive and useless hint! "Six men died ashore in a manner too traumatic to relate. I refuse to be specific about the means by which they died. All I am willing to tell you is that they fell into a rock chasm." It is difficult to imagine a more horrifying scene than six sailors ashore who plummet to their deaths in a chasm, toppling for many seconds through the air, and presumably killed by blunt force trauma when striking a hard surface at the bottom. One could easily imagine this being too traumatic an incident for an eyewitness to discuss– but in this case, he *does* discuss it. The actual trauma apparently comes from some even more horrible peripheral condition to which Johansen's reticence vaguely alludes. Here, as is so often the case in Lovecraft, a rift is created between the most horrible of describable things and the even more abominable reality lying beneath them.

12. Some Peculiarly Abominable Quality

"There was some peculiarly abominable quality about [the foreign crew] which made their destruction seem almost a duty, and Johansen shows ingenuous wonder at the charge of ruthlessness brought against his party during the court of inquiry." (CC 191-2)

This can be viewed as another instance of "the spirit of the thing" or "the general outline of the whole" that exceed all palpable traits. Despite the use of the word "quality" here, the narrator is not speaking of qualities in Hume's sense of a "bundle of qualities." The "peculiarly abominable quality" cannot take the form of a tangible adjective such as "red," or "evil" or "greedy," but is a sort of malign general atmosphere lying beyond all speech, and accessible only through the sort of allusion that the narrator utilizes here.

The difference between this passage and the description of the Cthulhu idol is the ethical dimension it brings into play. Just as individual substances can be reduced to bundles of qualities, so too can ethics be transformed into a "bundle of rules," as it often is. According to this procedure, people must be judged by their actions, not by some mythic underlying good or evil character. Yet experience teaches the opposite. We never judge people identically for the same actions, and this is not just for reasons of "hypocrisy." None of us is able to get away with the same things as others can; indeed, what makes each of us unique is the private range of normally forbidden or discouraged actions that we are able to engage in while still escaping punishment and sometimes even censure. In other words, for each person there is a certain "spirit of the thing" or "general outline of the whole" that precedes our piecemeal judgment of their individual actions. The reason this is not merely "hypocrisy" is that the charge of hypocrisy *presupposes* that the only thing that matters is an externally accessible set of norms to which all persons must be equally subject.

In the passage above, the Australian "court of inquiry" treats human action as reducible to a bundle of rules. To some extent this is necessary for society to function, and generally we do presume that mass slaughter of a ship's crew lies beyond the scope of what anyone should be able to get away with. "Getting away with murder" is a familiar slogan of outrage. But we have seen no evidence that Johansen is either murderous, insane, or morally corrupt in any way. In fact, the newspaper article stresses that he is "of some intelligence" (CC 188) and "a sober and worthy man" (CC 188-9). However vague the "peculiarly abominable quality" of the foreign crew might sound, it was sufficiently overwhelming that Johansen cannot even understand the charge of "ruthlessness" brought by the court of inquiry. He reacts instead with "ingenuous wonder," just as he would react if David Hume tried to comfort him by saying that Cthulhu is nothing more than octopus, dragon, and human spliced together. What Hume will forever miss, but what Edmund Husserl is unlikely to miss, is the "peculiarly abominable quality" lying in the heart of certain individual things.

13. An Acute Angle that Behaved as if it were Obtuse

"...and Johansen swears [Parker] was swallowed up by an angle of masonry which shouldn't have been there; an angle which was acute, but behaved as if it were obtuse." (CC 194)

To close our stylistic survey of "The Call of Cthulhu," we consider this troubling passage from late in the story, one of the most effective cases of Lovecraft undermining the bond between a thing and its traits. This happens in several different ways.

The difference between acute and obtuse angles is well known even to schoolchildren: an acute angle is less than ninety degrees and thus appears "closed," while an obtuse angle is greater than ninety degrees and thus appears "open" when compared with a right angle. Each type of angle has known geometrical properties, and following centuries of geometrical work there is every reason to suppose we have exhausted these properties. But here, Lovecraft introduces a problem. Not only is Cthulhu something over and above the three creatures he partially resembles, and not only does a foreign ship's crew have some "peculiarly abominable quality" that justifies their massacre outside all maritime law– we now find that even acute and obtuse angles must be something over and above their qualities. There seems to be a "spirit" of acute angles, a "general outline of the whole," which allows them to remain acute angles even in cases where they *behave* as if they were obtuse. Not since Pythagoras have geometrical entities been granted this sort of psychic potency, to the point that they have a deeper being over and above their measurable and experienceable traits.

Something else is disturbing about the passage as well. Namely, it is unclear how the mere fact of "behaving as obtuse" would allow an angle to "swallow up" an unwary sailor. Sketch the diagram of an obtuse angle for yourself, and you will see the difficulty in intuitively grasping what happened. If the phrase "she looked daggers at him" is an example of catachresis in language, a misapplication of a word to gain metaphorical effects, then the acute angle obtusely swallowing a sailor is a fine example of catachresis in geometry. We might as well say: "It was the number 21, but it behaved as though it were the number 6."

There are additional factors at play. For one thing, it is unclear why the strange angle in question should be made "of masonry," given the remote Pacific location of the island. But the word "masonry" is often associated in Lovecraft with the most sinister situations. For another thing, there is the fact that Johansen "swears" that this incident occurred, emphasizing the gap between Johansen the storyteller and the readers who might be expected to doubt the story of the strange acute angle, yet who are inclined to believe it nonetheless.

The Colour Out of Space

Lovecraft generally preferred British spellings to American ones, just as he mourned the defeat of King George III in the American Revolutionary War. Hence the use of the British spelling "colour" in the title of this story is a deliberate decision on Lovecraft's part. The story was written during the same period in 1927 as "The Case of Charles Dexter Ward," the brilliant novella that I am sorry to have to exclude from the present book. A government surveyor arrives in the wild hills west of Arkham, Massachusetts (a fictitious location), preparing for the construction of a reservoir in the area. He observes an area known among the locals as "the blasted heath" and finds that it deserves the description. The water of the new reservoir will eventually cover the area, a fact that becomes sickening for the reader after learning of what happened there late in the nineteenth century. The narrator does not observe the terrible events directly, since they occurred some decades in the past. Instead, he seeks out an aged recluse named Ammi Pierce, who provides information on the terrifying events of the past, just as the drunkard Zadok Allen will later do in "The Shadow Over Innsmouth."

In those strange days of the previous century, a meteorite landed on the property of the Nahum Gardner family, friends of Mr. Pierce. Initially there seemed no cause for alarm, though local scientists were unable to classify the material that came from space, and soon found that it had shriveled and vanished. The meteorite contaminates the Gardner property, gradually causing all plants and animals to turn grey and brittle. The family members slowly lose their minds, and die through some hideous form of physical degeneration. The strange warbling "colour" responsible for these events seems to be hiding in the well on the property. A team of local residents finally excavates the well (just as the narrator in Lovecraft's "The Shunned House" digs up an equally horrible cellar in Providence). Later that night the colour shoots off into space, but Ammi Pierce swears to have seen one small piece remain behind on earth. Upon hearing Pierce's story, the narrator returns to Boston and resigns his position on the reservoir project.

14. Chiaroscuro Gone Awry

"Upon everything was a haze of restlessness and oppression; a touch of the unreal and the grotesque, as if some vital element of perspective or chiaroscuro were awry." (CS 341)

By now we have seen that Lovecraft is immune to Wilsonian charges that adjectives such as "unreal" and "grotesque" mark the height of tasteless prose. These are not the heart of the matter stylistically, but simply add seasoning by alerting us to the narrator's personal despair over events brought to life elsewhere in the passage. For here the key to the passage is obviously found in its concluding words: "...as if some vital element of perspective or chiaroscuro were awry."

Chiaroscuro, of course, is the Italian Renaissance term for the interplay of light and dark in painting. Sometimes Leonardo da Vinci is credited with inventing the technique, sometimes Antonio da Correggio.[64] In this instance Lovecraft applies the term to the play of light and shadow not in artworks, but in reality itself. Just as geometrical relationships are a basic background component of the world, never questioned in the works of Homer, Shakespeare, Cervantes, Tolstoy, or even Kafka, we also take for granted that there are certain basic features of light and shadow on our planet. These usual features can be modified by artificial tricks such as colored gels and strobe lights, and are also briefly transformed by rare natural events such as solar eclipses. But such known distortions are trivial modifications of customary light in comparison with the situation Lovecraft describes west of Arkham. So too with perspective, another term pertaining to three-dimensional illusionist painting, in which distant objects become smaller due to the decreased angle of vision by which they are perceived. To imagine a distortion in the usual conditions of chiaroscuro or perspective, to imagine them as somehow "awry," is as difficult as to picture a city in which "the geometry is all wrong," and every bit as frightening. No linguistic description can do justice to such a situation, and hence Lovecraft can do nothing more than make vertical allusion to something beyond the bounds of perception and language.

Here we should mention how difficult it would be to do justice to Lovecraft in cinematic form. In one sense, any film based on literature would be nothing better than a translation of the original. But it would obviously be far easier to make an accurate film based on Austen, Dickens, Joyce, or even Kafka, than to present plausible visual images of Lovecraft's stories. Any film would be forced to commit itself to some distinct appearance of Cthulhu, even though Lovecraft's prose lets us know how impossible this is. The "peculiarly abominable quality" of the foreign ship crew would also have to take on some definite aspect. And any film of "The Colour Out of Space" would have no choice but to roll the dice on some specific version of distorted chiaroscuro and perspective. Some cinematic efforts would be more successful than others in visually capturing the bizarre notion of "chiaroscuro and perspective gone awry," but even in the best case, the most we could do would be to applaud in amusement at the director's jolly good effort. In the strict sense, any filmed version of Lovecraft would fall short of capturing his allusiveness.

15. The Reservoir Will Soon Be Built

"The reservoir will soon be built now... and nothing could bribe me to drink the new city water of Arkham." (CS 343)

Many effects of horror in Lovecraft occur when something arises from a concealed background into the forefront of our awareness. This happens for instance when we learn of anomalies in known geometrical laws or the structure of chiaroscuro and perspective. All these basic structures of the world become poignantly visible in the moment of their breakdown, just like Heidegger's broken hammers and tardy rail networks– though more threateningly so, given their deeper generality when compared with these specific everyday entities.

What is interesting about the passage above concerning the reservoir is that it produces the *opposite* movement. The events at the Gardner farmhouse now lie far in the past, and only Ammi Pierce seems to remember all the details. But if the Gardner family tragedy is dimmed from human memory, the causes of that tragedy are reportedly still with us. Ammi claims that when the colour shot off into space at the story's end, a small piece of it remained behind. The creeping desolation near the site, which grows by a small amount each year, lends credence to Ammi's fear that a small chip of colour still lurks malignantly in the blasted heath. The Gardner horror now retreats into the background not because it has vanished from memory, but because that horror will be incorporated into the unseen municipal infrastructure of Arkham, Massachusetts, infesting the water supply of the entire town. In Heideggerian terms, the "broken tool" of the Gardner family well is about to become an invisible tool silently relied upon in everyday life. In McLuhan's terms, what was once a horrible content will now become an invisible "medium" on which the whole of Arkham humanity must rely.

16. Colour Only by Analogy

"The colour, which resembled some of the bands in the meteor's strange spectrum, was almost impossible to describe; and it was only by analogy that they called it colour at all." (CS 345)

Colour now shares the same fate as geometry, chiaroscuro, and perspective. Three paragraphs earlier, faculty members from (fictional) Miskatonic University had arrived from Arkham to take samples from the strange meteorite. Laboratory testing revealed that "upon heating before the spectroscope it displayed shining bands unlike any known colours of the normal spectrum." (CS 344) The Gardner incident occurred in the 1880's, and given that spectral patterns would later be intimate keys to the quantum theory of Bohr and his colleagues, the most advanced twentieth-century physics is here under assault, several decades prior to being formulated.

The problem is not simply that a certain kind of material yields an unusual spectrum. Instead, the resulting colour itself is impossible to assimilate into the known visible spectrum. For "it was only by analogy that they called it colour at all," which sounds more like twisted Medieval sophistry than a phenomenon directly visible to the human eye. Here we have another impossible challenge for Hollywood filmmakers, since there is no conceivable way to put "colour by analogy" on film. Lovecraft does help us come to terms with this idea by offering a few augmenting and distracting subsidiary features. The colour had a "glossy" texture. Tapping the substance gave a vague impression of "both brittleness and hollowness." When struck forcefully with a hammer, "it burst with a nervous little pop," leaving nothing behind. (CS 345-6) We are asked to imagine a colour that is not quite a colour, that is "almost impossible to describe," and which in fact is a colour only by analogy– whatever that means. Hume is not challenged here by a vague general outline over and above the qualities it unifies, but is mocked from within: "When we think of the Gardner family meteorite, we only join four consistent ideas, *glossy*, *brittle*, *hollow*, and *strange color by means of a sort of analogy*, with which we were formerly acquainted."

17. Other Realms of Entity

"…[the meteorite had been a] lone, weird message from other universes and other realms of matter, force, and entity." (CS 346)

Here we have another sentence that would fail the Wilson test for good prose, and would even be condemned as the worst sort of pulp writing. Under other circumstances, that condemnation might be justified. For instance, imagine a science fiction story that *began* with the sentence above: "The meteorite was a lone, weird message from other universes and other realms of matter, force, and entity." Indeed, this sentence sounds like a good candidate for the famous "Dark and Stormy Night" contest for the worst story openings ever written.

But of course, it is *not* the opening sentence of the story. If it were, its words would be nothing more than unearned attempts to shock the reader's sensibility into accepting "other universes" from the start. The pen would outrun the mind, and the reader would feel cheated or even insulted by this amateurish effort. Instead, the sentence occurs six pages into a twenty-nine page story, and while it might seem more appropriate as a summarizing reminiscence in the final paragraph, it works perfectly well as a summary of the substance just vanished from the university laboratory where it was tested. To say that the meteorite belonged to "other universes and other realms of matter, force, and entity" is no longer just a case of the narrator blowing smoke–not now, after the laws governing the emission of spectra have been flagrantly violated by this disturbing piece of matter; not now, after its colour is shown to be colour "only by analogy"; not now, after it has "burst with a nervous little pop" and then vanished; not now, after lightning struck the meteorite impact site no fewer than six times during a thunderstorm.

In short, Lovecraft has already *earned* our belief with his sufficiently detailed account of the laboratory experiments and the baffling results they yielded. We are fully aware of the strange properties of this peculiar substance, even if most of them elude all comprehension. Lovecraft takes this opportunity to shift our attention from this single renegade object and focus instead on the horrifying super-cosmic environment where it originally made its home. No longer just a single aberrant object that landed in Massachusetts by accident, it has now become just one typical product of "other universes and other realms of matter, force, and entity." The vastness of our universe, with all the infinite marvels of its topography, is now reduced to a speck amidst countless other possible universes, each with its own laws of matter, force, geometry, chiaroscuro, and perspective, and each with its own laws of color spectra as well.

18. Not as Characteristic as They Ought to Be

"[Nahum] was never specific [about the footprints in the snow,] but appeared to think that they were not as characteristic of the anatomy and habits of squirrels and rabbits and foxes as they ought to be." (CS 347-8)

Far from being a bad stylist, Lovecraft often makes innovations that feel like technical breakthroughs of the sort Vasari finds in various Italian artists.[65] After seeing several examples of allusions to the unspeakable, we now have what might be described as an allusion to an allusion, resulting in an especially vivid effect of horror.

We begin with a familiar Lovecraftian gesture. The footprints are not as characteristic as they ought to be. Even this initial theme is enriched by a number of nuances, perhaps three in all.

First, there is the grouping of "squirrels and rabbits and foxes." These basically harmless and picturesque countryside animals often serve as emblems of pastoral comfort. Now linked together as a unit, they seem to have undergone some process of corruption or degeneration; moreover, they seem to have done so *jointly*. This suggests that the colour corrupts not individual animals, nor even entire species, but whole groups of species that seem to function as a single kind of object: the general squirrel-rabbit-fox entity now becomes a causal partner with the colour out of space, and thereby this three-species group becomes a real thing in a manner not normally the case. Second, there is the grouping together of "anatomy and habits," a typical and effective Lovecraftian move. Normally, there is such an immediate bond between any given creature and its character-istic footprints that we would not think to divide the two. But now, by depicting a breakdown in that relationship, Lovecraft makes us aware that something is amiss in the way that the anatomy and habits of the animals is reflected in their prints. Third, there is the additional frightening vagueness of the "ought" near the end of the passage– as if conceding that the relation between anatomy/habits and footprints is not an automatically binding rule, but a generally accepted regulative principle with a certain leeway for deviation. This would be disturbing enough even in a piece of naturalistic fiction.

But what really makes the passage interesting is that all these distortions of the relation between things and their qualities is neither witnessed directly by the narrator or Ammi Pierce, nor were they reported bluntly to Pierce by Nahum Gardner. Instead, we are simply told that Nahum *"appeared to think* that they were not as characteristic of the anatomy and habits of squirrels and rabbits and foxes as they ought to be." It is difficult to know exactly how we might infer from someone's evasive reticence that they had drawn such specific conclusions about a set of animal footprints. But Lovecraft somehow makes it work, piling allusion on allusion like a creepy old neighbor constructing a second basement beneath his already mysterious existing one.

The novelty of the technique is best shown by modifying one of our earlier passages to test it. For example, imagine that the Cthulhu idol in the previous story had not been witnessed directly by the narrator, but only by Nahum Gardner. The situation would yield something like this: "Nahum was never very specific about the appearance of the idol, but appeared to think that simultaneous pictures of an octopus, a dragon, and a human caricature were not entirely unfaithful to the spirit of the thing." Both the original Cthulhu passage and this modified version deal with a breakdown in the relation between objects and their manifestations, but only the latter adds a second level of inference or allusion to the proceedings.

19. An Expression Never Seen in a Woodchuck Before

"The proportions of [the woodchuck's] body seemed slightly altered in a way impossible to describe, while its face had taken on an expression which no one ever saw in a woodchuck before." (CS 348)

Here again we have a standard Lovecraftian trick with a small added twist. The standard trick is typically effective: the proportions of an animal body have been slightly altered. This in itself could be somewhat disturbing, since every animal is associated with a certain set of bodily proportions, just as the known universe is tacitly linked with a certain geometry, and the terrestrial world with certain rules of light and shadow. Given that there is something degenerate about the woodchuck's body shape, and that this certain something is "impossible to describe," we are in the same situation as with the footprints described in the previous section.

The additional step here moves in the direction of comedy. In the first place, woodchucks are automatically amusing in a way that squirrels and rabbits and foxes are not (even the phonetic structure of the name "woodchuck" has something comical about it). Try substituting one of these other animals into the passage above, and you will immediately feel the difference in effect. For instance: "...while its face had taken on an expression which no one ever saw in a fox before." Somehow the effect here is not quite as amusing. Tame squirrels are encountered with daily regularity in the United States, and it is not difficult to look them in the eyes and get some degree of an emotional reading on them. The same is true of rabbits to a lesser extent in the wild, but as pets they are quite physically accessible, easily touched and viewed from up close. And if foxes are somewhat stealthier and more elusive, numerous illustrations, photographs, and advertisements have long created a widespread public sense of what the face of a fox ought to look like. By contrast, woodchucks are solitary and live in underground burrows. Human contact with them is somewhat rare, and their non-descript faces seem to allow little range for emotional variability. Hence, the notion that variations in woodchuck facial expres-sions might serve as a gateway to horror seems to be a deliberate comical absurdity on Lovecraft's part.

But there is another element in this passage that is mildly comic and tragic at the same time, just as Socrates demands. I refer to the portion placed in italics: "while its face had taken on an expression *which no one ever saw* in a woodchuck before." On one level, it is purely absurd to appeal to some cultural consensus as to the range of normal woodchuck facial expressions, as if group consultations had been held on the topic and a diligent mental search for precedents were being conducted. Yet there is also something a bit unnerving here, since a collective mind or stock cultural unconscious is being appealed to over and above the sum total of individual experiences. It is not just one person feeling that there is something not quite right about the woodchuck's face, but the assembly of all human experience that reaches this verdict.

20. A Diseased Underlying Primary Tone

"No wholesome colours were anywhere to be seen except in the green grass and leafage; but everywhere those hectic and prismatic variants of some diseased, underlying primary tone without a place among the known tints of the earth." (CS 350)

From the tests at Miskatonic and the remarks of observers, we already know that the color from space is color "only by analogy." Hence it is no surprise to read further that it has no place among the known tints of the earth. What is new in this passage is the way in which the undefineable-analogical color becomes a source of chromatic diversity. Here we are not strictly in the realm of the deep and the hidden. The color out of space is easily visible to the naked eye, but is simply difficult to classify as a color in the strict sense. This color-by-analogy is now described as a "diseased, underlying primary tone." The notion of an underlying primary tone found beneath numerous specific tints would not be so shocking if found in an art history text describing the works of some old master. But when referring to nature it is mildly sinister, even a bit paranoia-inducing, to think of one deviant underlying tone unifying all others in systematic fashion. Besides which, that underlying tone is said to be "diseased," no longer value-neutral as might have seemed to be true in the laboratory.

From that diseased underlying primary tone there now branch off numerous "hectic and prismatic variants," a difficult notion to analyze. The word "prismatic" suggests a degree of continuity and nuance from the gradations of the original tone, thereby placing these minute variations almost beyond the power of perception. The word "hectic" suggests a great multitude of such variants, and an excessive energy in the way they are juxtaposed with one another in nature. But for the most part, the phrase "hectic and prismatic variants" also seems chosen precisely because it is unthinkable. After all, we would ruin the phrase if we literalized it as "numerous and continuous variations."

The other ingredient in the passage is found at the beginning: "No wholesome colours were anywhere to be seen except in the green grass and leafage..." Amidst general decay brought about by the diseased underlying primary tone of the colour from space, the grass and leafage in the area remains (for now) a fortress of chromatic sanity. Nature remains healthy, and this allows its diseased surroundings to appear even more degenerate by contrast.

21. Blasphemous-Looking Flowers

"The asters and goldenrod bloomed grey and distorted, and the roses and zinneas and hollyhocks in the front yard were such blasphemous-looking things that Nahum's eldest boy Zenas cut them down." (CS 352)

In this passage the effects of the colour from space are differentiated, by showing how it has different effects in specific types of flower. Unlike squirrels and rabbits and foxes, the flowers in the passage are divided into two groups, no matter how faint the difference seems to be. Nor does the narrator merely tells us that "some of the flowers were affected in one way, others in an even worse way," as might have been good enough to do the job. Instead, he speaks like a good amateur horticulturist. First, the asters and goldenrod "bloomed grey and distorted." The greyness is disturbing enough, since in their healthy state both of these flowers are unusually bright in their hues. As to the way in which they might be "distorted," we are not educated further, giving us a classic Lovecraftian vertical rift between some underlying reality and the incapacity of language to express it adequately.

Yet an even worse fate is reserved for the roses and zinneas and hollyhocks. These equally bright flowers did not merely bloom grey and distorted, but were "such blasphemous-looking things" that young Zenas felt moved to cut them down. Whatever inner fortitude the asters and goldenrods possessed that preserved them from an outright state of "blasphemy," the roses, zinneas, and hollyhocks were weak enough to succumb to the blasphemous forces. Here once again, Wilson would be wrong to find fault with use of the word "blasphemous." In psychological terms it vividly expresses the mental state of those who reacted to the sight of them, and in referential terms it succeeds in letting us know that the blasphemy in question cannot be expressed in an easily discernible list of qualities that might be communicated to us.

But the most interesting feature of this passage is the apparently arbitrary line it draws between two separate categories of flowers. We are left guessing what hidden structural properties might save asters and goldenrod from the worst of all floral destinies. Their fate is terrible enough, yet it might be called the "merest fringe" of bad possibilities for flowers, as we soon learn when Zenas cuts down the other three "blasphemous" ones. Here a hierarchy of disease is established, quite different from the democracy of chaos found in one of our earlier examples: "...items from India speak guardedly of serious native unrest toward the end of March. Voodoo orgies multiply in Haiti, and African outposts report ominous mutterings. American officers in the Philippines find certain tribes bothersome about this time, and New York policemen are mobbed by hysterical Levantines on the night of March 22-23." (CC 174) To rewrite this passage in the manner of the current one about flowers, we would have to do something like this: "There were reports of serious unrest and ominous mutterings in India, Haiti, and Africa, while events in the Philippines were so blasphemous that military action was required." Instead of doing this, the original passage on India, Haiti, Africa, the Philippines, and hysterical Levantines adopts a "flat ontology" in which all the manifestations of cosmic disorder seem to have roughly equal status.

22. An Inane Titter or Whisper

"Thaddeus went mad in September after a visit to the well. He had gone with a pail and had come back empty-handed, shrieking and waving his arms, and sometimes lapsing into an inane titter or whisper about 'the moving colours down there'." (CS 353)

Another classic Lovecraftian technique is to use the word "or" in order to treat two divergent realities as though they were familiar next-door neighbors in the continuum of being. We are accustomed to being asked if we prefer coffee or tea, apples or oranges, Democrats or Republicans, blondes or brunettes. But if we ask someone to choose between completely unrelated realities then we have entered the realm of surrealist comedy, as when my brother once jokingly asked: "Do you prefer peanut brittle, or Mr. Spock?" More troubling are the intermediate cases, where there is disjunction between two terms not comically unrelated, but far enough apart that we are forced to imagine an intermediate zone between the two. In this way, a kind of metaphor is created as a byproduct.

So it is when we are told that Thaddeus returns from the well, sometimes lapsing into a "titter or whisper." A titter is a nervous obstructed laugh, and is generally both shrill and nervewracking. A whisper is something quite the opposite in both respects. Thus, it is difficult to imagine a voice fluctuating indeterminately between a titter and a whisper, and even more difficult to conceive of a voice lying halfway between those two registers. Such a voice would be inherently monstrous, and when the narrator calls the voice "inane," this merely adds tension by expressing the negative reaction any observer would have to Thaddeus's new voice, without this inanity detracting in any way from the horror of it. This conjunction of loosely related cousins by use of the word "or" is so important in Lovecraft's toolbox that it ranks among the key ingredients of any would-be

Lovecraft parody. There could even be a party game called Invent a Lovecraftian Disjunction: "a thumping or scraping noise," "there was something vaguely frosty or humid about the air in the cellar," "the voice had a moaning or proselytizing tone," "the ground seemed to sink or waver."

As for the content of Thaddeus's report, Lovecraft often uses fragile sanity in his characters as an alibi for speaking in vague, clipped phrases about unutterable horrors. The phrase "the moving colours down there" would be a fine example of this technique. The very best example of this is probably Danforth's raving in "At the Mountains of Madness" about what he witnessed in Antarctica, and refuses to share with Professor Dyer when asked:

> He has on rare occasions whispered disjointed and irrespon-sible things about 'the black pit,' 'the carven rim,' 'the proto-shoggoths,' 'the windowless solids with five dimensions,' 'the nameless cylinder,' 'the elder pharos,' 'Yog-Sothoth,' 'the primal white jelly,' 'the colour out of space,' 'the wings,' 'the eyes in darkness,' 'the moon-ladder,' 'the original, the eternal, the undying,' and other bizarre conceptions... (MM 586)

Here just as with the "inane" titter or whisper of Thaddeus, the narrator takes a distance from what he reports (with the phrase "and other bizarre conceptions") while allowing us as readers to draw more radical conclusions. In cases where insanity is unavailable, rustic backwardness can be used to justify the needed clipped phrasing: "The common name applied to [the monsters] was 'those ones,' or 'the old ones,' though other terms had a local and transient use." (WD 418-9)

23. Uncannily Shrivelled or Compressed

"Then something struck the cows. Certain areas or sometimes the whole body would be uncannily shrivelled or compressed, and atrocious collapses or disintegrations were common." (CS 353)

This passage combines at least three Lovecraftian techniques already familiar to us. First, there are the sorts of disjunctions found in the previous section: "shriveled or compressed," "collapses or disintegrations" (à la "titter or whisper"). Second, there are the anti-Wilsonian adjectives before each disjunction, which serve as spices to emphasize the emotional state of those confronting them: "uncannily," "atrocious" (à la "*inane* titter or whisper"). Third, there is the deliberate choice of cows, which rank among the most banal of domestic animals. Cattle will face an even more terrible fate in "The Dunwich Horror," but here their role, like that of squirrels and their counterparts, is to emphasize the spread of horror over increasingly greater areas of the previously comfortable local environment, while further differentiating the cosmic disease by showing that it also has specific cow-symptoms to go with its woodchuck- and goldenrod-symptoms. The color spreads its malign influence, yet must always adapt to the local conditions of the host it infects. Like a classically trained musician, Lovecraft repeats his favorite motifs, but always with suitable variations and modifications breathing new life into the theme.

There remains the particular character of the disjunctions in the passage, which are especially well-chosen. "Uncannily shrivelled or compressed" surely does not mean that in some cases there was shriveling and in other cases compression. Although I have called these passages "disjunctions," that is true only in the grammatical sense. The two terms of a Lovecraftian disjunction never offer a choice between one or the other, but reveal both choices to be completely inadequate expressions of a single phenomenon. What the cows undergo is neither shriveling nor compression, but something found in a painful no-man's-land between the two, just as foreign to normal experience as the colour that does not belong among the known tints of the earth. As for "collapses or disintegrations," these might seem more closely akin. But when referring to the death of an organic being, both are so equally terrible that the effect is of two neighboring but distinct explosions. Nothing refutes Wilson's antipathy to emphastic adjectives better than this case. Imagine that the passage had simply said: "Certain areas or sometimes the whole body would be uncannily shrivelled or compressed, and collapses or disintegrations were common." All that has changed is the removal of the word "atrocious" before "collapses and disintegrations." There is now an imbalance; the final phrase after the comma suddenly feels too cold and clinical. We see animals die in a variety of ways on this planet, but never through collapse or disintegration. The only way the sentence can be made believable is by the narrator expressing his own disgust and shock at this means of death, which is indeed "atrocious."

24. A Fiendish and Unclean Suction

"Halted by some vague fear, he heard further sounds below. Indubitably there was a sort of heavy dragging, and a most detestably sticky noise as of some fiendish and unclean species of suction." (CS 357)

This is the scene where Ammi has just found Mrs. Gardner collapsing or shriveling or disintegrating in the attic. A clear hint is given that Ammi finished her off in a mercy killing: "There are things which cannot be mentioned, and what is done in common humanity is sometimes cruelly judged by the law," (CS 357) continuing the theme of moral obligation as irreducible to bundles of rules, just as in Johansen's belief that massacring the foreign ship crew was in some sense a duty. Descending the stairs, Ammi has the experience described in the passage above. The reader easily guesses that the heavily dragging object is Nahum, victim of the same fate as his feebleminded wife.

It took someone of Lovecraft's allusive talents to invent the description of a death so horrid despite being so deliberately lacking in detail. The drowning of witches, the burning of heretics, the impaling of Turks in Transylvania, the screams of cutpurses broken on the wheel in central Paris– all these scenes are easily outstripped by the barely intelligible death of Nahum Gardner. Along with the sticky noise there is the sound of "a feeble scratching on the floor." Nahum is now described almost as an inanimate object: "the death had been at it," perhaps the only time this bizarre phrase has occurred in the English language. Although nothing was visibly wrong with him half an hour earlier, "collapse, graying, and disintegration were already far advanced. There was a horrible brittleness, and dry fragments were scaling off." (CS 358) There follows a sort of conversation with this semi-animate Nahum, until finally Nahum is no more "because it [sic] had completely caved in." (CS 359) Collapse and disintegration, a brittleness leading to the scaling off of dry fragments, an eventual cave-in of the body: unusual means of death indeed, but Lovecraft has done enough work to earn our belief in them.

The most interesting part of the passage above is surely the concluding portion: "a most detestably sticky noise as of some fiendish and unclean species of suction." We already know that the adjective "detestably" escapes Wilsonian charges of excess, since it is merely the narrator's inevitable humane commentary on a horror earned elsewhere in the passage. So far we have spoken of Lovecraftian disjunctions using the word "or." We might wonder whether conjunctions with "and" have a similar effect, piling up two adjectives and demanding that the reader grope towards something lying midway between them. It is a worthy question, but not one that needs to be answered here. In the phrase "fiendish and unclean," "fiendish" simply doubles the work performed by "detestably": it is meta-commentary by the narrator to reassure us that he knows as well as we do how horrible this all sounds. That leaves the stripped-down nucleus of the passage, "unclean species of suction." At times like these, vulgar wiseacres always like to counter with phrases of the following sort: "as opposed to a *clean* species of suction?" In the present context, the answer is yes. That is exactly the work of the passage: to call our attention to the perfectly clean and natural character of most suction noises, which are now sadly tainted and rendered dubious by some horrid but indescribable undertone in the sound.

25. The Rural Tales are Queer

"The rural tales are queer. They might be even queerer if city men and college chemists could be interested enough to analyse the water from that disused well, or the grey dust that no wind ever seems to disperse. Botanists, too, ought to study the stunted flora on the borders of that spot..." (CS 367)

Oddly enough, we learn here that the queerness of the rural tales would be *increased* if chemists and botanists would do research in the area, flouting the usual principle that scientists are called in to *eliminate* rumor and superstition. Here we get a faint foretaste of something that becomes even more vivid as we progress through the great tales of Lovecraft. The usual opposition is between enlightened modernism and anti-modern obscurantism. Either the scientist dismisses the gullible fetishes of witch doctors and theosophists, or these mystics dismiss science as having access to nothing but a shallow version of a more terrible cosmic truth. Despite Lovecraft's alleged materialism (and he is certainly a materialist in part), his attitude to the problem is quite different. For Lovecraft, cult rituals and the scrawlings of Medieval Arab wizards stand in a perfect continuum of knowledge with the most advanced modern science.

It is generally true in Lovecraft's stories that the most advanced knowledge of cosmic truth belongs not to scientists, but to those who gain insight from direct contact with the more monstrous beings that fill his writings. An average middle-aged woman from early colonial New England becomes a cosmo-logical genius able to travel through non-Euclidean space. Degenerate crews of sailors gain insight into ultimate matters that initially escape even the leading scholars at Miskatonic University. In "The Whisperer in Darkness," Wilmarth the folklorist turns out to be more ignorant than the rustic tale-tellers he initially mocks. National media outlets write satires and parodies on supposedly fictitious alien attacks in villages, yet these incidents turn out to be perfectly genuine. The passage at the top of this section is one of the few where scientists are treated as more enlightened and trustworthy seekers of the same knowledge presented, in germ, in wild popular rumor. For the most part, Lovecraft has the scientists rushing to catch up with the occult devotees and the decadent sculptors.

The Dunwich Horror

This story was written in August 1928, and sold to *Weird Tales* for a mere $240, though at the time this was Lovecraft's most lucrative sale. Set in the fictional town of Dunwich, Massachusetts, it is one of the two great tales ("The Dreams in the Witch House" is the other) to be told by an omniscient third-person narrator rather than in the usual Poe-like first person. The tale begins with two of the finest pages of scene-setting prose ever written by Lovecraft– or anyone else. There follows a report that the disturbing albino Lavinia Whateley gave birth to a child of unknown paternity, in a local culture haunted by biological decay. Only later do we learn that there are in fact two children. The known child is the grotesque Wilbur, fearsomely ugly but intellectually and physically precocious. As Wilbur comes of age, he seeks access to the dreaded *Necronomicon* in the libraries of Miskatonic and Harvard, arousing the suspicion of academics in those places. Wilbur is eventually killed by a guard dog at Miskatonic while breaking into the library one night, with his corpse undergoing grisly disintegration in the presence of three faculty eyewitnesses. At about the same time his previously unknown brother, an invisible giant immeasurably more monstrous than Wilbur, emerges from the house to destroy a number of scattered farmhouses near Dunwich. The three Miskatonic faculty members eventually succeed in killing this brother on a nearby mountaintop, thereby saving the earth from being cleared off for the use of alien monsters.

The Lovecraft specialist S.T. Joshi expresses reservations about the story,[66] mostly because he thinks Lovecraft departs here from his usual "amoral" approach to the cosmos, in favor of a Christian model of the Whateley brothers as evil stellar beings fought by good humans. And certainly we must admit the Christian symbolism of the story: from the "immaculate conception" of Lavinia to the monster calling out for his father while dying high above the crowd. But these elements are clearly nothing more than grotesque parody, and do not constitute a true deviation from the amoral cosmos found in Lovecraft's other stories. My own objections stem rather from the comic book aspects of the hero Dr. Armitage, and the absurd ritualistic means by which the monster is finally slain. Otherwise, "The Dunwich Horror" is a riveting story wonderfully told, and one that is launched with the finest opening pages found anywhere in the stories.

26. Gnarled, Solitary Figures

"Without knowing why, one hesitates to ask directions from the gnarled, solitary figures spied now and then on crumbling doorsteps or on the sloping, rock-strewn meadows. Those figures are so silent and furtive that one feels somehow confronted by forbidden things, with which it would be better to have nothing to do." (DH 370)

This comes from the brilliant two-page opening of the story. Unlike many such passages in Lovecraft, it is purely atmospheric: there is no indication that any of these "gnarled, solitary figures" in the central Massachusetts countryside are in league with other-worldly beings– much less that they are actual hybrids having such beings for parents, as will turn out to be the case in Innsmouth. Nonetheless, the passage does suggest that something is deeply amiss with the region that might make it a suitable home for the horror we will soon see inflicted upon Dunwich.

"Without knowing why, one hesitates to ask directions…" The asking of directions is not always the first thing on the traveler's agenda, but Lovecraft has already made clear that one ends up in this area only by taking "the wrong fork" in the road. Directions are therefore needed, but one hesitates to ask these mysterious figures. Much like "the spirit of the thing" and "the general outline of the whole" lying behind the specific zoological properties of the Cthulhu idol, these elusive figures are known to be ominous not through some list of tangible qualities, but through some sort of grasp of their reality deeper than all surface qualities. But we have already covered the topic elsewhere. The key to this particular passage is as follows. Elusive malevolence is normally evoked by Lovecraft only in connection with specific monsters or idols or loathsome individuals or groups thereof. But here, an entire portion of Massachusetts seems imbued with sinister atmosphere, despite its merely peripheral connection with events that were centered in Dunwich alone. It is Lovecraft's first foray into "weird geography," "weird anthropology," or "weird sociology." But it will hardly be his last.

27. Almost Unnameable Violence and Perversity

"They have come to form a race by themselves, with the well-defined mental and physical stigmata of degeneracy and inbreeding. The average of their intelligence is woefully low, whilst their annals reek of overt viciousness and of half-hidden murders, incests, and deeds of almost unnameable violence and perversity." (DH 372)

Here the anthropological theme continues, and it will form one of the major background conditions of the story. In the decayed port of Innsmouth, biological degeneracy results from the grisly mating of humans and undersea creatures already marred by degeneracy in their own right, being neither fish nor frog. Here in Dunwich, however, the responsibility for the intellectual and physical degeneracy of the populace seems to be purely human; moreover, all of the inappropriate mating seems to have taken place entirely within Caucasian family trees. Lovecraft adds relief and drama to this appalling local decay by refusing to paint with too broad a brush. We learn that not *everyone* in Dunwich is reduced to inbred stupidity. After all, "some of the Whateleys and Bishops still send their eldest sons to Harvard and Miskatonic," and more generally, "the old gentry... have kept somewhat above the general level of decay." Yet such faint praise is overwhelmed by critique, since "many of the branches are sunk into the sordid populace so deeply that only their names remain as a key to the origin they disgrace." (DH 372) In addition to providing a sinister atmosphere for the story, such words also have a comic effect similar to that of the digressive rant about bad Providence architecture in "The Call of Cthulhu." In a story devoted to threats against earth-life from abysmal unknown creatures, our third-person narrator takes the time to engage in social snobbery and haughty diatribes about biological fitness. But while such harangues in Lovecraft usually have racist overtones, the history here has nothing to do with miscegenation, only with inbreeding and flat-out incest.

Also comical here is the reference to "the well-defined mental and physical stigmata of degeneracy and inbreeding," as though these were generally known to any educated person and require no explanation. Positing the non-obvious as the obvious is another frequent trick from Lovecraft's toolbox, found often in other contexts as well. Once again this device shifts our attention to the narrator himself, so deeply enmeshed in overwrought biological prejudices that most of us never take seriously. How the town annals might "reek of overt viciousness" is also unclear, but the narrator makes himself comical here as well, despite the sinister nature of the subject he describes. The murders and incests are "half-hidden," and other accompanying deeds are of a violence and perversity "almost unnameable." Given the risk that simple terms of inaccessibility such as "hidden" and "unnameable" might veer into clichés, Lovecraft senses that some qualification is needed. By calling them merely *half*-hidden and *almost* unnameable, the reader is given a partial handhold on these semi-concealed atrocities, which thereby seem to come closer to us despite the fact that no examples are given.

28. The Internal Organs of Sound-Production

"The strangeness [of the boy's speech] did not reside in what he said, or even in the simple idioms he used; but seemed vaguely linked with his intonation or with the internal organs that produced the spoken sounds." (DH 377)

Fresh ground is broken in the tales with the character of young Wilbur Whateley. In the story of Cthulhu, all the ostensible humans are actually human and we never have reason for physiological suspicion. While the various sailors in "The Call of Cthulhu" are subjected to racial and ethnic slurs, they are unmistakably human, no matter how low on the totem pole the narrator places them in social and genetic terms. In "The Colour Out of Space," the Gardner family is weakened and destroyed by the color in the well, but they too are absolutely human. With Wilbur Whateley, by contrast, we have the soon-to-be-classic Lovecraftian theme of a being who pretends to be human while concealing a much darker identity. In Lovecraft's tales the *voice* is often the first sign that something is amiss in a character's claim to humanity. As Houellebecq humorously puts it: "when a character sitting across from you places his hands on the table and emits a weak sucking noise, or when in another character's laugh you discern the nuance of a *cackle*, or bizarre insect stridulation, you know you are inside a Lovecraftian story."[67]

Other elements of the passage are classically Lovecraftian as well. The strangeness of Wilbur's speech "seems vaguely linked" with certain features, rather than being directly identifiable with them. In everyday life we encounter a range of intonations in the human voice, and rarely or never do these variable tones strike us as inhuman. Nor is there usually reason to question the means by which the voice is produced: as far as we know it is always a matter of lungs, larynx, tongue, and lips, except in those rare and obvious cases where drastic surgery forces the use of electronic aids. In Wilbur Whateley's case, however, something seems vaguely wrong with the intonation, and there must also be something strange in the timbre of his voice that suggests speech produced by organs other than those of human communication. In keeping with the basic theme of objects separated from their qualities, Wilbur's voice becomes a strange autonomous entity no longer identifiable with its equally strange surface intonation, and this leads to an implicit rupture between that voice and its antecedent physical basis.

29. The Sound Carpentry of a Demented Babbler

"There must have been prodigious reserves of strength in the old man to enable him to accomplish so much hard labour; and though he still babbled dementedly at times, his carpentry seemed to shew the effect of sound calculation." (DH 377)

It is typical of Lovecraft that he likes to position the reader to draw conclusions outstripping those of the narrator himself. Rather than simply telling us that something weird is going on, which would always give us the chance to disagree, Lovecraft has a talent for maneuvering us into becoming the very advocates of the weird, even as his own narrators retain a rationalist and skeptical posture. We often feel ourselves wanting to shout at the narrator and urge him to see what lies directly before his eyes. In the present case, given the advanced age of Old Whateley, we are stunned by the way in which the narrator unthinkingly ascribes "prodigious reserves of strength" to explain the vast amounts of work done on his property, especially given the widespread rumors that he practices wizardry. The narrator also seems to think nothing of the bizarre contrast between Whateley's demented babbling and the "effect of sound calculation" witnessed in his carpentry. For our own part, we as readers come to the obvious conclusion that Old Whately is receiving unseen assistance. The context makes it fairly clear that this assistance cannot possibly be human, given the isolated nature of the property and the fact that we seem to have a good sense of all the personae inhabiting the neighborhood. As a result, the narrator occupies a gullible or even comical stance while we the readers rush to draw much wilder conclusions, which nonetheless turn out to be more rational under the circumstances.

This frequent trick of Lovecraft seems to be derived from a hilarious passage of Poe's tale "The Black Cat." Having viciously hanged his beloved pet, the alcoholic narrator awakens to find his house on fire. Returning to the ruins the next day, he finds that the wall bears the image of a cat with a rope around its neck. At first, he is terrified by the sight:

> But at length reflection came to my aid. The cat, I remembered, had been hung in a garden adjacent to the house. Upon the alarm of the fire, this garden had been immediately filled by the crowd– by some one of whom the animal must have been cut from the tree and thrown, through an open window, into my chamber. This had probably been done with a view to arousing me from sleep. The falling of other walls had compressed the victim of my cruelty into the substance of the freshly spread plaster; the lime of which, with the flames, and the *ammonia* from the carcass, had then accomplished the portraiture as I saw it.[68]

No reader will accept this preposterous physical explanation, especially since the opening sentence is patently absurd ("But at length reflection came to my aid..."). In this way, we the readers are immediately positioned as greater believers in the supernatural than the narrator himself.

In fact, the easiest way to ruin the Lovecraft passage above is to have the narrator do our thinking for us. Imagine rewriting the passage as follows: "He seemed to have accomplished a surprising amount of hard labour for such an old man. And the carpentry seemed impossibly sound for someone still given to occasional demented babbling. Thus, I could only conclude that Old Whateley had not done the work himself. And given that there was no obvious human aid available in the vicinity, the only alternative was monstrous or supernatural assistance. I shuddered at the thought, but the conclusion was inescapable." This is a total failure of rhetoric, spelling something out in explicit terms that is best left for readers to gather for themselves. It is the rough equivalent of ruining a joke or magic trick by simultaneously explaining it to one's audience, or of destroying a love letter by converting all innuendo into explicit requests for favors.

30. Rhythmical Surging or Lapping

"The shapeless albino daughter and oddly bearded grandson stood by the bedside, whilst from the vacant abyss overhead there came a disquieting suggestion of rhythmical surging or lapping, as of the waves on some level beach." (DH 381)

We begin with the classic Lovecraftian disjunction in this passage: "rhythmical surging or lapping." The distance between surging and lapping is arguably less than that between titters and whispers, yet the gap remains great enough that the reader has a queasy feeling when trying to aim for a point midway between the two. The fruitless additional clarification, "as of the waves on some level beach," simply makes the surging or lapping even more grotesque: rather than leading us to identify the unknown thing upstairs with the ocean, it works in reverse, poisoning our faith in the ocean by linking it with monstrous things.

Furthermore, all of this is combined with a second Lovecraftian trick. What is heard from overhead is not directly a rhythmical surging or lapping, which would be disturbing enough. Instead, there is *"a disquieting suggestion* of rhythmical surging or lapping." We can only vaguely *hint* at the literal description, which is barely intelligible even when we reach it. We again have an allusion to an allusion– as if a second black hole were discovered at the core of a first one. The word "disquieting" creates a minimal problem here, since something can only be disquieting *for someone,* and third-person omniscient narrators generally do not take an emotional stand on what they observe. Nor is it conceivable that either Wilbur or even Lavinia Whateley would be "disquieted" by the sound in the overhead space. For this purpose, we are relieved to find that "Dr. Houghton of Aylesbury" is on the scene in a failed attempt to save Old Whateley's life, and surely it was he who gave such disquieting reports about the deathbed scene.

So far we have said nothing about "the vacant abyss overhead." In addition to the innate difficulty of imagining a sound that would resemble "surging or lapping," there is the additional fact that watery sounds of any sort have no natural place in the area above the downstairs room. What we already know about the space upstairs is far from reassuring. It is "lined with tall, firm shelving" (DH 378) where various forbidden books are carefully arranged. Observers of the upper floor "wondered why one of the upper windows had been made into a solid plank door... and no one could imagine why a cleated wooden runway was built from it up to the ground." (DH 378) The rare visitors to the house hear "odd sounds and footsteps" upstairs, including a fish-peddler who "thought he heard a horse stamping upstairs." (DH 379) The suggestion that the upper room houses cattle or horses, or some other animal capable of using "a cleated runway," forms a disturbing contrast with the rhythmical surging and lapping, so reminiscent of beaches.

Finally, a brief word is in order about the opening of the passage, with its reference to "the shapeless albino daughter and oddly bearded grandson." The effect of this is best discovered by simplifying it and witnessing the result. If we say merely "the albino daughter and bearded grandson," this sounds like a lurid line from Georg Trakl or some other expressionist poet of the Great War era. But expanding the first part into "*shapeless* albino daughter" not only gives an additional piece of information about Lavinia's appearance, it also shields the unnerving word "albino" from the wind, treating it as real by making it a rock upon which variable modifying adjectives might be placed. This remains necessary even though her albinism was asserted quite early in the story. As for "oddly bearded grandson," the effect is twofold. The word "oddly" both reminds us of Wilbur's young age and terribly precocious development, and once again positions the reaction of the narrator (or rather, of Dr. Houghton of Aylesbury) to make the description more believable– what is asserted is not only that young Wilbur had a beard, but that this fact had a rather disturbing effect on those who witnessed it.

31. The Mad Arab Abdul Alhazred

"…the dreaded volume kept under lock and key at the college library– the hideous *Necronomicon* of the mad Arab Abdul Alhazred in Olaus Wormius' Latin version, as printed in Spain in the seventeenth century." (DH 384)

The young Lovecraft had a taste for the exotic, and was fascinated quite early in life with the stories of *The Arabian Nights*. Already at the age of five, he adopted the name "Abdul Alhazred" as an alias, and later indulged this childhood name by making it one of the pillars of his adult mythos. This requires a suspension of linguistic disbelief, since "Abdul Alhazred" is simply ungrammatical Arabic. The "-ul" of "Abdul" and the "Al" of "Alhazred" are one and the same definite article, and should not be repeated as they were by Lovecraft; the name should simply be either "Abdul Hazred" or "Abd Alhazred." Another linguistic mistake is found in Lovecraft's frequently repeated fictional book title of von Junzt, *Unaussprechlichen Kulten* (borrowed by Lovecraft from Conan author Robert E. Howard). The title is in the dative case but lacks an appropriate preposition, and should be edited either to *Unaussprechliche Kulten* or *Von Unaussprechlichen Kulten*. But readers will easily forgive these small missteps.

In order to make his creatures more believable, Lovecraft tries to establish that they are not just unlucky emergences of the 1920's, but have long been known to humans through cryptic traditions, ancient lore, and forbidden books. Since no actual book ever produced by humankind is terrifying enough to do the trick, it is necessary to invent one. Hence the *Necronomicon*, sufficiently convincing as a fabrication that real librarians around the world often report requests for the book even today. Merely to assert the existence of such a book would border on an arbitrary pulp stunt, and thus Lovecraft tries to secure legitimacy for it through a variety of means. One is to remind us continually that copies exist in various libraries. Since Miskatonic University is fictitious, this institution is not quite enough to do the job, and thus Lovecraft assures us (falsely) that Harvard's real-life Widener Library also has a heavily guarded copy. All of the Miskatonic faculty members and graduate students we meet in the tales seem no less acquainted with the *Necronomicon* than they might be with Thucydides or Plutarch. Lovecraft also adopts a "strength in numbers" approach by regularly smuggling the *Necromicon* into his stories amidst an army of fictional peer volumes, as in this passage from "The Haunter of the Dark":

> He had himself read many of [the old books]– a Latin version of the abhorred *Necronomicon*, the sinister *Liber Ivonis*, the infamous *Cultes des Goules* of Comte d'Erlette, the *Unaussprechlichen Kulten* of von Junzt, and old Ludvig Prinn's hellish *De Vermis Mysteriis*... the Pnakotic Manuscripts, the *Book of Dyzan*, and a crumbling volume in wholly unidenti-

fiable characters yet shudderingly reognisable to the occult student. (HD 792)

The *Necromicon* is also made more real by referring to the existence of translations: "Olaus Wormius' Latin version, as printed in Spain in the seventeenth century." Instead of being merely asserted, the book is thereby shown to have affected a wide range of historical actors, thereby soliciting further belief from the reader. With its reality quasi-established even further thanks to repeated references by Lovecraft and his circle of authorial friends, the *Necronomicon* appears again and again as a historical and intellectual anchor in his tales. It contains descriptions of the Old Ones and instructions for summoning them, assembled by the mad Arab of Yemen who worshipped blasphemous deities, explored various subterranean cities in the Arab lands, and eventually died in Damascus early in the eighth century under worse-than-mysterious circumstances.

32. A Grotesque Trip to Harvard

"He had heard, meanwhile, of Whateley's grotesque trip to Cambridge, and of his frantic efforts to borrow or copy from *Necronomicon* at the Widener Library." (DH 387)

Having already spent seventeen pages as a central personage in the story, the monstrous Wilbur looms large as we move towards the climax. He is a fictional character, seeking an evil fictional book at fictional Miskatonic University, and his strangeness dominates the fictional town of Dunwich. Wilbur will now gain added reality by crossing over into the co-ordinates of our everyday world, as if the bones of J.R.R. Tolkien's elves and hobbits were one day found in crypts beneath Stonehenge. Having been denied the opportunity to borrow the *Necronomicon* from the Miskatonic Library, Wilbur replies: "Wal, all right, ef ye feel that way abaout it. Maybe Harvard wun't be so fussy as you." (DH 386) Young Wilbur certainly must have turned heads in Cambridge, Massachusetts upon arrival, since he is described as "almost eight feet tall, and carrying a cheap new valise from Osborn's general store... [a] dark and goatish gargoyle." (DH 384)

Now, let's remove the word "grotesque" from the passage (as Edmund Wilson might prefer), and see what happens: "He had heard, meanwhile, of Whateley's trip to Cambridge, and of his frantic efforts to borrow or copy from *Necronomicon* at the Widener Library." While this might seem to work reasonably well, the mere assertion of an eight-foot cretin strolling blithely onto the Harvard campus has something a bit pulpish about it. It seems unlikely that such a visit could occur without disruptively negative consequences from the environing populace. By adding the word "grotesque," the narrator is making a helpful concession to our disbelief, as if to say: "Yes, I realize how absurd this sounds, but Wilbur actually did follow through on his threat to travel to Harvard." Of Armitage we learn only that "he had heard" of Wilbur's trip to Cambridge, a comical abbreviation of what must have been lengthy and terrified gossip about the visit. All we learn of the details of the incident at Harvard, whose librarians had been warned in advance by Armitage, is that "Wilbur had been shockingly nervous at Cambridge; anxious for the book, yet almost equally anxious to get home again, as if he feared the results of being away too long." (DH 387-8)

We have seen that the mixing of the fictitious and the real is a stock Lovecraftian technique, one that adds bulk and credibility to his stories. The squatters near the Cthulhu orgy are called descendants of Lafitte's men. The narrators in "The Colour Out of Space" and "The Shadow Over Innsmouth" both repair to Boston after their ordeals in fictional towns, and the latter then returns for his senior year at the eminently real Oberlin College. In "The Case of Charles Dexter Ward," Joseph Curwen keeps his copy of "the forbidden *Necronomicon*" alongside real books such as

"Hermes Trismegistus in Menard's edition," and works of Albertus Magnus, Raymond Lully, Roger Bacon, and "mediaeval Jews and Arabs... in profusion." (CW 225)

33. Trite and Not Wholly Accurate

"It would be trite and not wholly accurate to say that no human pen could describe it, but one may properly say that it could not be vividly visualized by anyone whose ideas of aspect and contour are too closely bound up with the common life-forms of this planet and of the three known dimensions." (DH 389)

This is one of the greatest and most important of all Lovecraft passages. Since it was already analyzed in Part One, we can cover it briefly here. What is described in this passage is the dead body of Wilbur after he is killed by the guard dog that had always hated him. No longer shielded by clothing, the body is repulsive in its strangeness. A total ruination of the passage could be achieved by replacing this entire passage with: "No human pen could describe it." This would not only be a bland literary cliché, it would also give us no guidance or allusion as to the specific *manner* in which the corpse resists description. Instead, Lovecraft holds the cliché at a distance by calling it trite and not wholly accurate, while lingering as close to the edge of indescribability as possible. The closing portion of the passage is delightfully ludicrous: "it could not be vividly visualized by anyone whose ideas of aspect and contour are too closely bound up with the common life-forms of this planet and of the three known dimensions." Oh, if only my ideas of aspect and contour were not so closely bound up with common life-forms and the known three dimensions!

Following this "vertical" allusion to an unspeakable "general outline" of the body, Lovecraft turns to his second and horizontal technique, so cubist or Husserlian in flavor, by multiplying an absurd number of concrete features that are nearly impossible to unify into a single entity: "the back was piebald with yellow and black, and dimly suggested the squamous covering of certain snakes"; "from the abdomen a score of longish green-grey tentacles with red sucking mouths protruded limply. Their arrangement was odd, and seemed to follow the symmetries of some cosmic geometry unknown to the earth or solar system"; "the limbs... terminated in ridgy-veined pads that were neither hoofs nor claws"; "its tail and tentacles rhythmically changed colour, as if from some circulatory cause normal to the non-human side of its ancestry". While not exactly beyond the power of vision, the sheer massing of such images overwhelms the reader's imagination, and a patient artist indeed would be required to depict such a body with even the remotest degree of accuracy.

34. Adjudged a Sort of Diary

"An almost interminable manuscript in strange characters, written in a huge ledger and adjudged a sort of diary because of the spacing and the variations in ink and penmanship, presented a baffling puzzle..." (DH 391-2)

After his death, it is found that Wilbur's home is filled with numerous strange books, including the one described above. In a wonderful irony, all are sent to the very place where Wilbur was killed by the guard dog: the Miskatonic University Library. The long, strange book described in the passage, filled with myste-rious characters adds additional atmosphere to the story. But the really interesting part of this passage is: "adjudged a sort of diary because of the spacing and the variations in ink and penmanship." It is not surprising to think that each genre of personal writing has certain distinctive features that give external clues as to its nature. Normally this is not even an issue, since most handwritten documents are not written in code, so that the content of the document in question lets us know what it is. Yet given that its transferral into code makes the content seem highly foreign (though the document later turns out to be written in English) we are forced to rely on certain formal properties of the document in determining what it is. If we simply read a historical diary in straightforward fashion, we may not be consciously aware of any particular traits of spacing or "variations in ink and penmanship," but the scholars at Miskatonic seem unnaturally alert to such subtle clues.

We thus return to Lovecraft's primary stylistic theme: the separation of an object from its qualities. The usual easy link between a diary and its outward qualities is disrupted, since the linguistic content is shielded from view by the use of code while the more purely physical features of the diary remain visible. The diary-content vanishes behind the inscrutable code that shields it, yet it leaves behind a specific type of spacing and particular variations in ink and penmanship, all of these traits imbued with the flavor of an underlying diary-object. There is even something a bit disturbing about this passage, though ostensibly it only reports the conclusions of a team of scholars. But we might imagine a similar passage referring to a voice heard in the night speaking in a foreign tongue: "An almost interminable speech in a foreign language could be heard from the fog below, adjudged a sort of promise because of certain undertones in the voice and due to the spacing of the words and the almost pleading rhythm of the pauses." In this way it might even be possible to discover a universal verbal structure of promises. Yet the ability to make such inferences seems uncanny, to say the least.

As for how to ruin the passage, the easiest method would be to provide too much detail as to how the scholarly inference was achieved: "An almost interminable manuscript in strange characters, written in a huge ledger, was adjudged a sort of diary because of the spacing and the variations in ink and penmanship.

Forensic records compiled by the Miskatonic faculty of Criminal Justice showed that line spacing in diaries normally averages between 0.4 and 0.6 cm, more than the average for handwritten texts; Wilbur's ledger averaged line spacings of 0.57 cm, more within the range for diaries than for normal books of prose. Up to seven different kinds of black ink and four or five of blue were found in the ledger, suggesting that it was compiled over a long period of time in precisely the manner one would expect of a diary; the gradually evolving style of penmanship also suggested a lengthy period of composition." This level of detail is both boring and unnecessary. More importantly, it deprives us of the allusion to uncanny power of vague scholarly inference hinted in the original passage.

35. Saracenic Wizards

"Armitage had an idea that the alphabet might be something esoterically used by certain forbidden cults which have come down from old times, and which may have inherited many forms and traditions from the wizards of the Saracenic world." (DH 398)

The initial part of the passage ("Armitage had an idea that the alphabet might be something esoterically used by certain forbidden cults") is a somewhat weaker form of the previous passage about the spacing, ink, and penmanship of diaries. Nothing tells us explicitly what caused Armitage to "adjudge" this fact, but clearly there must be certain features of the alphabet that gave the old scholar this idea.

But the most striking part of the passage is the closing flourish "the wizards of the Saracenic world." The word "Saracen" is a quaint, old-fashioned way to describe the Arabs, and in recent times has come to be viewed as vaguely insulting. Still, it is effective in placing us mentally in a Medieval frame of mind, since this was the era when the term was most widely in use. The same holds for "wizards," another word with associations of medieval times or outright fantasy. It is not a word generally associated with the Arab world, where if forced to choose we would probably go with "magicians," a term often associated in the Biblical lands with false prophets.

If we were to replace the words in the passage above with "the magicians of the Arab world," we would damage the passage without quite ruining it, since "magician" and "Arab" would still sound sufficiently fresh or exotic in the context of this story from Protestant New England. To ruin the phrase outright we could change "of the Saracenic world" to the rather non-poetic "Middle East." The phrase "the magicians of the Middle East" sounds vaguely ridiculous in a Lovecraftian context. Unlike with "Saracenic world," it is difficult to find a boring equivalent for "wizard," since no matter what this profession might be called, it is inherently associated with enchanting and marvellous things. But more importantly, by using the phrase "wizards of the Saracenic world," Lovecraft is simply employing a trick already outlined by Aristotle in *Poetics* XXII, where he notes that good diction should be "clear" but "not mean." That is to say, it should contain some use of metaphor or rare words, but not enough to turn the passage into a riddle:

> Diction becomes distinguished and non-prosaic by the use of unfamiliar terms, i.e. strange words, metaphors, lengthened forms, and everything that deviates from the ordinary modes of speech. But a whole statement in such terms will be either a riddle or a barbarism, a riddle if made up of metaphors, a barbarism if made up of strange words. The very nature of a riddle is this, to describe a fact in an impossible combination of words (which cannot be done with the real names for things, but can be with their metaphorical substitutes); e.g. 'I saw a man glue brass on another with fire,' and the like. The corresponding use of strange words results in a barbarism. A

certain admixture, accordingly, of unfamiliar terms is necessary. These, the strange word, the metaphor, the ornamental equivalent, &c., will save the language from seeming mean and prosaic, while the ordinary words in it will secure the requisite clearness.[69]

In the passage at the head of this section, the phrase "which may have inherited many forms and traditions from the wizards of the Saracenic world" is effective because the unusual character of "wizards" and "Saracenic" is buffered and diluted by the prosaic "inherited many forms and traditions." Following Aristotle, we can change this passage into a *riddle* by substituting metaphors for the literal portion ("bore the legacy of the picture's frames and grandmother's yarns of the wizards of the Saracenic world") or into a *barbarism* by substituting strange words ("were bequeathed the die and praxis of the wizards of the Saracenic world"). Lovecraft avoids these extremes here, and thereby passes the test established in Aristotle's *Poetics*.

36. Massachusetts State Police

"Opinions were divided as to notifying the Massachusetts State Police, and the negative finally won. There were things involved which simply could not be believed by those who had seen a sample, as indeed was made clear during certain subsequent investigations." (DH 401-2)

One recurring structural problem for Lovecraft is how to explain why events as bizarre as those described in his stories would not quickly gain public attention through the police or the mass media. This problem is addressed in a number of different ways in the tales. In some stories there is university involvement and perhaps a bit of police work ("The Colour Out of Space," "The Dreams in the Witch House.") In another, government forces do in fact overpower and destroy the threatening monsters, though without informing the public ("The Shadow Over Innsmouth"). In one story ("The Dunwich Horror") the media is told what is happening but treats it as a ludicrous joke or delusion. In another instance ("The Whisperer in Darkness") the initial event of monstrous corpses witnessed in the flooding river is dismissed in the newspapers as a misunderstanding, while later events are purposely suppressed by Wilmarth and Akeley, the two uncorrupted humans who know what is really happening. Two stories ("At the Mountains of Madness," "The Shadow Over Innsmouth") are explicitly framed as public warnings, while in the case of one other tale ("The Shadow Out of Time") it is left to the narrator's son to decide if the story should be publicized. In short, Lovecraft tackles this problem from every possible angle. The only thing we never see in the great tales is the public as a whole involved in an ongoing horror, in the manner of "King Kong" or "Godzilla." Lovecraft must have found such a theme difficult to handle without degenerating into monster movie vulgarity. But the notion of the mass public confronted with rips in the fabric of reality is not unworkable, and other writers with different gifts might make it work. Here we find one of the voluntary limits of Lovecraft's literary vision, just as the complete absence of love affairs is characteristic of his stories. A Lovecraftian love story is not quite unthinkable, though it could prove highly distracting, and would also not be a good fit with what we know of him as a human character.

The strange thing about the passage at the head of this section is that the decision *not* to inform the State Police is rendered completely irrelevant just one page later. Upon arriving in Dunwich, the three Miskatonic faculty members are "apprised of a party of State Police which had come from Aylesbury that morning in response to the first telephone reports of the Frye tragedy... There had been five of them in a car, but now the car stood empty near the ruins in the Frye yard." (DH 403) The police seem to have gone down into the glen, where the invisible monster with the barrel-shaped footprints now lurks, and we are left to infer that the officers have been annihilated.

That leaves only the mildly comical closing words: "as indeed was made clear during certain subsequent investigations." The narrator does not go into detail, but merely alludes to the failure of the State Police to understand certain matters during subsequent investigations of the horror. But given the likely fate of the five officers who entered the glen, it seems unlikely that the Massachusetts State Police will have rejected the story entirely.

37. A Ghastly, Infra-Bass Timbre

"It is almost erroneous to call them *sounds* at all, since so much of their ghastly, infra-bass timbre spoke to dim seats of consciousness and terror far subtler than the ear; yet one must do so, since their form was indisputably though vaguely that of half-articulate *words*." (DH 411)

Having already encountered a type of color that is color "only by analogy," we are now faced with *sounds* having a similarly elusive quality. They were "deep, cracked, raucous vocal sounds... [and] the vocal organs of man can yield no such acoustic perversions." (DH 411) Like the colour out of space, the sounds from the mountain peak are not withdrawn from human access. They are perfectly accessible to us, yet are somehow sufficiently disturbing as not to be easily grasped or categorized as sound in a normal sense. We have heard of negative theologies, but Lovecraft excels in something else altogether: negative *psychology*. "It was a color, but really only by way of analogy... It was a sound, but not really in the usual sense of sound."

But here as usual, the description is not *entirely* negative: the old "not describable by any human pen" maneuver was already dismissed by Lovecraft as trite, and he meant it. Instead, Lovecraft always gives us some indication of where to look for the elusive reality even as he undercuts his own descriptions. The phrase "infra-bass timbre" is one such instance. Here we are told that we are looking for a sound somewhere in the bass range, but are also warned in advance that it is not *quite* bass. Rather, it is "infra-bass," as if exceeding the normal acoustic range of the human ear. The additional fact of being called a "*ghastly* infra-bass timbre" is a tactic familiar to us by now. Lovecraft cannot make a soundless sound believable without sharing our initial disbelief as to its existence, and by telling us it is "ghastly" he reassures us that his own reaction of disbelief mirrors our own. And besides, the sound speaks "to dim seats of consciousness and terror far subtler than the ear," primitive senses that we may not even have known we possessed. Despite the highly primitive character of the sounds, they take the form of words. Yet even this is somewhat dubious, since they are words "indisputably though vaguely," a wonderful pairing of adverbs that normally do not travel together.

Having seen what Lovecraft can achieve by introducing colors and sounds that are only barely colors and sounds, it is tempting to wonder what he might do with the other senses: "It is almost erroneous to call them *flavours* at all, since so much of their ghastly, sub-salty savour spoke to dim seats of consciousness and terror far subtler than the tongue; yet one must do so, since their form was indisputably though vaguely that of degenerate spices." Or this: "The smell was almost impossible to describe; and it was only by analogy that they called it an odour at all." Perhaps the technique could be extended beyond the five senses into the realm of everyday objects in general: "It is almost erroneous to call them *steel girders* at all, since so much of their ghastly tensile resilience spoke to dim seats of consciousness and terror far subtler than the muscles; yet one must do so, since their form was indisputably though vaguely that of support columns." At worst, this method could degenerate into easy polemical cheap shots, as in the first sentence of a possible very harsh book review: "This book is almost impossible to describe; and it is only by analogy that I call it a book at all." Or a heartless pedant indulging himself in a viciously cruel break-up: "It is only by analogy that I call you a woman at all."

The Whisperer in Darkness

This story was completed in September 1930, more than two years after the writing of "The Dunwich Horror." In the meantime, Lovecraft was involved with divorce proceedings in Rhode Island, and with sightseeing trips as distant as South Carolina, Virginia, and Quebec. He had also begun a correspondence with *Conan the Cimmerian* author and Texas native Robert E. Howard; this lasted until Howard's suicide, nine months prior to Lovecraft's own death from cancer. *Weird Tales* purchased "The Whisperer in Darkness" for $350, a substantial increase over Lovecraft's previous personal record of $240 for "The Dunwich Horror."

In this story Lovecraft returns to the first-person narrative style, in the character of Albert N. Wilmarth. He is an instructor of literature at Miskatonic University, whose faculty must rank among the most talented and unlucky of any in the history of world academia. The state of Vermont undergoes terrible flooding in November 1927. Numerous witnesses spot disturbing corpses in the floods, and swear they are other than human. This leads to wider reports of the sighting of strange creatures on other occasions in various portions of New England. A lively debate is ignited in three New England newspapers, with Wilmarth adopting a skeptical-rational stance and a mocking tone against those who believe in the various myths and monstrous sightings. As a result of these exchanges, Wilmarth receives a letter from a reader named Henry Akeley, who resides near Brattleboro, Vermont. This letter results in a chilling correspondence that turns Wilmarth into an unwilling believer that crab-like fungoid creatures from outer space haunt the hills of Vermont, where they mine a special stone found on no other planet. Wilmarth eventually travels to Brattleboro, unaware that Akeley has already been subdued by the aliens, his brain removed from his body and placed in a metal cylinder for transport to Yuggoth (known to us today as Pluto). Wilmarth barely escapes the same fate as Akeley, by rushing from the house in terror and speeding away in an automobile.

38. Gorges Shunned by the Wolves

"These [hidden monstrous] beings were seldom glimpsed, but evidences of their presence were reported by those who had ventured farther than usual up the slopes of certain mountains or into certain deep, steep-sided gorges that even the wolves shunned." (WD 417)

Lovecraft the person was by no means anti-science or anti-enlightenment. Nonetheless, his stories suggest that when science and enlightenment are pushed far enough, they yield conclusions alarmingly similar to those already anticipated by mystics and theosophists. This ragged avant garde of cutting-edge visionaries even includes uneducated ship crews of exotic sailors, even though Lovecraft's prudish narrators dismiss them as inferior beings. In one case the ranks of the enlightened elite even admit a witch: "a mediocre old woman of the seventeenth century [who achieves] an insight into mathematical depths perhaps beyond the utmost modern delvings of Planck, Heisenberg, Einstein, and de Sitter." (WH 656) But in some cases superior knowledge even belongs to animals, such as the wolves in the passage above. Given that wolves are normally considered fearless, their avoidance of "certain deep, steep-sided gorges" seems cause for genuine alarm about those places.

Enlightened, rational humans scoff at all hidden or occult qualities, and offer palpable evidence for their conclusions. In this way, enlightened humans are able to reject many of the gullible superstitions of the past. But by the same stroke they also become over-intellectualized, which means that they are sadly mesmerized by the surface qualities of things. Only when these qualities go terribly awry, such as when we witness indescribable idols or "colours only by analogy," or hear some "ghastly, infra-bass timbre," do we slowly become attuned to the fact that the fault-lines of the cosmos have ruptured. Animals, by contrast, seem to have deeper if more erratic contact with the essence of things. It is a well-known trope of both life and literature that shifty, stealthy people are often recognized by barking or growling pets before humans notice anything wrong with these individuals. In "The Colour Out of Space," (CS 357) horses respond badly to certain events at the Gardner farm, recognizing more vividly than we do that something is not right in the vicinity. In "The Dunwich Horror," Wilbur is so hated by local pets that he is forced to carry firearms: "Dogs abhorred the boy, and he was always obliged to take various defensive measures against their barking menace." (DH 377) In "The Shadow Over Innsmouth," we learn from the station agent that the residents of Innsmouth are not popular with animals either: "Animals hate 'em– they used to have lots of horse trouble before autos came in." (SI 591) And perhaps the best example of all, the one where the dogs really have it more right than humans, is found in "At the Mountains of Madness." Speaking of the dogs' reaction to the recently excavated animal-vegetable Elder Things, Professor Lake radios as follows: "Have brought all [specimens] to the surface, leading off dogs to distance. They cannot stand the things." (MM 499) Lake should have listened to the dogs. The Elder Things soon awaken from eons-long sleep and slaughter everyone, humans and dogs alike. In fact, I can think of no passage in Lovecraft's stories where animals guess incorrectly. Their instinctive reactions tunnel through the deceptive outer surfaces of things and make vague contact with the things themselves.

39. Accident Rather than Design

"Most people simply knew that certain hilly regions were considered as highly unhealthy, unprofitable, and generally unlucky to live in, and that the farther one kept from them the better off one usually was. In time the ruts of custom and economic interest became so deeply cut in approved places that there was no longer any reason for going outside them, and the haunted hills were left deserted by accident rather than by design." (WD 419-20)

Like a composer of fugues, Lovecraft continues to weave a small number of basic stylistic elements into unprecedented combinations. Here, the first sentence is a familiar element augmented by the new technique of the second.

Like wolves, dogs, and horses, humans are also sometimes granted sub-verbal knowledge of the malevolent character of things. This passage provides us with such a case. There are not simply one or two locations felt to be harmful, but the more vague and general "certain hilly regions." No specific reason is given for avoiding these locations, other than the unspoken sense that they are "highly unhealthy, unprofitable, and generally unlucky to live in." And best of all, "the farther one kept from them the better off one usually was." We already know from an earlier example that this sentence can be ruined by making it too specific. For instance: "Most people knew that certain hilly regions were scenes of disappearances and outright murders. Two such regions in particular saw seventeen deaths in the period from 1750-1800 alone. There were forty-six additional cases of people who returned from these regions not dead, but in a mental state approaching insanity, and wracked with a strange type of fever." One problem with this parody version of the sentence is that such details of human doom are never as frightening as the vague sense of a deeper, more ineffable fate. Another problem is that tangible disasters of this sort would be recognized by the forces of rational enlightenment, viewed as too extreme to be tolerated, and met with collective investigation and probable law enforcement action or public health measures. But keeping the baleful effects of these hilly regions vague allows us to be all the more terrified by the possible consequences of visiting them, while also explaining why the situation was allowed to continue unchallenged. Vague feelings about these malevolent regions can always be explained away as empty superstition. And in fact, this is usually the fate of rural wisdom in Lovecraft's stories: ridicule and dismissal by urban authority, which generally turns out to be less realistic than the hazy rustic fear of farmers, horses, and wolves.

But the key to this passage is really the second sentence. It is a novelty in Lovecraft's prose, and if memory serves it is the only such passage in his works. What originally took the form of vague but no doubt justified fears is reflected in the choice of settlement locations in the Vermont hills. And given that settlement generally builds on pre-existing settlement, the further development of Vermont habitation and industry ("the ruts of custom and economic interest") unknowingly ratify the initial fear of certain malignant regions by continuing to avoid them through habit rather than fear. In short, the entire demographic layout of modern-day Vermont turns out to be grounded in the "irrational" fears of its early countryside folk. In this sense, not only do peasants, sailors, theosophists, horses and wolves have better cosmic knowledge than enlightened scientists. Instead, even sheer demographic fact reflects greater wisdom than our most hyper-conscious politicians and professors of literature.

This passage might also be viewed as a variant of the one on the reservoir in section 15 above. In that case, unconscious urban infrastructure is on the verge of incorporating the monstrous colour of the Garden farm into the water supply of Arkham. In the present instance, human infrastructure has tacitly obeyed the whispers of a terrified rustic populace and gotten into the habit of *excluding* vague horrors from its realm. The reservoir builders of Arkham ought to have taken a cue from the early builders and civilizers of Vermont.

40. Too Sanely Prosaic

"The more I laughed at such theories, the more these stubborn friends asseverated them; adding that even without the heritage of legend the recent reports were too clear, consistent, detailed, and sanely prosaic in manner of telling, to be completely ignored." (WD 421)

The theories in question concern "the real existence of some queer elder earth-race, driven to hiding after the advent and dominance of mankind." (WD 421) In this story they are initially (and wrongly) debunked not by means of physics and chemistry, but by the less exact tools of anthropology. The amateur folklorist Wilmarth opens fire on these wild Vermont theorists by pointing to similar myths recurring in Greece, Wales, Ireland, and the Himalayan regions. (WD 420) Henry Akeley, who began as a skeptic himself before encountering actual traces of the creatures, cites as reasons for his former skepticism "the standard authorities such as Tylor, Lubbock, Frazer, Quatrefages, Murray, Osborn, Keith, Boule, G. Elliot Smith, and so on." (WD 423) All the weight of collected debunker's enlightenment in the social sciences is brought to bear on the ostensibly naïve fantasies of the believers in mysterious Vermont hill creatures.

The counter-weaponry of Wilmarth's "stubborn friends" seems flimsy enough, but given the usual logic of Lovecraft's stories, we know they will prove decisive. Namely, "the recent reports were too clear, consistent, detailed, and sanely prosaic in manner of telling, to be completely ignored." (WD 421)

Since my teenaged years I have often found significant philosophical insight in the baseball writings of the author Bill James (now a consultant for the Boston Red Sox), whose influence on an entire generation of American writers cannot be overstated. After rating 1930's star Jimmie Foxx as the best first baseman in the sport other than Lou Gehrig, James relates the following anecdote. The talent scout known as Home Run Baker became lost one day in rural Maryland. Spotting a boy plowing a field with a mule, he stopped and asked the boy the directions to the nearest town. Young Jimmie Foxx supposedly said "over that way," and picked up the plow with one arm, pointing at the next town with it. This display of strength led Baker to ask Foxx if he played baseball, and the rest is a matter of American sports history. James concedes that the story sounds like a fake: "the anecdote is easily recognizable as apocryphal– yet when you walk it through, the story has no improbable elements."[70] In those days of underdeveloped highways, someone like Baker might easily have become lost in the Maryland backwoods. Star baseball players were often discovered by scouts through sheer accident in that rather disorganized era. The plows of the day were by no means too heavy for a robust young man to lift with one arm, and it would be quite typical of a cocky, athletic teenager to show off his strength by doing so. And once that happened, almost any scout would be sufficiently impressed to ask young Foxx if he played baseball. James concludes: "What marks the story as improbable is not its facts, but its form. There is something you can't put your finger on; the story is too pat, too well-formed. And that tells us something about how we distinguish truth from falsehood in our everyday experience."[71]

Here, with the phrase "there is something you can't put your finger on," James is just one step short of Lovecraft himself. We can almost imagine Jimmie Foxx as a Lovecraftian hybrid along the lines of Wilbur Whateley, half human and half Old One. We can even imagine a Lovecraft story entitled "The Case of Jimmie Foxx," which might include a passage running as follows:

Home Run Baker was almost ashamed to report his misgivings about the encounter. Although there was nothing impossible or even improbable in the young boy's lifting of the plow, certain vague aberrations in the *manner* of lifting had left Baker with a disturbing impression. Although he refused to give explicit details, Baker seemed to feel that there was something unnaturally torsive or vibratory in the action of the boy's muscles. And whereas objects lifted from the ground tend to move in a roughly parabolic path rather than a vertical one, Baker seemed to think that under certain conditions, there was something tending toward the *ellipsoid* in the arm motions he witnessed. Naturally, these feelings were viewed by the locals as digressively subtle, and Baker's reservations were generally ignored. The old baseball scout began to drink heavily and was increasingly shunned, while young Foxx continued his rise through the semi-professional leagues of the Eastern Shore.

Returning to the topic at hand, when James speaks of "something you can't put your finger on," he is referring to certain background subtleties in the structure of tales. We cannot put our finger on these subtleties any better than Bill James, but Wilmarth's friends seem able to do so, since they argue that "the recent reports were too clear, consistent, detailed, and sanely prosaic in manner of telling, to be completely ignored." Beneath the content of any communication lie certain modulations of rhetorical subtlety that have more weight in our determination of truth, falsity, and reality than does any explicit judgment about content.

41. A Damnably Suggestive Power

"Glancing at these pictures as I took them from the envelope, I felt a curious sense of fright and nearness to forbidden things; for in spite of the vagueness of most of them, they had a damnably suggestive power..." (WD 427)

Although we have already discussed these sorts of statements before, this passage is a Lovecraft classic, and deserves to be recorded. The photographs sent by Akeley to Wilmarth are vague indeed, but now as ever, they are not so vague that Lovecraft leaves us completely in the dark as to their contents. The first shows a footprint, of which Wilmarth reports that he "can scarcely describe it save to say that it was hideously crab-like, and that there seemed to be some ambiguity about its direction." (WD 428) By now we have learned not to be dismissive of the word "hideously," which is simply Lovecraft's way of expressing solidarity with the reader's bewilderment, while giving a signal as to Wilmarth's own increasingly troubled state of mind. Taken in isolation, a crab-like footprint might simply be the stuff of pulp fiction. What is truly Lovecraftian is the bizarre added remark that it seems to have some ambiguity of direction. Here the usual immediate bond between a footprint and its definite pointing in one particular direction is broken; the footprint becomes an aimless carnal impression in the earth, its purpose unknown. And quite apart from the lack of purposive direction, the description of the print itself leaves us queasy: "From a central pad, pairs of saw-toothed nippers projected in opposite directions..." (WD 428)

The second photograph simply depicts "a druid-like circle of standing stones on the summit of a wild hill" (WD 428) No footprints are clearly visible here, and the real highlight of this passage is Wilmarth's wonderfully vague inference that "the extreme remoteness of the place was apparent from the veritable sea of tenantless mountains which formed the background and stretched away toward a misty horizon." (WD 428) This explicit deduction of the photograph's location, drawn from subsidiary hints of its design, further display Lovecraft's obsessive tendency to speak openly of connections and junctions that are normally left in an unstated rhetorical or perceptual background. Again we find a precedent for this in Poe, who is Lovecraft's primary ancestor in style no less than in content. In Poe's well-known tale "The Fall of the House of Usher," the narrator observes

Roderick's painting of a long and ominous tunnel. As we are told, in a manner foreshadowing that of Wilmarth:

> Certain accessory portions of the design served well to convey the idea that this excavation lay at an exceeding depth below the surface of the earth. No outlet was observed in any portion of its vast extent, and no torch, or other artificial source of light was discernible; yet a flood of intense rays rolled throughout, and bathed the whole in a ghastly and inappropriate splendor.[72]

From the merest pictorial data, the surrounding conditions of the image are subtly inferred. The febrile imaginations of Poe and Lovecraft bring these subterranean regions to the surface, where the reader can contemplate them.

The third photograph of "damnably suggestive power" depicts a black stone found by Akeley in the woods; bizarrely and amusingly, Akeley's "bust of Milton" can also be seen in the photo, in what amounts to a self-parody of Lovecraft's frequent trick of providing classical-historical bulk to his contemporary imaginative fantasies. And within this damnably suggestive photo we find that the black stone itself is also a damnably suggestive object. "The thing... [had] a somewhat irregularly curved surface of one by two feet; but to say anything definite about that surface, or about the general shape of the whole mass, almost defies the power of language. What outlandish geometrical principles had guided its cutting –for artificially cut it surely was– I could not even begin to guess..." (WD 428-9) This too is classic Lovecraft, as is his description of another photograph, "which seemed to bear traces of strange and unwholesome tenancy." (WD 429) What these traces might be we are never told, but as we have seen often enough in Lovecraft, the inability or unwillingness to tell us is usually the very point.

Here once more, we should take note of another gesture that we have noted as typical of Lovecraft: the piling of allusion on top of allusion. As if it were not bad enough that the shape of the black stone "almost defies the power of language," the stone is depicted only in a "vague, but damnably suggestive" photograph. The technique could have been pushed even further, to Level 3, if Akeley had not sent the photographs to Wilmarth, but only *described* them with the usual Lovecraftian hesitations and qualifications: "I can also say that on my desk are some photographs– vague, but damnably suggestive. One of them is of a black stone, and though this picture almost defies the power of language, I can say that certain outlandish geometrical principles seem to have guided the cutting of it." It could even be pushed to Level 4, if Wilmarth were only describing the letter to us rather than entering it verbatim into the story: "Akeley's letter showed signs of increased agitation. In it, he described certain vague but damnably suggestive photographs of a black stone found in the woods. Though he swore that this stone nearly exceeded the descriptive powers of language, he did say that it seemed to have been cut according to unknown and outlandish geometrical principles." Perhaps pushing our luck, we could even advance to Level 5, by having Wilmarth feel uncertain as to whether he had even remembered this terrible letter properly: "Given the nervous turmoil instilled by the events that followed, one might doubt –as I myself have doubted– whether my memory of Akeley's latter is accurate, or merely the result of certain hectic dismemberments in the connective associations of memory. Nonetheless, I am vaguely yet palpably sure that Akeley's letter described certain damnably suggestive photographs of a black stone found in the woods. As if in a dream, I seem to recall his swearing that the stone nearly exceeded the descriptive powers of language, though I also dimly recollect a further statement that it seemed to have been cut according to unknown and outlandish geometrical principles." The exercise is amusing, but going any further than this would probably yield diminishing results, for us as for Lovecraft himself.

42. Absorbing Zoological Conjectures

"For one thing, we also decided that these [crab-like] morbidities and the hellish Himalayan *Mi-Go* were one and the same order of incarnated nightmare. There were also absorbing zoölogical conjectures, which I would have referred to Professor Dexter in my own college but for Akeley's imperative command to tell no one of the matter before us." (WD 431)

This is Wilmarth's compact summary of a lengthy period of correspondence with Akeley– during which, as we ominously learn, "once in a while a letter would be lost, so that we would have to retrace our ground and perform considerable laborious copying." (WD 430) Lovecraft is wise to report the conclusion about the *Mi-Go* in summary form, since it is difficult to imagine any protracted dialogue of five or six pages between Akeley and Wilmarth making a sufficiently persuasive case to bring the reader on board. As for the use of adjectives, Edmund Wilson's preferred non-purple phrasing might run as follows: "For one thing, we also decided that the Vermont creatures and the Himalayan *Mi-Go* were one and the same species." Instead, Lovecraft spices up the sentence with "morbidities," "hellish," and "incarnated nightmare." He deserves high marks for doing so. By this point in the story, the reader is impressed enough by the same evidence that eroded Wilmarth's inveterate skepticism that we need not be *forced* into belief by raving, assertive adjectives. The structure of the story has already brought us into the fold, and to hear of the "morbidities" in Vermont, the "hellish" monsters in the Himalayas, and then to hear both of these described as "one and the same order of hellish nightmare" makes Wilmarth more rather than less convincing.

Paradoxically, a more objective and less emotional description would put us *closer* to the realm of pulp, as discussed earlier when we considered "Some Notes on Interplanetary Fiction." Lovecraft would surely have been appalled, for example, by the miserable second sentence of L. Ron Hubbard's *Battlefield Earth*: "The hairy paws of the Chamco brothers hung suspended above the broad keys of the laser-bash game."[73] This is a mere assertion, dropped on our heads from nowhere like a sack of cement, and Hubbard merely attempts to impose it upon us by fiat. What Lovecraft does is completely different: he registers the tension between Wilmarth's previous set of beliefs and the new horror he is now forced to acknowledge in the hills of Vermont. The pain of such tension can only be registered with such words as "morbidities," "hellish," and "incarnate nightmare." These adjectives do not clumsily produce an effect in their own right, but merely emphasize work already done elsewhere.

Finally and most interestingly, there is the matter of the "absorbing zoölogical conjectures" made by Akeley and Wilmarth. Again this notion is more effective when left vague as it is here. It would not be impossible to expand at length on these zoological notions (Lovecraft often follows allusive hints with cubistic attempts to deliver the goods in person), but sometimes it is better if these things are left unspoken. Along with the unstated vagueness of these conjectures, they are insulated from professional scrutiny by the fact that Akeley forbids Wilmarth from consulting Professor Dexter or anyone else. While on the surface this might seem to undermine the credibility of these conjectures, it also serves to put them in a more favorable light by making them seem like the best available knowledge under the circumstances. In literary terms, it also prevents meddling outsiders from interfering with the tightly orchestrated two-person show of Akeley and Wilmarth, which dominates the story.

43. The Accursed Buzzing

"The second voice, however, was the real crux of the thing–
for this was the accursed *buzzing* which had no likeness to
humanity despite the human words which it uttered in good
English grammar and a scholarly accent." (WD 432)

Having succeeded in describing the allusions within allusions of
the photographs, with their "vague but damnably suggestive"
character, Lovecraft now shifts to phonograph recordings. It is
almost preposterous that Akeley would have been able to sneak
up close enough to the creatures to record their voices, and that
is probably why Lovecraft left the phonograph for last, in an
effort to prepare us for taking it seriously. Now, it may seem like
a phonograph record should count as direct evidence of a conversation, and thus as anything other than "vague" and
"suggestive." But Lovecraft does effective work in undercutting
the reliability of the recording just enough to give it the same
allusion-within-allusion structure as the photographs. First, there
is the fact that Wilmarth does not own the machine himself, but
has to borrow it from the college administration building,
suggesting some degree of unfamiliarity with how phonographs
work. Second, we are told that Akeley's "recording phonograph
and dictaphone had not worked uniformly well," aside from
which there was "the remote and muffled nature of the
overheard ritual; so that the actual speech secured was very
fragmentary." (WD 432) This is emphasized by the frequent
ellipses in the transcript of the recording prepared by Akeley.

Just as the vague and damnably suggestive photographs
served as a gateway onto the monstrously allusive geometry of
the black stone, the "remote and muffled" nature of the phonograph generates a cloud of doubt through which we encounter
something even worse than the oddly cut stone: namely, a *buzzing*
sound formed into the words of human speech. Already, we
encountered irregularities in the voice of Wilbur Whateley that

raised serious suspicions. But in Wilbur's case there were also crudities of grammar and dialect accompanying the distortions of voice. In the present case, however, the loathsome buzzing voice speaks "in good English grammar and a scholarly accent." In short, all the outward features of the voice are socially impeccable. It speaks the King's English, and comes from a higher caste of intellectual breeding than normally heard in an average voice. The "scholarly accent" ought to be even more reassuring, given the physically non-threatening behavior of scholars under most conditions. But there is one small problem. Despite its polished grammar and accent, the voice sounds like "a morbid echo winging its way across unimaginable abysses from unimaginable outer hells." (WD 434) It does not help in the least that the buzzing creature is answered in a "mellow Bostonian voice" by the words: "Iä! Shub-Niggurath! The Goat with a Thousand Young!" (WD 434) The normal bonds that implicitly link good accent and grammar with a genteel underlying persona, and the Bostonian accent with flinty and pragmatic but basically benevolent New England intelligence, are now completely shattered. We learn that good outward vocal poise can be linked with morbid echoes from unimaginable outer hells.

44. The Drone of Some Loathsome, Gigantic Insect

"But though that voice is always in my ears, I have not even yet been able to analyse it well enough for a graphic description. It was like the drone of some loathsome, gigantic insect ponderously shaped into the articulate speech of an alien species, and I am perfectly certain that the organs producing it can have no resemblance to the vocal organs of man, or indeed to those of any of the mammalia." (WD 434)

There is more to be said about this voice. It does not lie entirely beyond all description, since we have already heard that it approximated the sound of buzzing. But now Lovecraft becomes even more exact. A loathsome, gigantic insect is already a terrible image, but even worse is to imagine the "drone" of this insect "ponderously shaped" into an alien's articulate speech. The word "ponderously" lets us know that such shaping is not easy, and hence the translation from drone into alien speech seems not to be exact, and we can almost feel the tension between the two as we read. There is a drone-like residue lingering in that speech— which furthermore is described as *alien* rather than human speech, creating yet another layer of imperfect translatability between the buzzing creature and ostensible humanity. Despite its correct English grammar and scholarly accent, its voice contains droning overtones and separate hints of an alien intelligent species. Its ability to mimic our grammar and scholarly intonations is apparently not matched by an equal ability to copy the basic sound of the earthly human vocal tones.

This is precisely what terrifies Wilmarth. He continues the passage above by saying that the buzzing voice contained "singularities of timbre, range, and overtones which placed this phenomenon wholly outside the sphere of humanity and earth-life." (WD 434) Whereas the "ghastly, infra-bass timbre" heard at the end of "The Dunwich Horror" yielded a sound that was not really a sound, much like the color that was not really a color, here we have a more earthly distortion. The buzzing voice most definitely falls within the range of sounds; Wilmarth never questions this. But while undeniably a sound, it remains terrifying through its "singularities of timbre, range, and overtones." It is one of the classic Lovecraftian gestures, breaking up the usual relation between a voice and its features by invoking bizarre variations on those features that cannot possibly belong to man, or indeed to those of any of the mammalia. This initially cautious limited claim ("No *mammal* could have made such a sound! Of that I am sure!") quickly expands to the assertion that the buzzing voice lies "wholly outside the sphere of humanity and earth-life." When the second long snippet of the buzzing voice is heard, Wilmarth feels "a sharp intensification of that feeling of blasphemous infinity which had struck me during the shorter and earlier passage." (WD 435) Wilmarth then sits in a stupor and stares, as the recording comically ends "during an unusually clear speech of the human and Bostonian voice," (WD 435) which we were earlier told belonged to "a man of greater cultivation" (WD 432) than most of the Vermont locals.

45. The Pride of Memory

"But here is the substance of the text, carefully transcribed from a memory in which I take some pride." (WD 445)

The entire story is dominated by the consultation and presentation of evidence: letters, photographs, phonographic recordings, transcripts, and even the black stone itself. The irony, however, is that by story's end none of these things remain in Wilmarth's possession. The Fungi from Yuggoth apparently succeed in capturing or subduing Akeley, and then deceive Wilmarth into coming to Brattleboro and bringing all of the evidence along with him, under the pretext that it will be needed for the purposes of consultation (though the reader is not tricked along with him, knowing in advance that Wilmarth is being led into a trap). This device is necessary to prevent the police and media from becoming involved in the story as it approaches its conclusion, though it does create the problem of how to base an entire story on the supposedly verbatim recounting of evidence that no longer exists.

All that can be done is to give the reader repeated reassurances that Wilmarth is absolutely sure that he remembers everything correctly. For example, before the remarkable text of Akeley's first letter is given, we read as follows: "It is no longer in my possession, but my memory holds almost every word of its portentous message," (WD 422) and by quickly changing the subject to affirmations of the sanity of Akeley, we are given no further opportunity to doubt Wilmarth's mnemonic prowess. Later, before giving us the transcript of the phonograph record, Wilmarth tells us: "I will present it here in full as I remember it– and I am fairly confident that I know it correctly by heart, not only from reading the transcript, but from playing the record itself over and over again. It is not a thing which one might readily forget!" (WD 432-433) In a subtle but effective maneuver, Wilmarth also briefly places himself on the level of the reader by glancing through the transcript before playing the recording. Yet he does not remain on our level for long, for in answer to doubters who "profess to find nothing but cheap imposture or madness" in the buzzing voice, Wilmarth responds: *"could they have heard the thing itself... I know they would think differently."* (WD 434) If only they knew. If only they could have heard the thing itself.

46. Reactions and Rhythm-Responses

"Word-choice, spelling– all were subtly different. And with my academic sensitiveness to prose style, I could trace profound divergences in his commonest reactions and rhythm-responses." (WD 449)

This passage would be another good candidate for the longed-for Socratic union of comic and tragic. The comedy unfolds here on two different levels. First, there is the fact that despite recognizing great differences in Akeley's latest letter, Wilmarth remains fool enough to travel to Brattleboro and even to take all of the precious physical evidence with him. This is perhaps the most extreme case in the great tales in which Lovecraft allows the reader to be shrewder than the narrator, more committed to the reality and the subterfuges of the alien creatures than Wilmarth. As readers we feel like children at one of those schoolhouse puppet shows, watching the Prince puppet come onto the stage and say: "I think I'll go take a nap in the forest," as we the children vainly shout: "No! No! Don't go in the forest!" For we have just seen the Evil Dragon puppet enter that forest to set an ambush for him. In this respect, Wilmarth is already comical, even though what he finds at Akeley's farmhouse will be the very antithesis of comedy.

Second, there are the absurdly mannered and pretentious claims of the passage itself. While it may be true that university instructors in literature have better than average sensitivity to variations in normal prose style, the point is too subtle to be taken for granted so matter-of-factly, as if it were tangibly comparable to the ability to juggle or cook a good chili. More specifically, it may be questioned not only whether anyone has the ability to "trace profound divergences in [someone's] commonest reactions and rhythm-responses," but even whether this means anything definite at all. Or rather, it is not an entirely "meaningless" claim, but more along the lines of the claim to see with one's own eyes a colour that is colour only by analogy. An individual prose style is normally identified with a bundle of traits that it exhibits, but here the relation between the style and its features breaks down. "Profound divergences" are noticed in the "reactions and rhythm-responses" associated with the style of "Akeley" in this letter. But ironically, we the readers are even more sensitive than Wilmarth to the shift in prose style, to the point that surely none of us would travel to Brattleboro after reading such a letter. Just as all readers probably suspect, Akeley has been subdued or captured, and the letter is typed (for the first time) precisely because Akeley's handwriting style cannot be convincingly mimicked by the creatures or their corrupted human minions.

47. Obscure Secrets and Immemorial Survivals

"As we passed out of Brattleboro my sense of constraint and foreboding increased, for a vague quality in the hill-crowded countryside with its towering, threatening, close-pressing green and granite slopes hinted at obscure secrets and immemorial survivals which might or might not be hostile to mankind." (WD 454)

Lovecraft is a skilled landscape painter in words, though for obvious reasons his range of color is restricted to various shades of dark. In the opening travelogue of "The Dunwich Horror," the Antarctic scenes of "At the Mountains of Madness," and the description of the hemmed-in swampy geography near Innsmouth, Lovecraft has a talent for depicting certain geographic locales as suitable homes for impending horror. There is nothing in his stories to suggest a *literal* link between the two. Inanimate landscapes themselves are not corrupted by the other-worldly beings, unless they happen to become contaminated by the brittling influence of the colour out of space. Instead, the landscapes simply provide an ominous background for events soon to unfold in them.

The landscape described above is even more Lovecraftian than most. There is a "vague quality" in the Vermont countryside that causes him to feel constraint and foreboding. The surrounding slopes merely "hint" at something, and what they hint at are "obscure secrets" and "immemorial survivals," which in turn may or may not prove to be harmful. As for the possible ruination of this passage, we have already practiced making passages overly literal, replacing vague hints with ultimately disap-pointing details. For the sake of variety, we can try to ruin the present description in a different manner. One of the unspoken features of this description is that Wilmarth joins us on the same level of ignorance. The hills seem to be hinting at something, though none of us know exactly what. At other times in

Lovecraft, as in Wilmarth's foolish decision to travel to Brattleboro at pseudo-Akeley's request, the readers are allowed to be wiser than the narrator. But what can never possibly succeed, in a Lovecraftian framework, is to have the narrator know *more* than we do. Consider the following possible stylistic abomination: "I know full well which obscure secrets were hinted by the hill-crowded countryside with its towering, threatening, close-pressing green and granite slopes. But I do not care to share that information with the reader." It is hard to imagine a less Lovecraftian tone than this fruitless and impotent snobbery.

48. Half-Imaginary Rhythm or Vibration

"The room beyond was darkened, as I had known before; and as I entered it I noticed that the queer odour was stronger there. There likewise appeared to be some faint, half-imaginary rhythm or vibration in the air." (WD 459)

The fact that the queer odour becomes stronger as Wilmarth enters the room is not especially interesting, since it merely provides a clue that Akeley is in fact pseudo-Akeley, which most readers have probably already guessed. The real point of interest in the passage, of course, is found in the concluding portion: "some faint, half-imaginary rhythm or vibration in the air." We have already encountered these deliberately vague descriptions of sound in the case of voices, in the "ghastly, infra-bass timbre" emanating from Wilbur's giant invisible brother, or in the less vague but more disturbing buzzing sound lurking behind the perfect grammar and scholarly accent of the phonograph record. Always a player of stylistic fugues, Lovecraft now varies the theme by divorcing the strangeness of sound from any voice at all. The mere physical presence of the Fungi from Yuggoth (recognized by the reader, if not by Wilmarth himself) is apparently enough to cause a sense of rhythm or vibration in the air–

and let us remember, this sense is only "faint" and "half-imaginary." Though this point is never clearly explained in the story, the September 6, 1928 letter from pseudo-Akeley gives sufficient hints to allow us to form a general idea. As the impostor puts it to the visiting Wilmarth:

> The Outer Beings are... members of a cosmos-wide race of which all other life-forms are merely degenerate variants. They are more vegetable than animal, if these sorts of terms can be applied to the sort of matter composing them, and have a somewhat fungoid structure; though the presence of a chlorophyll-like substance and a very singular nutritive system differentiate them altogether from the true cormo-phytic fungi. Indeed, the type is composed of a form of matter totally alien to our part of space– with electrons having a totally different vibration-rate. (WD 447)

When reading these words we shake our heads once again at Wilmarth's decision to travel to Brattleboro, as well as the decision of the creatures to reveal this much of their nature to someone who might have chosen not to come at all. But the passage does give us a suitably "vague," "half-imaginary" sense of why there might be a strange rhythm or vibration in the air. Electrons with a totally different vibration-rate could well provide the answer.

49. Mercifully Cloaked

"...I started with loathing when told of the monstrous nuclear chaos beyond angled space which the *Necronomicon* had mercifully cloaked under the name of Azathoth." (WD 464)

With this passage, Lovecraft reaches a new peak of technical achievement. Edmund Wilson, brilliant critic though he was, would presumably have seen nothing here besides boyish outbursts concerning alternative worlds. But in doing so, he would merely occupy the same crabby, benighted niche of an old academic art critic rejecting the stunning grey tangle of Jackson Pollock's *Number 14*. Having already been through numerous comparable preliminary statements, we are in a position to appreciate the passage above all the more deeply.

First, we can simplify things by handling "I started with loathing" separately. We are now quite familiar with these anti-Wilsonian exclamations by Lovecraft. They always have a twofold structure. First, they help convince us of whatever bizarre subject matter is under discussion, since the narrator thereby reassures us that he himself also finds them strange or horrible or completely implausible, and that he still has no choice but to believe anyway. Second, they place the spotlight on the mental state of the narrator himself, which is comical insofar as the agent is reduced to a greater sincerity than we are, and tragic insofar as we too experience the cosmos-threatening information that led him onto such disturbing emotional terrain.

What we are now left with is the following phrase: "the monstrous nuclear chaos beyond angled space which the *Necronomicon* had mercifully cloaked under the name of Azathoth." Here Lovecraft shows his wizardry as a prose stylist by stacking up not two, not three, but *four* allusions in the same passage. We can consider them one-by-one in the form of a list:

1. The idea that the dreaded, fearsome, forbidden *Necronomicon* of the mad Arab Abdul Alhazred might serve as an agent of mercy is troubling indeed. In that case, what would a *merciless* book look like? In any case, we are asked to believe that this evil fictitious book, a manual of the Outer Beings containing hints on how to summon them to a precious planet that they would love to destroy, is in fact a benevolent comforter shielding us from *even darker* truths. Having expended all possible efforts in

various stories to make us shudder whenever this book is mentioned, Lovecraft now effectively lets us know that the *Necronomicon* is the "merest fringe" of existing evils.

2. The ultimate horror, we learn, was "mercifully cloaked" by the *Necronomicon* under the name of "Azathoth." There is little mercy in this name, and even less information. In "The Dreams in the Witch House" we will encounter more information but even less mercy, since there we read that Azathoth is at "the throne of Chaos where the thin flutes pipe mindlessly," (WH 664) and that "the mindless entity Azathoth... rules all time and space from a curiously environed black throne at the centre of Chaos." (WH 674) The same story speaks further of "the spiral black vortices of that ultimate void of Chaos wherein reigns the mindless daemon-sultan Azathoth" (WH 686). And in a final spasm of ecstatic prose in his very late story "The Haunter of the Dark," Lovecraft tells us of "Ultimate Chaos, at whose centre sprawls the blind idiot god Azathoth, Lord of All Things, encircled by his flopping horde of mindless and amorphous dancers, and lulled by the thin monotonous piping of a daemoniac flute held in nameless paws." (HD 802) Please keep in mind that even this wild Lovecraftian outburst is still packaged as a "merciful" version of cosmic truth.

3. All of this lies "beyond angled space," an allusion even less visualizable than that of an acute angle with obtuse behavior, since by definition such entities still belong to the realm of palpable and intelligible geometric angles, whatever inconsistency there might be between their appearance and their behavior.

4. Passing beyond the blind idiot God encircled by a flopping horde of mindless and amorphous dancers, beyond all angled space, and beyond all "merciful cloaking" of these realities by the unspeakable *Necronomicon*, we arrive at last

at "monstrous nuclear chaos." What this might entail, we can only guess vaguely based on our common schoolhouse understanding of how the atomic nucleus functions. But given that the Azathoth legends are termed a merciful cloaking of underlying chaotic reality, by analogy we are led to shudder.

It took Lovecraft several major stories to get to the point where he could pull off a sentence of this refined complexity, whatever its surface appearance of adolescent self-indulgence. The idea that Lovecraft is outclassed as a stylist by the likes of Proust or Joyce (two of Wilson's favorites) is not an idea to which I can assent. The opposite claim seems closer to the truth.

50. The Horror of Inference

"As I said before, there was nothing of actual visual horror about [the objects]. The trouble was in what they led one to infer." (WD 479)

The obvious fascination of this passage is that it can be interpreted as Lovecraft reflecting on his own force and technique as a writer. There are indeed cases of direct sensory horror in Lovecraft: the color that is color only by analogy, the infra-bass timbre that should not really be called sound. But more often, we find loose qualities trembling at the surface of perception, announcing their bondage to some deeper hidden entity that can only be vaguely named.

In the present case, the inference in question is somewhat disappointing. The final sentence, which serves as grounds for the ultimate inference, is as follows: "For the things in the chair, perfect to the last, subtle detail of microscopic resemblance, were the face and hands of Henry Wentworth Akeley." (WD 480) Wilmarth has spent the night in Akeley's house and engaged in some conversation with him. "Akeley" sits motionless in his chair, with a sickly appearance, speaking only in a whisper. There is a strange odour much stronger near Akeley than elsewhere, along with the aforementioned rhythm or vibration in the air. Later, as Wilmarth eavesdrops on a larger conversation from upstairs, there is some indication that Akeley's brain has been removed from his body and that he speaks instead from one of the metallic cannisters, ready for transport beyond the earth. All these things lead the reader to conclude long before the end of the story that Akeley is in fact pseudo-Akeley. In this respect, Wilmarth's terrible inference comes far too late to frighten us. Lovecraft already used the technique of keeping Wilmarth more skeptical and naïve than we are in order to maneuver us into position to be greater advocates of the weird than the narrator himself. Lovecraft cannot now have it both ways and ask us to be surprised *along with* Wilmarth. This unconvincing ending makes an unfortunate pair with the unusually weak opening paragraph of the story. The opening gives us a series of hysterical out-of-context statements by Wilmarth about his sudden bolting from Akeley's home and his departure from the property. This use of the *in medias res* technique is a bit cheap, and ruins a golden opportunity to begin the story instead with the brilliantly deadpan second paragraph: "The whole matter began, so far as I am concerned, with the historic and unprecedented Vermont floods of November 3, 1927. I was then, as now, an instructor of literature at Miskatonic University in Arkham, Massachusetts, and an enthusiastic amateur student of Massachusetts folklore..." (WD 415) This would rank among Lovecraft's greatest story openings– if only it were an opening.

More generally, however, the passage at the head of this section could be taken as a summary of Lovecraft's entire procedure as a writer: "As I said before, there was nothing of actual visual horror about [the objects]. The trouble was in what they led one to infer." But even the inferences cannot be put into literal form. Surface qualities hint vaguely at some underlying entity. But that entity itself turns out to be vague, and often mercifully cloaks some deeper and darker truth. We never reach a final layer of horror for Lovecraft, since even the "monstrous nuclear chaos" cloaked by the name of Azathoth is not something we can comprehend.

At the Mountains of Madness

This story was written in early 1931, only to be rejected by the previously receptive *Weird Tales*. It was finally published in 1936 by *Astounding Stories,* in serial form, so that Lovecraft did at least live to see it in print. With its bleak Antarctic setting and catalog of scientifically described horrors, it is the favorite Lovecraft story of many readers. It would easily rank as my favorite as well, if not that the entire second half of the story seems like a very bad idea. In my view, the story should have ended with Dyer and Danforth witnessing the Cyclopean city from the air and returning to the campsite in a state of horror and hysteria. The final sixty pages of city exploration undermine the city's innate architectural horror by bringing it too close, and they also spiral into an overly detailed historical account of the creatures that sounds too much like the backstory for someone's role-playing game campaign. The final lesson of the urban exploration seems to be that the Elder Things are more like us than we might have expected. They too have a historical cycle of flourishing and decadence, and they too can be the victims of murder. But all of these details undermine Lovecraft's primary gift, which is to poise his creatures forever on the very brink of knowability.

The first half of the story, by contrast, is perhaps the most brilliant thing Lovecraft ever wrote. A team of Miskatonic University professors and graduate students is assembled for an Antarctic expedition. An ingenious drill invented by Professor Pabodie of the Geology Department allows for deeper borings than on previous Antarctic expeditions. Professor Lake (Biology) soon turns almost mutinous after discovering what he believes to be fossils of strange footprints, though expedition commander Professor Dyer (Geology) dismisses them as normal markings not unlike others already known to his discipline. Lake asserts his instincts against Dyer's reservations, and takes a side-expedition by aircraft hundreds of miles from the main camp. His gamble initially pays off in a series of staggering scientific discoveries. Among other things, he finds a mountain range much higher than the Himalayas. But even more important is a wondrous cache of fossils from an impossibly early date, including a number of giant, barrel-shaped things that Lake takes to be highly advanced marine radiata. These discoveries are dramatically relayed in a series of radio conversations between the three separate camps of the expedition. Lake is astonished, excited, and perhaps a bit alarmed to discover that the barrel-shaped organisms, which seem to lie midway between the animal and vegetable kingdoms, are what made the strange footprints discovered earlier in the story. The specimens are brought into camp despite the ferocious barking of the dogs, who cannot stand the fossils (always a bad sign in a Lovecraft story). A terrible storm then arises, accompanied by a long period of radio silence. The remaining team with Dyer decides to investigate the silence, and flies to the camp of Professor Lake. All humans and dogs are found slaughtered, except that one human and one dog seem to be missing. The deaths of the humans seem to have occurred in especially grisly fashion: stripped of internal tissues and sprinkled lightly with salt. As usual, the reader guesses the truth well before the narrator, for the killers are later determined to be the "radiata" themselves, which turn out to be archetypal Lovecraftian beings: the Elder Things. Dyer and the graduate student Danforth then make an aerial expedition that leads first to a stunning description of architecture from the air, and then to a detailed exploration story that I have already criticized as bland, distracting, and unfortunate.

51. A Certain Strangeness of Technique

"The hitherto withheld photographs, both ordinary and aerial, will count in my favour; for they are damnably vivid and graphic. Still, they will be doubted because of the great lengths to which clever fakery can be carried. The ink drawings, of course, will be jeered at as obvious impostures; notwithstanding a certain strangeness of technique which art experts ought to remark and puzzle over." (MM 481)

This passage is obviously the stylistic descendant of the "vague but damnably suggestive" photographs of "The Whisperer in Darkness." Even the language is similar, since Dyer describes his Antarctic photographs as "damnably vivid and graphic." In a strange reversal of fortune, however, the photographs will turn out to be less valuable as evidence than the mere ink drawings are. After all, photographs can always be touched up with "clever fakery" to look like the real thing. The ink drawings initially seem to be in a weaker position, likely to be "jeered at as obvious impostures." Yet these drawings have something in their favor that even the photographs do not: "a certain strangeness of technique."

The *technique* of a number of ink drawings now seems to be a greater testament to veracity than either the content of the drawings or any aspect of the photographs. Normally there is an immediate bond between the "technique" of a drawing and what it depicts. But in Dyer's case there seems to be something amiss in that bond. We are first led to wonder what relation a *non-*strange technique of drawing would have to its subject matter. Is there something embedded in the normal *technique* of inkwork that makes it inherently less reliable than a photograph, as opposed to the simple fact that it is ink rather than a direct visual image? And if so, what is it about this new and strange technique that cuts against the grain of suspicion and impels us to recognize that such apparent impostures are proven to be true on the basis of the technique and nothing else? The odd technique of the drawings, after all, is not that of alien races, nor even of avant garde human artists, but of a mere professor of geology and one of his graduate students. Their pen techniques are influenced neither by aspirations toward artistic innovation, nor by the wish to perpetrate a fraud. Instead, the simple pressure of reality itself forces that technique to shift in the direction of the strange. Dyer notes that "art experts ought to remark and puzzle" over it. In a daringly bizarre inversion of the usual procedures of evidence, the truth of the Antarctic reports may be decided not by biologists or by detectives able to discern photographic fraud, but by art historians.

52. Not Unlike Ripple Effects

"These fragments [of slate] came from a point to the westward, near the Queen Alexandra Range; and Lake, as a biologist, seemed to find their curious marking unusually puzzling and provocative, though to my geological eye it looked not unlike some of the ripple effects reasonably common in the sedimentary rocks." (MM 488)

The usual role of scientists in Lovecraft stories is to conduct tests that lead nowhere, and then to shrug in puzzlement. He depicts scientists as generally on the right track, but rarely as far advanced as various lower-ranking humans (foreign sailors, theosophists, witches, mad Arabs) who have somehow been granted more direct insight into reality. In the passage above, we have something different: here, for the first and perhaps only time, Lovecraft stages a scientific controversy in the heart of one of his stories. The biologist senses the trace of moving life forms in the rock, while the geologist is less impressed by what seem to him like typical slate formations. In the end the biologist is right, though this scientific vindication costs him his life in grisly fashion.

The philosopher Bruno Latour has written at great length about controversy in science.[74] Once a fact is apparently established, it is treated as a solid and sleek "black box" without internal parts and without a history. As Latour puts it: "Who refers to Lavoisier's paper when writing the formula H_2O for water?"[75] This formula for water is now established as an apparently obvious datum. The same holds for most of our geological knowledge about rock (though geology has not even existed as a science for very long, and had to be largely created from scratch by Lyell[76]). Certain medical symptoms directly indicate certain diseases; certain subtle flavors separate great wine from "plonk." Normally there is an immediate bond between the object and its qualities, and this is how normal science progresses: by improving our detailed mastery of the catalog of delineable features associated with any given object.

A scientific controversy is something different. Here, some challenging new object or phenomenon confronts us, and requires us to rethink the very relation between any given thing and its qualities. At stake in the present case is a dispute over certain visible signs in the rock. It is described as a "curious marking," and earlier at greater length as "a queer triangular, striated marking about a foot in greatest diameter" (MM 488) For Dyer there is nothing special about this marking, which seems to belong to the known family of "ripple effects." In effect, the doomed Professor Lake performs what is actually a work of metaphor, taking qualities normally assigned to geological processes and transferring them to some vaguely sensed underlying causal and non-geological agent. Instead of Verlaine's "Your soul is like a painter's landscape...," Lake gives us "The unknown creature's footprint is like a ripple-effect ..." The qualities seem familiar to a geologist, but his rival transfers them to a different and still unknown object. What Kuhn calls "normal science" is brought to a halt, and we are on the verge of what he calls instead a paradigm shift,[77] in which the mere jostling of daily qualitative improvement comes to a close as a new object juts up through the heart of existing science.

Lake's obsession is both unremitting and completely on target. For those who know Lovecraft, the following passage is already cause for alarm: "It seems [Lake] had pondered a great deal, and with alarmingly radical daring, over that triangular striated marking in the slate; reading into it certain contradictions in Nature and geological period which whetted his curiosity to the utmost..." (MM 489) Lake is deeply committed to further "borings and blastings" (MM 489) and Dyer finally must relent and let him do as he pleases, even though the rock showing the marks "was of so vastly ancient a date –Cambrian if not actually pre-Cambrian– as to preclude the probable existence not only of all highly evolved life, but of any life at all above the unicellular or at most the trilobite stage." (MM 490) A contrast is drawn between the two scientists. Dyer "blackboxes" the relation between the markings and their presumed underlying cause: "since slate is no more than a metamorphic formation into which a sedimentary stratum is pressed, and since the pressure itself produces odd distorting effects on any markings which may exist, I saw no reason for extreme wonder over the striated depression." (MM 488) By contrast, Lake has the more typically Lovecraftian experience of a rift between objects and qualities, though he experiences this in slow-paced and halting fashion, working by instinct.

53. Widely Separated Bases

"In the morning I had a three-cornered wireless talk with Lake and Capt. Douglas at their widely separated bases..." (MM 494)

Much of the action in "The Whisperer in Darkness" took place through the mail, in the fascinating correspondence between Akeley and Wilmarth. Lovecraft handled that correspondence superbly, but of course there was already a long tradition of epistolary novels that provided him with numerous models: Bram Stroker's *Dracula*,[78] for instance. The innovation in "At the Mountains of Madness" is that much of the key information in the story is shared via three-way radio conversation. We as readers are present with Dyer, the narrator. Lake has flown several hundred miles to the northwest on his ill-fated pursuit of additional fossils. Back at McMurdo Sound, Captain Douglas and his crew are manning the *Arkham* and shepherding the supply cache. From McMurdo Sound, reports on the expedition are relayed back to the wider world, giving a certain degree of public visibility to everything that happens on the trip (though some of the worse events later need to be censored).

The discoveries reported by Lake over the radio become increasingly exciting and awe-inspiring. We have already heard that the mountains beneath which Lake is camped may equal the Himalayas in height (MM 491). On those mountains they witness "queer skyline effects– regular sections of cubes clinging to highest peaks," (MM 492) which we as readers correctly sense cannot be natural formations. The mountains seem to be "pre-Cambrian slate," (MM 492) giving an air of abysmal antiquity to the new findings. Then come the further biological discoveries that can be left to the next section. The radio goes dead, and initially this is thought to be a result of the punishing Antarctic storm that hits Dyer's camp that night no less than Lake's. But upon investigation, it is discovered that Lake's entire party is dead.

Whereas letters are obviously indirect forms of communication, radio lies paradoxically somewhere between the direct and the indirect. In one sense radio move at the speed of light, allowing conversations to occur in real time. But in another sense, with the inevitable crackling and the interweaving of vague oscillating drones, radio is an eerie medium– as anyone knows who spent a childhood falling asleep to distant radio shows at night.

The wireless conversation allows the scientific discoveries made by Lake to be made immediately known to the outside world, while the distance the radio covers protects survivors from the horrible fate of the Lake party. It is also interesting to note that, whereas in most Lovecraft stories evidence is laughed off or doubted by credible outside authorities, this seems highly unlikely to happen here. True enough, Dyer worries aloud on the first pages of the story that: "it is an unfortunate fact that relatively obscure men like myself and my associates, connected only with a small university, have little chance of making an impression where matters of a wildly bizarre or highly contro-versial nature are concerned." (MM 481) Yet the reader somehow feels that the collected evidence will be perfectly persuasive. Such qualifying statements as Dyer's serve to emphasize the utterly strange character of the events witnessed in the Antarctic, but we as readers do not genuinely feel that the reports of the Miskatonic exploration party will be dismissed in the manner he fears. Quite the contrary– as Dyer and Danforth's initial censorship policy seems to acknowledge.

54. An Einstein of Biology

"Emphasise importance of discovery in press. Will mean to biology what Einstein has meant to mathematics and physics." (MM 497)

In 1905, the young Swiss patent officer Albert Einstein had what is often described as his *annus mirabilis*, publishing four pathbreaking articles in the *Annalen der Physik*. In the first, Einstein explained the so-called photoelectric effect and black body radiation by proposing that light comes in small bundles or quanta, thereby extending Max Planck's earlier work on the theory of heat, and setting the table for Niels Bohr's quantum theory of electron orbits. In the second, Einstein's discussion of Brownian motion in liquids gave persuasive evidence for the existence of atoms, which until then had been defended by a limited pro-atomist camp in the scientific world. In the third, Einstein revealed his theory of special relativity, which further disproved the existence of an "ether" filling empty space, and also established the speed of light as a constant for all frames of reference– a direct challenge to Isaac Newton's assumption that immediate action at a distance was possible in the case of gravity. In the fourth, Einstein gave his famous equation $E=mc^2$, demonstrating the equivalence of matter and energy and thereby planting the seed for the later development of atomic weaponry. In 1916, after more than a decade of further struggle, Einstein published his general theory of relativity, which explained important anomalies in the orbit of Mercury that were inexplicable in the terms of Newton's classic *Principia*. This led to a more sweeping theory in which gravity was redefined as the curvature of space. Supporting observations for this theory, made by Sir Arthur Stanley Eddington during a 1919 eclipse, made Einstein a global celebrity.

This brief summary of Einstein's achievements highlights the revolutionary force of his insights in multiple areas of physics (but not really in mathematics, despite Professor Lake's misleading claim in the passage above). The post-Einsteinian physical universe was vastly different from that of 1904. In the passage that concerns us here, Professor Lake implicitly asks us to consider *Lake himself* as the Einstein of biology. Charles Darwin already has a good claim to occupy that position, and with his field-altering theory of evolution Darwin sets the bar very high for anyone who would claim to be the new Einstein of the biological sciences. Yet never for a moment do we as readers doubt Lake's claim. The report over the wireless tells us that his team member Fowler discovered that the "triangular striated prints" (MM 497) found earlier in ancient slate was also found in identical form in much later Comanchian sandstone and limestone, suggesting a rather non-Darwinian durability of a single species over appalling stretches of geological time. As if establishing his worthy pedigree for such a major discovery, Lake remarks drily and telegraphically: "joins up with my previous work and amplifies conclusions." (MM 497) The upshot of the discovery is that it "appears to indicate, as I suspected, that earth has seen whole cycle or cycles of organic life before known one that begins with Archaeozoic cells." (MM 497) The further question is how such advanced evolution could occur so quickly given the rather primitive state of the planet in those earliest eons, and the faint implication is made that there must be an extraterrestrial origin for these earliest living earth-beings. Given these conclusions, Lake's request to "emphasise importance of discovery in press" seems like anything but empty self-promotion.

And yet, these claims to Einsteinian stature are made *before* the final and most chilling discovery. At 10:15 p.m., Lake announces the discovery of "monstrous barrel-shaped fossil of wholly unknown nature; probably vegetable unless overgrown specimen of wholly unknown marine radiata." (MM 498) A super-Einsteinian moment occurs in the following hour: "11:30 p.m. Attention Dyer, Pabodie, Douglas. Matter of highest –I might say transcendent– importance. *Arkham* must relay to Kingsport Head Station at once. Strange barrel growth is the Archaean thing that left prints in rock." (MM 498) This latter point is perhaps less a theoretical discovery than a terrifying practical breakthrough, since the barrel growths (a.k.a. The Elder Things) soon wipe out Lake and his entire party. It could mean to politics and military science what Einstein meant to physics and Darwin and Lake to biology.

55. Tough as Leather, but Flexible

"10:15 p.m. Important discovery. Orrendorf and Watkins, working underground with light, found monstrous barrel-shaped fossil of wholly unknown nature; probably vegetable unless overgrown specimen of unknown marine radiata... Tough as leather, but astonishing flexibility retained in places." (MM 498)

Of interest here is the final sentence: "Tough as leather, but astonishing flexibility retained in places." We have had several encounters with Lovecraftian disjunctions: e.g., "inane titter or whisper." As remarked on those occasions, such disjunctions in Lovecraft never offer a clean choice between two discrete alternatives, but try to zero in on some barely describable third option that the two given words serve to establish as their elusive midpoint. For example, the voice of Nahum's newly insane young son is something between a titter and a whisper, whatever that might mean– and beyond that, it is inane. But with the final sentence in the passage above, what we have is a more explicit conjunction. In its simplest form, the phrase could be reduced to this: "tough and flexible." By changing it to "tough *but* flexible," Lovecraft asks us to consider a spirit of paradoxical contrast between these two adjectives. As a result, we are left in a situation not unlike that of the inane titter or whisper. We might say that the barrel-shaped fossils display "inane toughness and flexibility," just as the description of Nahum's son might have been reworded as follows: "he spoke in a titter, but in whispering fashion."

"Tough but flexible" is then further explained. "Tough as leather" sounds like a very high standard of toughness, until we remember that these are utterly primeval fossils, for which something as loose as a "leathery" texture sounds as soft as gelatin. As for the second part of the sentence, the point that the flexibility is "astonishing" performs the usual dual function of all such amazement-adjectives in Lovecraft: they make the unlikely seem plausible by having the narrator express surprise on our behalf, while also cluing us into Professor's Lake state of mind and thereby making him visible as a sincere intentional agent (more a tragic than a comic one, in this case). Finally, the added qualification "astonishing flexibility retained *in places*" adds a note of circumspect precision, making the unlikely conjunction of toughness and flexibility in a fossil seem more plausible by confining it to a limited physical extent.

56. A Curiously Vegetable Symmetry

"Cannot yet assign positively to animal or vegetable kingdom, but odds now favour animal. Probably represents incredibly advanced evolution of radiata without loss of certain primitive features... Symmetry is curiously vegetable-like, suggesting vegetable's essentially up-and-down structure rather than animal's fore-and-aft structure. " (MM 500)

A set of monstrous, barrel-shaped fossils is found underground in the Antarctic. Though older than even the most ancient protozoa of primeval biology, the fossils are only as tough as leather, and even then it is leather of a somewhat flexible sort. We now learn further that the identity of the creatures wavers midway between the animal and vegetable kingdoms, though "odds now favour animal," the feeblest expression of certitude one can imagine. The strange thing is that this uncertainty seems to be based solely on a visual inspection of anatomy. For two pages earlier, Lake had reported: "Strange barrel growth is the Archaean thing that left prints in rocks." (MM 498) Since the leaving of prints in fossilized rock seems directly associated with locomotion, the fact that Lake can say only that "odds now favour animal" is disturbing indeed. It is not a mere epistemo-logical wavering between animal and vegetable based on insufficient evidence, but an uncertainty suggesting that the motion of giant vegetables across the earth's surface is now regarded as thinkable.

The second sentence represents a preposterous attempt to recuperate the shocking fossil cache into the existing knowledge of biology. In the first place, "incredibly advanced evolution of radiata" seems like a palpably absurd notion. Radially symmetrical creatures such as jellyfish and starfish belong to this group, and their highly primitive nature seems utterly incompatible with the highly complicated anatomy described at MM 499-500. It becomes even more absurd after the passage a few pages later that will be covered in the next section. For this reason, the throwaway clause "without loss of certain primitive features" is the height of comedy. It would be like saying that a certain new flavor of ice cream is "an incredibly advanced version of vanilla, without the loss of a certain underlying blandness." Aside from this, we the readers know full well that these creatures will turn out to be something much worse than highly complicated jellyfish.

The third and final sentence is a fine example of Lovecraft's talent for using objective scientific description as a stylistic agent of horror. In the first place, the sentence is *informative*: it might never have occurred to most readers that there is a basic difference between vegetable and animal symmetries, other than those who happen to have had some sort of botanical or zoological training. But once the point is so objectively stated, it becomes immediately disconcerting. For we already know that these barrel-shaped entities seem to have the power of locomotion, given the striated trackings they left in ancient fossils. The idea of a creature with basically vegetable symmetry, lacking the "animal's fore-and-aft structure" but still moving about on the earth, is a terrible image to contemplate.

57. Excessively Primitive and Archaic in Some Respects

"The nervous system was so complex and highly developed as to leave Lake aghast. Though excessively primitive and archaic in some respects, the thing had a set of ganglial centres and connectives arguing the very extremes of specialized development. Its five-lobed brain was surprisingly advanced..." (MM 503)

This passage is interesting both in its own right and in view of what comes next. These "incredibly advanced evolutions of radiata" are indeed so incredibly advanced that they have five-lobed brains, despite their curiously vegetable symmetry. The science talk weighs ever more heavily on the reader. Despite the possibly vegetable structure of the fossil "the thing had a set of ganglial centres and connectives arguing the very extremes of specialized development." The word "arguing" here helps to create a slight gap between the visible phenomenon of the ganglial centres/connectives and the extremes of specialized development. Rather than one leading obviously and immediately to the other, the link is a more tenuous one of rational suggestion and inference. This deabsolutizing of the link between phenomenon and conclusion is even rather amusing, given that no one who hears about ganglial centres and connectives in a vegetable-looking organism will doubt that we are in the presence of an abominably intelligent creature.

Even more troubling, however, is that the physical structure of the nervous system suggests to Lake that these creatures must have had a sensory-perceptual structure unlike any other we know. As Dyer summarizes Lake's findings: "...there were signs of a sensory equipment... involving factors alien to any other terrestrial organism. Probably it had more than five senses, so that its habits could not be predicted from any existing analogy." (MM 503) From a color that is a color only by analogy, we have advanced to a creature that senses in a manner outstripping all possible analogy, despite the immediately visible nervous system lying bare on an Antarctic dissection table. The dissection scene becomes all the more unbearable when Dyer gratuitously adds that "it must, Lake thought, have been a creature of keen sensitiveness and delicately differentiated functions in its primal world; much like the ants and bees of today." (MM 503) The final touch about ants and bees makes matters even worse, by vaguely suggesting that there may be something akin to swarms or colonies in the societies of these barrel-shaped monstrosities.

The taxonomical contradictions begin to mass, in a manner that is surely unprecedented in literature: "to give [the fossil] a name at this stage was mere folly. It looked like a radiate, but was clearly something more. It was partly vegetable, but had three-fourths of the essentials of animal structure." (MM 503) It seemed to have originated in the sea, judging from its symmetry and "certain other attributes," (MM 503) whatever those might be. Yet in a crowning absurdity, this evident marine origin leads to a puzzling tension with the *wings* of the creature which, "after all, held a persistent suggestion of the aerial." (MM 503) To say the least! Even worse is that Lake and Dyer seem fully aware of the resemblance between these creatures and those referred to in the dreaded *Necronomicon*. Still one step worse is the fact of their friendship with their Miskatonic colleague Wilmarth from "The Whisperer in Darkness," and their additional familiarity with the octopus-dragon-human monster of our opening tale. Lake jams it all together into a single nondescript sentence over the radio, telling us that the fossils are "also like prehistoric folklore things Wilmarth has spoken of– Cthulhu cult appendages, etc." (MM 500)

Although much of Lovecraft's style involves allusions in depth to indescribable realities withdrawing from all linguistic, perceptual, and even cognitive access, the descriptions of the barrel-shaped monsters also generate perplexity on the fully accessible plane of empirical sensory data. The dissection report works again like a cubist painting, with numerous jostling planes jammed together along a single surface– all of them completely visible, yet never quite fitting together as a whole. This is why I have also pointed to a marked Husserlian element in Lovecraft's writing along with the more widely defended Kantian reading. In a certain sense there is nothing strictly "noumenal" about the barrel-shaped creatures. Every one of their features is exactly described, yet in combination these features are so monstrous and incompatible that they cannot easily be bundled together in a Humean arsenal of qualities.

58. An Amplified World of Lurking Horrors

"Thenceforward the ten of us –but the student Danforth and I above all others– were to face a hideously amplified world of lurking horrors which nothing can erase from our emotions, and which we would refrain from sharing with mankind in general if we could." (MM 506)

The turning point referred to here is the four-and-a-half-hour airplane flight made by Dyer and nine others to the site of the Lake party, which has fallen out of radio communication during the storm. The flight will include the devastating mirage of what later turns out to be a real Cyclopean city, as well as the painful sight of the campsite itself, filled with mutilated and partially devoured corpses and a ghastly series of upright snow-graves containing damaged specimens of the barrel-like fossils.

Lovecraft uses several techniques to lend credence to the near-mental breakdowns hinted at in the passage above. First, he makes it a terrible experience shared by no fewer than *ten* people, thereby placing it beyond the possibility of individual or small-group delusion. Second, he creates a gradation of disturbance by adding "the student Danforth and I above all others," adding some internal contrast to the ten-man continuum of insanity by hinting at the special emotional challenges faced by two members of the group, he himself being one of them. Ultimately, we will hear that Danforth was pressed to even further extremes of weakened sanity by a final sight witnessed by himself alone and not by Dyer. Third, there is the fact that just prior to the passage above, Dyer had said of the airplane flight that "it marked my loss, at the age of fifty-four, of all that peace and balance which the normal mind possesses through its accustomed conception of external Nature and Nature's laws." (MM 506) No highly strung and impressionable young man like the student Danforth, Dyer has enjoyed fifty-four years on the earth– years whose adult portion was presumably made up of relatively plodding academic routine, given the professional obscurity to which he laid claim on the story's first page. The bulk of those fifty-four years of normal, sane existence is shattered by the events of the flight. An even greater bulk of human experience, made up of billions of individuals and thousands of years of zoologically non-fabulous collective history, is about to be shattered by Dyer's lengthy public report on the Antarctic wastes, which "we would refrain from sharing with mankind in general if we could." But unfortunately that is not an option, given that "the coming Starkweather-Moore expedition" plans to return to the region, "despite the warnings I have issued since our return from the Antarctic." (MM 483)

The key phrase of the passage, however, is this: "a hideously amplified world of lurking horrors." We are already well-practiced enough to treat the word "hideously" in appreciative, non-Wilsonian fashion. That leaves us with the honed-down remnant, "an amplified world of lurking horrors." This is one case where the adjectives *are* asked to do most of the work, since without them we are left with this bland and ineffective opening: "Thenceforward the ten of us –but the student Danforth and I above all others– were to face a world of horrors which nothing can erase from our emotions..." To say that they faced "a world of horrors" does little to move the reader's imagination, and even resembles the mere assertions found in pulp. But along come the adjectives to save us, for once. The fact that the horrors are "lurking" shows that they are not just strident recent incidents in the Antarctic, but subterranean background threats secretly with us since the dawn of human history. And the fact that the world they compose is "amplified" implies that traces of the horror are already faintly visible in our midst, and will now merely be made more explicit.

59. Truncated Cones

"There were truncated cones, sometimes terraced or fluted, surmounted by tall cylindrical shafts here and there bulbously enlarged and often capped with tiers of thinnish scalloped discs; and strange, beetling, table-like constructions suggesting piles of multitudinous rectangular slabs or circular plates or five-pointed stars with each one overlapping the one beneath." (MM 508-9)

This passage is one of Lovecraft's greatest, combining his two primary weird stylistic tricks of (a) allusion in depth and (b) maddening clutter along the surface. Much as with the detailed balancing of the various animal and vegetable features of the Elder Things, the *primary* effort here is not to allude to mysterious things hidden in the depths beyond the sensory and linguistic world. Instead, Lovecraft makes use of the opposite and essentially cubist/Husserlian technique of crowding the surface of reality with numerous unmanageable details and descriptions. In this way we begin to realize that the object in question, though by no means hidden or withdrawn from cognition, is something over and above the total abundance of features. For nothing could be more absurd than a Humean treatment of the same scene: "When we think of a Cyclopean Antarctic city, we only join five consistent ideas, with which we were formerly acquainted– *truncated cones, tall cylindrical shafts, thinnish scalloped discs, beetling table-like constructions,* and *multitudinous rectangular slabs.*"

The reason for Hume's failure here is not only because each of these elements needs further analysis into each of its sub-components. The more important reason is that the city has a total effect not reducible to a sum total of architectural sub-units. That said, we should also say that along with the cubist surface effect of too many images colliding and failing to combine neatly in a bundle, each of the elements in the description also alludes to the indescribable in its own right. Imagine that we were to take the passage above and brutally strip it down to the following: "There were cones, shafts, discs, plates, and slabs." Such minimalism might be elegant in another context, but this is simply not a Lovecraftian sentence. Minimalism allows only that what you see is what you get. But for Lovecraft, what you get is always far more than can be seen. Hence the nearly unvisualizable hysteria of such phrases as "truncated cones, sometimes terraced or fluted," "thinnish scalloped discs," and best of all, "strange, beetling, table-like constructions suggesting piles of multitudinous rectangular slabs." And take note, the strange, beetling table-like constructions merely *suggest* piles of multitudinous rectangular slabs. If you were hoping to find piles of multitudinous rectangular slabs in person, you have apparently come to the wrong place. With each new story, Lovecraft becomes ever more complicated and daring in his mounting up of increasingly delirious descriptive effects.

60. Letting Hints Stand for Actual Facts

"It is only with vast hesitancy and repugnance that I let my mind go back to Lake's camp and what we really found there–and to that other thing beyond the frightful mountain wall. I am constantly tempted to shirk the details, and to let hints stand for actual facts and ineluctable deductions." (MM 514)

In a sense this passage is somewhat comical, since what Dyer describes as a "temptation" is long since a *fait accompli*. Where in

Lovecraft does the narrator *not* shirk the details and "let hints stand for actual facts and ineluctable deductions"? Indeed, the only time when this *fails* to happen is in cases such as the preceding architectural description, in which the opposite technique is utilized: not hints, but the brute force of excessive concrete descriptions that cannot be integrated in any usual convenient way.

At the close of "The Whisperer in Darkness," we also saw the manner in which inference, rather than directly accessible terrifying subject matter, is the true stuff of horror. The frightening thing was not seeing the replica of Akeley's face and hands lying in a chair, but the accompanying inference that rather than speaking with the real Akeley earlier in the evening, Wilmarth had actually been in conversation with a fungoid creature passing itself off as Akeley. In this respect, hints are generally even *more* terrifying than the real thing. This adds a paradoxical note to Dyer's remarks in the passage at the head of this section, since replacing facts and deductions with hints might lead to an even more horrifying situation– just as the neurotic symptoms from which one suffers prior to a talking-cure are perhaps more debilitating than the actual *knowledge* that you were seduced by your nursemaid at the age of three. In fact, we might even rewrite this passage more truly by having Dyer make the opposite claim: "I am constantly tempted to provide the full details, and to let actual facts and ineluctable deductions stand for hints and allusions." In some ways, nothing is *less* horrifying than those brass-knuckled materialist doctrines that say there is nothing more to the mind than the physical mechanism of the brain.

61. Tin Cans Pried Open in Unlikely Ways

"Then, too, there was the upsetting of the larder, the disappearance of certain staples, and the jarringly comical heap of tin cans pried open in the most unlikely ways and at the most unlikely places." (MM 517)

We have already seen cases of Lovecraft ripping asunder our usual assumptions about the most basic features of the perceptions of color and sound. We have seen him introduce uncertainty into the most basic representational features of photographs and voice recordings in order to yield vague but "damnably suggestive" images rather than pieces of directly legible physical evidence. In the passage above, Lovecraft extends this feature into the sphere of pragmatic action. Through some combination of innate features of the human mind and the sheer force of training and habit, it seems obvious to all of us how a tin can ought to be opened. Normally a can has one lid that is clearly meant to be opened, or at worst we are able to choose indifferently between one end of the cylinder or the other. By bringing the Elder Things into the sphere of practical goods found at Lake's ill-fated campsite, Lovecraft raises the possibility of a potentially infinite number of alternative ways to deal with any object of praxis. The thought of even the most violent cosmic beings tearing open tin cans in ineffective fashion is immediately comical to readers, despite the setting of inhuman mass murder. Following his usual technique, Lovecraft tries to persuade readers by expressing solidarity with their likely reactions to what is described, since he himself calls the heap of butchered tin cans "jarringly comical." He makes the wise authorial decision not to tell us exactly *how* the opening of tin cans occurred "in the most unlikely ways and at the most unlikely places," since it is hard to think of more than a few alternative possibilities; these would all come up short, along with being quickly exhausted and leading to tedium. But by leaving the details unstated, Lovecraft lets us rest with our vague worry and alarm over how the bizarre opening of tin cans might have been attempted.

He even extends the theme to other cases of incompetence by the monsters in coming to grips with human utensils. We hear, for example, of the "spatter-fringed ink-blots on certain pieces of paper," perhaps Lovecraft's anticipatory parody of the slowly emerging abstract art of his times. We hear of "evidences of curious alien fumbling and experimentation around the planes and all other mechanical devices both at the camp and at the boring." We have a "profusion of scattered matches, intact, broken, or spent," unlikely to be the human work of any nationality. And finally, various tent-cloths and fur suits show the signs of "peculiar and unorthodox slashings." (MM 517) Our everyday handling of practical items may seem like a simple matter, even cause for boredom. But by generating examples of comical ineptitude in such handling, Lovecraft creates a new fissure between objects and the normal way in which they are unthinkingly manipulated by us journeyman humans.

62. Guesses Forbidden by Sanity

"I will not be so naïve as to deny that each of us may have harboured wild guesses which sanity forbade him to formulate completely." (MM 518)

Here again, Dyer repeats the notion that hints, guesses, and allusions are a bulwark for sanity against the terrors of literal truth. This is an exact inversion of the philosophy expressed in the opening sentences of the Cthulhu story: "The most merciful thing in the world, I think, is the inability of the human mind to correlate all its contents. We live on a placid island of ignorance in the midst of black seas of infinity, and it was not meant that we should voyage far." (CC 167) As the Cthulhu passage has it, the literal level inhabited by mainstream scientists and of critics such as Edmund Wilson is our guarantee of sanity, while allusive suggestions and hints are the root of true horror. This accurately reflects Lovecraft's general philosophy of horror, which resembles that of Poe in its credo that suggestion is the site of the terrible rather than of sanity. The same is true in "The Whisperer in Darkness," where the vague and the damnably suggestive are always treated as worse than the literal truth.

But "At the Mountains of Madness" seems to take the opposite tack. Dyer always holds that oblique suggestion is for the sane, while the literal is only for those willing to risk full-blown insanity. He would prefer to leave things at the level of hint ("Trust me, you don't want to go to the Antarctic. If only you knew…"), but is forced by the dangerous aims of the Starkweather-Moore expedition to file a literal report on what was found in the Lake campsite and the city beyond the nearby mountains. If we were to replace Dyer's characteristic attitude with that of Wilmarth (it is comical that they are personally acquainted, and that Dyer refers to him as "that unpleasantly erudite folklorist Wilmarth," MM 508) we might end up with the opposite procedure. Rather than Dyer saying that he prefers to give hints but is forced to tell the bald-faced ugly truth, he might say that he would prefer to tell his story in literal pulp fiction style, but that in order to prevent the Starkweather-Moore party from traveling, he is forced to use the grotesque allusions and hints that characterize Lovecraft's style at its best. It can be read as a challenge in advance to the Edmund Wilsons who might interpret Dyer's accurate account of events as a bad piece of *Weird Tales* writing. In order to scare them all into belief, Dyer (i.e., Lovecraft) is forced to become a vague yet damnably suggestive stylist.

63. Worse Than Formless

"I thought again of... the daemoniac plateau of Leng, of the Mi-Go, or Abominable Snow-Men of the Himalayas, of the Pnakotic Manuscripts with their pre-human implications, of the Cthulhu cult, of the *Necronomicon*, and of the Hyperborean legends of formless Tsathoggua and the worse than formless star-spawn associated with that semi-entity." (MM 524)

In the first instance, what we have here is a case of Lovecraft trying to add bulk and credibility to a survey of his fictional geography by including two real-world myths in the list: those of the Abominable Snow-Men of the Himalayas and the Hyperborean people said to live much further to the north than Ancient Greece. The rest are the creations of Lovecraft himself, or perhaps the joint work of Lovecraft and his circle of literary friends. Adding further bulk to the list is the fact that Dyer and Danforth are later able to falsify an *incorrect* assumption about one of these places. While it is often suggested (within Lovecraft's own stories) that the plateau of Leng lies somewhere in Central Asia, Dyer seems able to conclude definitively that Leng is none other than the terrain where he and Danforth find the Cyclopean Antarctic city. This establishes a modicum of scientific-critical spirit in Dyer's relation to the list of places, as if to let us know that he is not so credulous as to swallow everything whole. The list also continues the accelerating process by which Lovecraft begins to weave his various stories together into a single tapestry, with the inclusion of Cthulhu and of Wilbur Whateley's much-prized *Necronomicon*, which we have seen is stocked even in Harvard's prestigious Widener Library. Furthermore, Lovecraft uses the stylistic device of beginning the list with simpler or more credible items, all the better to lure us into taking seriously the final, utterly raving clause: "the Hyperborean legends of formless Tsathoggua and the worse than formless star-spawn associated with that semi-entity."

In fact, this clause bears a closer look. First, we see that Lovecraft's own fabrication of the Tsathoggua legend is credited instead to the Hyperborean people who are mentioned in real-life history at least as early as Herodotus. This adds desired bulk and credibility to what would otherwise be a stylistically comical passage. "Formless Tsathoggua" sounds bad enough, with its vague similarity to Lovecraft's "blind idiot God Azathoth." But then formless Tsathoggua is made to sound like a pillar of sanity at the merest fringes of the darkness, despite being described in chilling fashion as a "semi-entity." For he must be a gentle old uncle in comparison with the *worse than formless* star-spawn associated with him. These even worse creatures are "vague yet damnably suggestive" for three reasons. First, they are associated with a semi-entity. Second, while the semi-entity is merely formless, they themselves are "worse" than formless. Third, they are described bizarrely as "star-spawn," and we the readers are unsure whether to take this merely in the metaphorical sense of "coming from other solar systems," or more literally as if they were actually *generated* by stars, in much the same fashion as chemical elements.

The Shadow Over Innsmouth

Joshi rightly says of this story that "Lovecraft never achieved a greater atmosphere of insidious decay than in 'The Shadow Over Innsmouth': one can almost smell the overwhelming stench of fish, see the physical anomalies of the inhabitants, and perceive the century-long dilapidation of an entire town in the story's evocative prose."[79] It was written late in 1931, and first published in book form in 1936, accompanied by four disappointing woodcuts by Frank Utpatel, done in a pop expressionist style with a few hints of pop cubism.

The young narrator has just completed his junior year at Oberlin College and is making a tour of New England. He wishes to travel from (the real) Newburyport to (the fictitious) Arkham, but finds the train fare too expensive. A station agent suggests that he take the bus, but warns that it passes through Innsmouth, a town long shunned by the residents of Newburyport. The narrator learns various intriguing things about Innsmouth from the station agent, then visits both the library and the local Historical Society to learn even more; in the latter place he sees a fiendish gold tiara decorated with sinister aquatic reliefs that is said to come from Innsmouth. The next day he finds himself alone on the bus to Innsmouth, driven by one Joe Sargent, whose physical deformities suggest some sort of biological degeneration. Eventually the narrator discovers that a good portion of the Innsmouth populace is marked by similar degenerate features: "the Innsmouth look," he calls it. After some exploration of the town, the narrator eventually lures local drunkard Zadok Allen to the waterfront, and spends two hours loosening up the elderly man with bootleg liquor. Eventually, Allen recites the wild history of a pact between Obed Marsh (a key figure in early Innsmouth) and a strange group of Pacific islanders. Marsh seems to have persuaded the townspeople to abandon Christianity for a pagan cult known as the Esoteric Order of Dagon, and to have ordered a number of families to mate with certain hybrid sea-creatures. Suddenly, Old Zadok screams that their conversation has been witnessed from the reef far offshore, and warns the narrator to run.

Our narrator is not inclined to believe Old Zadok's story. But upon returning to the bus pickup point he is told, unconvincingly, that the bus has broken down and that he will have to spend the night in the Gilman House, the dismal Innsmouth hotel where strange conversations have been overheard by past visitors. During the night, there is an attempted break-in of the narrator's hotel room. He manages to flee through two adjoining rooms and leap to the roof of a warehouse below. From there he succeeds in escaping from Innsmouth, first by mimicking the "shambling" gait of local residents, then by following an abandoned railway and leaping across a perilous gap on a bridge. Outside the town, he observes a huge party of pursuers attempting to track him down. As they cross the railroad tracks not far in front of him, he catches a full glimpse of their inhuman bodies and sickening gait and attire. The narrator faints. Awakening the next morning, he leaves the area and reports the events to authorities. As we learned at the beginning of the tale, the Federal government eventually attacks the town after a seven-month investigation, demolishes many of its buildings, and torpedoes the offshore reef. Numerous Innsmouth residents vanish into concentration camps, but even liberal groups allow this to pass quietly once they are allowed to see the prisoners in person. The story ends with the narrator concluding that he himself is descended from these fish-frog-human hybrids along one of his family branches. As time passes, his eyes look increasingly like the typical unblinking eyes of Innsmouth. He considers suicide, but by story's end appears to have resolved to make common cause with the fish-frogs, who have not been entirely eradicated by the Federal forces.

64. Passive and Reticent Liberal Organisations

"Complaints from many liberal organisations were met with long confidential discussions, and representatives were taken on trips to certain camps and prisons. As a result, these societies became surprisingly passive and reticent." (SI 587)

A large Federal force makes a major raid on Innsmouth: "Uninquiring souls let this occurrence pass as one of the major clashes in a spasmodic war on liquor. Keener news-followers, however, wondered at the prodigious number of arrests, the abnormally large force of men used in making them, and the secrecy surrounding the disposal of the prisoners." (SI 587) When vast numbers of arrestees seem to vanish, liberal groups take a stand on behalf of human rights. But after being brought in for consultations and personal inspection of the prisoners, even these liberals grow silent. This happens at the very beginning of the story, at a time when we have not yet seen the residents of Innsmouth for ourselves. As soon as we do, we recall this opening paragraph and are no longer surprised at the passivity and reticence of the liberal organisations, not blaming them at all for reaching their humanitarian limits. Indeed, if anything makes us wonder, it is the fact that the arrestees were imprisoned rather than shot, since we later learn from Old Zadok that the creatures are immortal unless they die by violence.

In most of Lovecraft's stories, the terrible truth is known only to a small number of people, and is either purposely shielded from the public for their own good, or offered to the public and met with disbelief (as is the case with the mocking story about Dunwich tall tales picked up by the Associated Press at DH 394). "The Shadow Over Innsmouth" is the only case in Lovecraft where government conspiracy organizes a cover-up so deep, and so justified, that even liberal and humanitarian groups tacitly approve the use of concentration camps. The danger in "At the Mountains of Madness" is that the authorities know too little, and are in danger of learning too much. In the case of Innsmouth things work in reverse: the authorities already know too much, and prefer that the public should continue to know very little.

65. A Slopping-Like Voice

"It was foreign talk, he thought, but he said the bad thing about it was the kind of voice that sometimes spoke. It sounded so unnatural –slopping-like, he said– that he didn't dare undress and go to sleep." (SI 592)

This is the station agent informing the narrator of the chilling experience of a factory inspector who stayed at the Gilman House, the only hotel in Innsmouth. The agent's purpose is to discourage the narrator from staying there as well, advising that he remain for the night in Newburyport and take the 10 AM bus to Innsmouth, followed by the 8 PM service to Arkham. This warning prepares us effectively for events the next evening in Innsmouth, when Joe Sargent fakes mechanical trouble with his bus. This forces the narrator to stay in the Gilman House, where all efforts are made to kill him during the night.

The most interesting notion in the passage, of course, is the "slopping-like" voice, a good fit with the generally sinister marine characteristics of the Innsmouth residents. In Lovecraft's other great tales the monsters often have an extraterrestrial feel. Here, however, the creatures of Innsmouth are purely of this earth; or rather, of the seas that cover three-quarters of the earth. Rather than being zoologically remote from what we already know, they represent an obscenely crossbred jumble of human, fish, and frog– three species normally kept entirely separate where issues of mating are concerned. The narrator remarks of bus driver Joe Sargent, almost as an afterthought: "A certain greasiness about the follow increased my dislike. He was evidently given to working or lounging around the fish docks, and carried with him much of their characteristic smell." (SI 598)

This along with other typical Innsmouth features –unblinking eyes, vaguely elliptical heads, clumsy hands, gigantic feet– help depict Innsmouth humans as already vaguely displaying the obvious traits of fish and frogs.

But the slopping-like voice is also interesting on purely technical stylistic grounds. For the description of the voice is really just a concealed version of Lovecraftian disjunctions such as "titter or whisper," but here with one of the terms left implicit. Notice that the station agent does not say the following: "he said the voice from next door almost escaped the power of language to describe, but it seemed to have certain features of a slopping sound." This would be the classic sort of Lovecraftian allusion to the unnameable. Instead, Lovecraft comes out and tells us directly that the voice was slopping (though qualified faintly as "slopping-*like*"). The problem is not that the features of the voice are too deep to be described, but that this reasonably clear description is hard to integrate with the other accessible aspect of the situation: the fact that we are dealing with a human voice, which rarely or never has slopping undertones. Thus the passage could be rewritten like this: "It was foreign talk, he thought, but he said the bad thing about it was the *slopping or human* voice that sometimes spoke." Here we have a classic Lovecraftian disjunction, but an imbalanced one, since there is little that is surprising about overhearing a human-sounding voice in a conversation. Thus, we are really being asked to aim our attention at vocal tones midway between those of a normal human and those of slopping sounds. This is nowhere near as difficult as imagining a color that is color only by analogy, yet the effect leaves us uneasy nonetheless.

66. An Unknown Racial or National Stream

"All other art objects I had ever seen either belonged to some known racial or national stream, or else were consciously modernistic defiances of every recognized stream. This tiara was neither. It clearly belonged to some settled technique of infinite maturity and perfection, yet that technique was utterly remote from any... which I had ever heard of or seen exemplified." (SI 595)

The first sentence is beautifully constructed, and pulls the neat trick of placing all known human cultures on the same level as all anti-traditional modernisms. While such modernisms generally present themselves as daring revolutions against all precedent, this sentence portrays them instead as locked with tradition in a dialectic of mere defiance. The role of exotic "other" to all human history is thereby stripped from modernism and given to the strange tiara in the display case, which clearly belongs to an established historical culture, though one previously unknown to us all. Human culture and human modernistic rebellion now seem equally prosaic in comparison with Innsmouth-look jewelry.

This is a typical Lovecraftian gesture. Often in his stories, we encounter objects that are utterly startling in their novelty, yet which are nonetheless recognizable as belonging to a distinct and otherworldly style. Our attention is thereby shifted from the surface content of such objects to whatever barely detectable regularities in its structure alert us that they belong to a settled tradition. Any one of us might be able to give rough descriptions of the style of Thomas Aquinas, Cézanne, or Trakl; in so doing, we would probably discuss some of the things they frequently talk about or visually depict, as well as a few basic features of how their works are generally organized. Yet this obviously becomes impossible when we are dealing with completely unfamiliar, even otherworldly content, since for us this will elude any exact description. Nonetheless, certain structural regularities might be vaguely recognizable. We all know a similar experience from travel. As an American I cannot quite put my finger on what it felt like to spend my first week in Egypt, Japan, or India. Along with the obvious surface differences between these places and the United States, there are certain tacit rules and usages that one subtly learns to observe. This layer of vague and unstated regularities is what we find embodied in the tiara.

More than this, the item is inherently disturbing in its own right. For one thing, it seems to be "designed for a head of almost freakishly elliptoid outline." (SI 595) For another, the narrator finds that after some minutes of looking at it, "the monotonously aquatic nature of the reliefs became almost sinister." (SI 595) These understandable worries are surrounded by chunks of familiar high-grade Lovecraftian allusion. For example: "the patterns all hinted of remote secrets and unimaginable abysses in time and space" (SI 595). And this: "Among these reliefs were fabulous monsters of abhorrent grotesqueness and malignity –half ichthyic and half bachtrian in suggestion– which one could not dissociate from a certain haunting and uncomfortable sense of pseudo-memory." (SI 595) Once these tentative allusions have been ventured, Lovecraft takes his usual extra step into an outright frenzy of cosmological panic: "At times I fancied that every contour of these blasphemous fish-frogs was overflowing with the ultimate quintessence of unknown and inhuman evil." (SI 596) But only "at times," of course; the narrator must not push his luck.

67. Frankly Tentative

"In odd contrast to the tiara's aspect was its brief and prosy history as related by Miss Tilton. It had been pawned for a ridiculous sum at a shop in State Street in 1873, by a drunken Innsmouth man shortly afterward killed in a brawl... It was labelled as of probable East-Indian or Indo-Chinese provenance, though the attribution was frankly tentative." (SI 596)

Lovecraft takes a great risk with this passage, but succeeds in bringing things off. The structure here is that of two contrasts followed by a crowning allusion. The narrator is allowed into the display room of the Newburyport Historical Society, since the hour is "not outrageously late," (SI 594) thereby letting us know that it is *almost* too late in the evening to be visiting a historical museum. An "ancient gentlewoman" (SI 594) named Miss Anna Tilton is the curator of the collection. Nearly all of the handful of female characters in Lovecraft are either monstrous or deformed, making Miss Tilton an unusual exception. She seems reasonably intelligent, and dedicated enough to her historical curatorship, while also showing a touch of petty snobbery: "her own attitude toward shadowed Innsmouth –which she had never seen– was one of disgust at a community slipping far down the cultural scale." (SI 596) The snobbery is also quite irrelevant, for we soon discover that slippage on the social ladder is the least of Innsmouth's troubles. Miss Tilton interprets the tiara as being part of "some exotic pirate hoard" (SI 596), as if pirates and tropical nations were sufficient to explain a freakishly elliptical tiara with monotonous aquatic reliefs belonging to no known racial or national stream. To top it off, she relates the "brief and prosy history" (SI 596) of an object sufficiently bizarre to make the narrator "literally gasp at the strange, unearthly splendour of the alien, opulent phantasy that rested there on a purple velvet cushion." (595) At the very least, Miss Tilton seems to be rather insensitive to the inherent strangeness of the thing.

The second contrast, however, is that between the narrator's description of Miss Tilton's story and the actual content of the story. "Prosy" is hardly the first word that comes to mind when we read the following: "It had been pawned for a ridiculous sum at a shop in State Street in 1873, by a drunken Innsmouth man shortly afterward killed in a brawl. The Society had acquired it directly from the pawnbroker…" We hear further of "insistent offers of purchase at a high price which the Marshes began to make as soon as they knew of its presence, and which they repeated to this day despite the Society's unvarying determination not to sell." To call this dramatic and mysterious story "prosy" is a variation on Poe's purposely ridiculous explanation of the silhouette of the hanged black cat. It positions the reader to make far weirder deductions than the narrator is prepared to make so far. Yet it also makes the narrator somewhat comical, since we immediately and permanently disagree with his verdict of prosiness. And given that "prosy" might also refer to a bland tone in Miss Tilton's telling of the story, it makes her comical as well. The prosaic social snobbery of an ancient gentlewoman with historical interests is a remarkable tone in which to describe the actions of pawnbrokers and drunken men killed in brawls.

That leaves us with the final part of the passage: "[The tiara] was labelled as of probable East-Indian or Indo-Chinese provenance, though the attribution was frankly tentative." The narrator has already told us that the item clearly belongs to no known racial or national stream. The Newburyport Historical Society apparently disagrees, thinking in their parochial fashion that those wild East Indians or Indo-Chinese might well have come up with such an unearthly thing. Yet somewhat comically, they seem to agree faintly with the narrator, since "[their] attribution [is] frankly tentative." Something about the classification is obviously not quite right, though the Society does not seem too bothered by the fact, and the narrator does not seem especially judgmental about it.

68. Biological Degeneration

"[Joe Sargent's] oddities certainly did not look Asiatic, Polynesian, Levantine, or negroid, yet I could see why the people found him alien. I myself would have thought of biological degeneration rather than alienage." (SI 598)

The bus driver Joe Sargent is perhaps the most loathsome of Lovecraft's basically humanoid characters. But Sargent's repulsiveness is not simply the collective result of a bundle of repulsive qualities: "even before I noticed any details, there swept over me a wave of spontaneous aversion which could be neither checked nor explained." (SI 597) And further, "it suddenly struck me as very natural that the local people should not wish to ride on a bus owned and driven by this man..." (SI 597) The initial wave of spontaneous aversion links the narrator in fellowship with all the horses, dogs, and wolves in Lovecraft, who also make their evaluations with spontaneously accurate likes and dislikes of this kind. But when Sargent exits the drug store, the narrator tries to zero in more exactly on the visible qualities linked with this aversion. On closer examination, what he finds is a stoop-shouldered man about thirty-five years old, dressed in shabby civilian clothes. But the worst part is this:

He had a narrow head, bulging, watery blue eyes that seemed never to wink, a flat nose, a receding forehead and chin, and singularly undeveloped ears. His long, thick lip and coarse-pored, grayish cheeks seemed almost beardless except for some sparse yellow hairs that straggled and curled in irregular patches; and in places the surface seemed queerly irregular, as if peeling from some cutaneous disease. (SI 597-8)

Sargent's hands and feet are also inordinately large. He walks with a shambling gait, and does not seem very welcoming to the narrator, the only passenger to board the bus. Throughout the ride to Innsmouth, "the silent driver's bent, rigid back and narrow head became more and more hateful." (SI 599)

The interesting part of the passage above is that Sargent's oddities "did not look Asiatic, Polynesian, Levantine, or negroid," especially when we consider the previous reflections on the unknown nationality of the tiara. For it might also be said that most humans seem to fit ethnically within some known racial or national stream. Yet there is no evidence that the people of Newburyport ever made specific claims that Sargent was either of Asian, Polynesian, Levantine, or African ancestry. Instead, we may safely assume that the populace viewed Sargent in much the same way as the narrator viewed the tiara– as belonging to some *unknown* racial or national stream. This contrasts with the narrator's own half-true opinion, which is that Sargent's physical anomalies result not from foreignness but from "biological degeneration." In the eyes of the narrator, Sargent would appear to belong to a known earthly race (presumably Caucasian) in a state of inbred genetic decline. Here we find Lovecraft's two main stylistic techniques, embodied in the two different theories of Sargent's appearance. The towns-people take the allusive approach of viewing Sargent as a member of some mysterious unknown race, while the narrator takes him for just another Caucasian like so many others in Massachusetts, but one whose surface qualities happen to be undergoing degeneration. The townspeople treat Sargent like an indescribable Cthulhu idol, while the narrator views him as a Cyclopean Antarctic city with bizarre qualities clustered confusingly alongside one another. The two perspectives on Sargent mirror the two major axes of Lovecraftian style.

69. A Nightmare Without Qualities

"...burning into my brain the momentary conception of nightmare which was all the more maddening because analysis could not shew a single nightmarish quality about it." (SI 602)

This ranks among the greatest of Lovecraft's tacitly anti-Humean passages. The shock of what the narrator saw while passing the church cannot be traced to any particular horrific quality. Instead, the horror lies at a level somewhere deeper than the qualities of the thing. And given that the terrible sight was witnessed only in momentary fashion, the sub-qualitative nightmare must have been instantly accessible rather than reached through long and nervous reflection.

The narrator tries to downplay the sensation by blaming his own state of mind: "had I been in a steadier mood I would have found nothing whatever of terror in it." (SI 602) Yet this seems laughably improbable once we hear further details: the narrator had seen another exotic tiara, which "had supplied namelessly sinister qualities to the indeterminate face and robed, shambling form beneath it." (SI 602) It seems rather unlikely that a "steadier mood" would have done much to deaden the horror of this sight. Nor is it very credible when the narrator tries to explain away the "shuddering touch of evil pseudo-memory" (SI 602) linked with the incident by asking rhetorically: "was it not natural that a local mystery cult should adopt among its regimentals an unique type of head-dress made familiar to the people in some strange way...?" (SI 602-3). Yet again, we the readers are maneuvered into being less rationalist and reductionist than Lovecraft himself. By making feeble cases for reductive explanations, he weakens them all the more.

In that momentary flash he had also subconsciously determined that the robed and shambling figure in the tiara was "clearly... the pastor." (SI 602) This "pastor" will later be seen among the monstrous entities hunting the narrator down on the country roads leading out of Innsmouth. The image of this religious leader makes us laugh again a few pages later, when the narrator learns about Innsmouth religious life from the out-of-town grocery store boy: "[The] churches were very odd– all violently disavowed by their respective denominations elsewhere, and apparently using the queerest kind of ceremonials and clerical vestments. Their creeds were heterodox and mysterious, involving hints of certain transformations leading to bodily immortality –of a sort– on this earth." (SI 604-5) And with a wonderful closing flourish: "The youth's own pastor –Dr. Wallace of Asbury M.E. Church in Arkham– had gravely urged him not to join any church in Innsmouth." (SI 605) Much like dogs, horses, and wolves, the churches and clergy of Massachusetts seem to have an instinctive insight into the dangerous peculiarities of the town.

70. Basic Osseous Features

"Only a very rare affliction, of course, could bring about such vast and radical anatomical changes in a single individual after maturity– changes involving osseous features as basic as the shape of the skull..." (SI 605)

This passage comes from the narrator's summary of his conversation with the young grocery clerk, so heartlessly transferred to Innsmouth by his employer. At issue is whether or not the so-called "Innsmouth look" is the result of a disease. The two interlocutors reach no conclusion on the issue, though we later come to learn that the hybrid children are born with a human appearance but gradually take on more of the fish-frog traits as the years go by, until eventually they disappear full-time into the sea.

In this passage we have a cold and clinical description of physical changes that would be matters of the greatest possible horror if witnessed directly. Strictly speaking, it would be *medically impossible* for changes of this sort to occur on so vast a scale as witnessed in Innsmouth. Hence the phrase "Only a very rare affliction..." is a piece of understatement that makes the narrator sound comically pedantic despite his vaguely touching air of humane concern for the locals. The second salient feature of the passage is the qualifier "after maturity," which adds a strange note of limitation to the claims of rarity for the hypothesized disease– as if vast anatomical changes of the Innsmouth sort were somehow plausible even *prior* to reaching the age of adulthood.

And then we have the concluding phrase, surely never uttered before by any speaker of the English language: "osseous features as basic as the shape of the skull." The first cause for either comedy or unease (or a bit of both) is the use of the plural, as though the human body were characterized by an entire class of osseous features, some of them especially basic. It makes little difference that this is probably true. Admittedly, the human form might have evolved in any number of different ways along paths of evolution distinct from those it actually took. When McLuhan says that "the medium is the message," he means that we are so stupefied by the content of television shows that we fail to notice the basic features of television as a background medium. And just as we usually do not take explicit notice of the Kantian categories operating in our various perceptions, it is even more the case that the human skeletal structure is a medium taken for granted, to the point that we would be immediately horrified by any sudden changes in our bones, or those of our comrades. The shape of the skull, in particular, hits very close to home, since no piece of bone lies closer to what we regard as the seat of our very selves.

71. Stark Raving

"Iä! Iä! Cthulhu fhtagn! Ph'nglui mglw'nafh Cthulhu R'lyeh wgah-nagl fhtagn– Old Zadok was fast lapsing into stark raving." (SI 622)

The phrase in italics is the typical unpronounceable formula uttered or chanted by devotees of the Cthulhu Cult. Thus, it ties the Innsmouth story together with the remainder of Lovecraft's mythos in especially direct fashion. After uttering these words, Old Zadok seems like much more than the town drunk. We must now conclude that he is either a partial member of the heterodox religions holding sway in the town, or (more likely) someone who picked up a good deal of the religion through his youthful upbringing there. Otherwise, this is the familiar case in which the reader is maneuvered into making more radical deductions than the narrator himself. It is especially comical in the sense that the narrator seems to think that his phrase "stark raving" is some sort of devastating dismissal, when it is actually a rather tame understatement. It is something much worse than raving, after all. There is also the strange fact that rather than merely telling us that Old Zadok fell into stark raving, the narrator is able to record the exact pattern of the barely coherent sounds uttered by the old man, which has a further comical effect.

Old Zadok has been plied with bootleg whiskey for more than two hours, with the narrator attempting to pump him for as much information as possible. Despite the comic-terrible effect of the sudden string of Cthulu Cult oaths, the situation is really rather moving in human terms. The old man is calling up memories from deep in his childhood, hinting that human sacrifices were offered to the sea in order to acquire gold and various "knick-knacks." At one point Zadok even begins moaning, as tears stream down his face. He admits to having taken the first two Oaths of Dagon, but hints terribly at a grisly third oath: "but I wudn't take the third Oath– I'd a died ruther'n take that." (SI

622) The narrator himself is not left unmoved: "Poor old soul– to what pitiful depths of hallucination had his liquor, plus his hatred of the decay, alienage, and disease around him, brought that fertile, imaginative brain." (SI 622)

72. A Nucleus of Historic Allegory

"Later I might sift the tale and extract some nucleus of historic allegory; just now I wished to put it out of my head." (SI 625)

The story told by Old Zadok concerned the history of Innsmouth both before and after Obed Marsh instituted the Esoteric Order of Dagon, leading to a drastic upsurge in wealth for the town. When Marsh was eventually jailed, the undersea creatures attacked the town and freed him. Forced interbreeding with the fish-frog hybrids became widespread in the town, and thus began the long process of apparent genetic decay. Old Zadok also claims that a *shoggoth* is being readied beneath the sea for a planned assault on land-dwelling humans. (SI 624) Readers of "At the Mountains of Madness" will recall that shoggoths are "multicellular protoplasmic masses capable of moulding their tissues into all sorts of temporary organs under hypnotic influence," and are also described poetically as "viscous masses." (MM 541) They move with the speed of a freight train and kill their victims by decapitation. Unlike the narrator, the reader feels inclined to believe every word of Old Zadok's story, which seems heated but not distorted by his consumption of the bootleg whiskey.

As usual in Lovecraft, the narrator's reaction is more skeptical: "Puerile though the story was, old Zadok's insane earnestness and horror had communicated to me a mounting unrest which joined with my earlier sense of loathing for the town and its blight of intangible shadow." (SI 625) A split is thereby generated between the content of Old Zadok's tale and his manner of telling it. The narrator absolutely rejects the content as "puerile," but is deeply affected by the old man's *manner* of telling the story. That leaves the question of what to do with the content of the tale. The reader has no reason to doubt a word of it– we are in a Lovecraft story, after all. Yet the narrator is only willing to concede, with a cautious pedantry that is faintly ludicrous under the circumstances, that there must be "some nucleus of historic allegory" in the tale. Though this Oberlin student has just heard a terrifying tale from a screaming, moaning, and crying drunkard who makes a raving outburst in a bizarre foreign tongue, and though the student has spent an entire day feeling (correctly) an ominous sense of dread in this degenerate little seaport, he already has eggheadish plans for some anthropological sifting of the tale once he returns to more comfortable surroundings. Here as so often, Lovecraft proves the Socratic thesis that the same person ought to be able to write both comedy and tragedy. I am not among those who claim Lovecraft is not scary, since I find his tales frightening indeed. But even so, I often find a smile on my face during even the most frightening parts of his tales, due precisely to sentences such as the one above: "Later I might sift the tale and extract some nucleus of historic allegory; just now I wished to put it out of my head."

73. Loose-Syllabled Croakings

"A moment later I felt less sure that the deeper sounds were voices, since the apparent hoarse barkings and loose-syllabled croakings bore so little resemblance to recognized human speech." (SI 630)

The narrator is stuck in the Gilman House for the night. This is where a visiting factory inspector once heard a "slopping-like" voice in a nearby room that prevented him from falling asleep. But the narrator's situation is even more appalling than that. Someone has already tried to enter his room with a passkey, both through the main door and from the two adjoining rooms. A stealthy creaking is heard in the hallway and on the stairs. When the narrator jumps out of bed and attempts to turn on the overhead light, he finds that the power has been cut– the final signal of what now seems to be (and is) a massive conspiracy against him.

But our concern here is with the voices he hears outside the room, which are not quite voices– or perhaps they are voices "only by analogy." As concerns the "slopping-like" voice heard in the same hotel by the factory inspector, we saw that it could be treated as a classic Lovecraftian disjunction with one of the terms left implicit. We were essentially being asked to aim our attention at something midway between a human voice and a slopping sound. In the present case there seems to be a conjunction of barkings *and* croakings. Now, this could be read as meaning that there are two separate monstrous species in the hallway, one that barks and another that croaks. Nothing in the text prevents such an interpretation. But for me at least, the more natural way to read the passage is to imagine the barkings and croakings as emanating from one and the same throat. And since these two kinds of sounds are normally associated with two utterly different sorts of animals, attention is immediately shifted from the palpable tones themselves towards the unknown vocal organs of a mysterious species somehow capable of modulating betweens barks and croaks.

But we need to account for the more expansive versions of the phrases that Lovecraft gives us. First we have "hoarse" barkings, which does as well as any adjective in preventing us from reading through the barkings too quickly, by modifying them in somewhat unusual fashion. Our attention is held a bit longer than would otherwise have been the case, as we run through the exercise of *hoarsening* the barks in our minds. Since even the shrieks of monkeys are sometimes described as hoarse, this is not especially difficult. But a more ornate effort is demanded of our attempts to imagine "loose-syllabled croakings," and here we have a more classic Lovecraftian maneuver. Croaking usually does not occur in syllables when heard in frogs, and thus we are already reminded that we need to consider the sound as lying midway between a croak and a human voice. And as for "loose-syllabled," this would be an unnerving concept even if a *human* voice were involved. Normally we do not think of the syllables of our speech as packed together in especially tight fashion anyway. But in the present case, the rhythm of the croaking must intersperse gaps between the syllables in chilling fashion.

74. A Crouching, Shambling Gait

"Their features were indistinguishable, but their crouching, shambling gait was abominably repellent. And worst of all, I perceived that one figure was strangely robed, and unmistakably surmounted by a tall tiara of a design altogether familiar." (SI 636)

The second sentence immediately harks back to the abominable "pastor" viewed briefly through the rectangular doorway earlier in the story. Presumably the robed figure is the very same entity as the one viewed there, but in any case the two share all essential features. The use of ceremonial human clothing by these monstrous beings heightens the repulsion of their physique. Nor does the clothing always take the form of ritual vestments: the narrator later observes that one of the creatures "was clad in a ghoulishly humped black coat and striped trousers, and had a man's felt hat perched on the shapeless thing that answered for a head..." (SI 646)

But the key to this passage comes in the first sentence, with its reference to the "crouching shambling gait" of the Innsmouth natives– one of the most powerful images in Lovecraft's writing. The narrator first noticed this "shambling" trait in Newburyport that same morning, when three unkempt men left Joe Sargent's bus and "clumsily shambled out and began walking up State Street in silent, almost furtive fashion." (SI 597) In Innsmouth itself he has witnessed plenty of shambling, and when fleeing the port he is forced to "carefully and imitatively shamble" (SI 640) through lit intersections in case he is observed, a gait he otherwise maligns for its "dog-like sub-humanness" (SI 641), usually found in shambling figures too given to "croaking and jabbering in some hateful gutteral patois." (SI 641)

The first point to acknowledge is that it is somewhat difficult to imitate this shambling gait. With so many of Lovecraft's descriptions of physical, musical, and chromatic anomalies, no direct imitation or visualization is possible even in principle. This point does not quite apply here, since we all have some notion of what "shambling" might look like, and I myself have made some progress in attempting to imitate the Innsmouth walk. It is simply very difficult to achieve this effect, given the structural limitations of our normal human gait. Any effort to shamble generally fails on sheer pragmatic grounds; we find it difficult to achieve a sufficiently repellent effect when doing so, though the story's narrator seems to have succeeded at the task. Ultimately the shambling gait occupies roughly the same position in our minds as the "slopping" voice. Here too, slopping is not a truly allusive concept in its own right. After all, we can imagine a slopping voice in principle. It is simply difficult to attain this effect with our own voices when we try, and it is probable that only a highly skilled actor could do so with regularity.

75. A Disturbing Suggestion of Undulant Motion

"What I saw –or fancied I saw– was a disturbing suggestion of undulant motion far to the south; a suggestion which led me to conclude that a very large horde must be pouring out of the city along the level Ipswich Road... it undulated too much, and glistened too brightly in the rays of the now westering moon. There was a suggestion of sound, too..." (SI 643)

Although many different things seem to be going on this passage, for our purposes there are really just two. The first is a very clear example of an object being separated from its qualities. None of the creatures are visible at this distance, yet their tangible features are there for the taking, and those features serve perfectly well to "suggest" the underlying reality that rules them. Far to the south there is excessive glistening of moonlight, accompanied by suggestions of undulant motion and even sound. The horror is not these qualities themselves, but rather that which they lead us to infer: a mob of pursuers in all their "dog-like sub-humanness." The second thing that happens at such a great distance is that we are not even dealing with individual monsters, but only with the horde as a whole. What undulates and glistens is the horde, not the invisible single beings. So too, the suggestion of sound cannot be a suggestion of individual voices. This yields troubling suggestions of a group mentality or purpose as embodied in a mass physical existence of the horde, as if a single body were shared by all. This unified horde-object would be no more visible if it were directly before us; indeed it would even be less so, since at close range we could only be distracted by the specific details of its individual creatures.

When the narrator later does view the horde at close range, the effect is not so picturesque as in the passage above: "I saw them in a limitless stream –flopping, hopping, croaking, bleating– surging inhumanly through the spectral moonlight in a grotesque, malignant saraband of fantastic nightmare." (SI 646) The entire second half of this sentence is mere spice added to the work already done by "flopping, hopping, croaking, bleating." This phrase is a masterful Lovecraftian example of either conjunction or disjunction, depending on whether we think that different subspecies of monster do each of these four things, or whether all represent the modulations of a single type of creature.

The Dreams in the Witch House

"The Dreams in the Witch House" is the only great tale other than "The Dunwich Horror" to use an omniscient third-person narrator rather than the usual first-person participant. Accordingly, the tone is calmer and cooler than in most of the other stories. Here Lovecraft tries his hand at a tale of New England witchcraft, in a rather successful effort at integrating that genre with his own expanding mythos. Miskatonic University student Walter Gilman wishes to rent a room in the same Arkham house inhabited centuries ago by a witch named Keziah Mason. His course of study at the university covers such apparently far-flung disciplines as non-Euclidean geometry, quantum theory, and folklore. But these fields turn out to be united, since witchcraft is merely a faster means of access to truths approached vaguely by the pathbreaking discoveries of early twentieth century mathematics and physics. Keziah and her repulsive familiar, a rat-like entity named "Brown Jenkin," visit Gilman too often in his sleep, and take him on numerous trips that seem to lie in extra-dimensional space. Keziah and Brown Jenkin also pay obsequious attention to a towering black man named Nyarlathotep, who is mistaken for ethnically African by casual witnesses, though his facial features seem to be entirely Caucasian. In fact, Nyarlathotep is not just an unusual human, but is one of the most dreaded beings referred to in the *Necronomicon*.

Gilman's nightly distractions lead to failure in his studies, despite his quickly advancing grasp of non-Euclidean geometry. At the climax of the story, Gilman fails to prevent the sacrifice of a human infant at a grotesque Walpurgis Night ceremony held in some unknown abstract space. He does manage to kick Brown Jenkin over a railing and into a deep abyss, though the abominable little animal survives and soon takes its revenge. One night Brown Jenkin tunnels into the body of the sleeping Gilman, devours his heart, then tunnels out the other side.

76. Utmost Modern Delvings

"Gilman... knew he wanted to be in the building where some circumstance had more or less suddenly given a mediocre woman of the seventeenth century an insight into mathematical depths perhaps beyond the utmost modern delvings of Planck, Heisenberg, Einstein, and de Sitter." (WH 656)

One of the crowning perversities of Lovecraft's vision is found in his treatment of the relation between science and the occult. In the usual comic book version of the Enlightenment, brave scientists swept away the cobwebs and shed light into the darkness. Goblins, trolls, and alchemists are banished from the world forever, as the scientists exterminate such phantasms to make room for explanatory factors having nothing deep or ghostly about them. But Lovecraft views science differently. Far from making a *contrast* with witches, monsters, folklore, and obscure idiot deities surrounded by flopping hordes of mindless and amorphous dancers, the sciences tend generally in the same direction as all these less prestigious disciplines. In this way, Planck and Einstein are joined in spiritual fraternity with such anti-Enlightenment riffraff as Paracelsus, von Junzt and Abdul Alhazred.

This actually marks a return to the vision recorded in the opening of "The Call of Cthulhu." Science is not a destroyer of irrational illusions, but a dangerous probe into truths too terrifying for rationality to withstand. If witches should be burned, then perhaps scientists should as well, and *for the same reason*: both are direct threats to the sanity of earth-life. But far from treating occult knowledge as a primitive and incipient form of full-fledged science (alchemy and magic are sometimes viewed this way) Lovecraft generally favors the short-cuts of the occult over the slow and tentative progress of the sciences. Witchcraft gives Keziah Mason, basically "a mediocre woman of the seventeenth century," a mathematical knowledge far exceeding that of the early twentieth century's most revolutionary intellects. In his associations with Keziah and Brown Jenkin, Gilman acquires an education far beyond anything offered by Miskatonic University.

Otherwise, "utmost modern delvings" is one of the finest phrases found anywhere in Lovecraft. The passage would be gravely harmed if it were rewritten as follows: "mathematical depths perhaps beyond the most advanced researches of Planck, Heisenberg, Einstein, and de Sitter." In this revised version the diction is too "mean," in Aristotle's sense, whereas Lovecraft's use of the unexpected words "utmost" and "delvings" lends a certain dignity and beauty to the passage.

77. Quaintly Called Brown Jenkin

"That object [was] no larger than a good-sized rat and [was] quaintly called by the townspeople 'Brown Jenkin'... Witnesses said it had long hair and the shape of a rat, but that its sharp-toothed, bearded face was evilly human while its paws were like tiny human hands." (WH 658)

One of the ironies of Lovecraft's fiction is that, for all his special efforts to create unthinkable, unnameable, extraterrestrial fiends of complete originality in world literature, one of his most effective villainous beings is strongly rooted in known European tradition. The concept of a witch's familiar, in circulation since at least the Middle Ages, is that of an animal or other being that serves as the assistant and alter ego of the witch herself. If Lovecraft had offered us a ghost or an elf as one of his ghastliest monsters, the effect would be little more surprising.

Brown Jenkin is not one of those Lovecraftian creatures that is withdrawn from the power of language into some monstrous nuclear chaos cloaked under the name of Azathoth, or any such layering of concealment and innuendo. Instead, Brown Jenkin is more like the Cyclopean Antarctic city, an essentially cubist beast made up of an excessive number of juxtaposed qualities that do not exceed our cognitive grasp individually, but that fail to come together jointly. Here once more, it is amusing to describe the little beast in the language of David Hume: "When we think of Brown Jenkin, we only join five consistent ideas, *rat, long hair, sharp teeth, bearded human face,* and *hand-like paws,* with which we were formerly acquainted." This absurd attempt fails for the same reason that it fails in all other cases. We could perhaps weather the sharp teeth or the hand-like paws, if just barely. But the combination of all these features points to a fundamentally cubistic confusion of jostling planes of quality.

Another nice feature of this passage is the way in which the creature's name is introduced: it was *"quaintly* called by the townspeople 'Brown Jenkin'." Usually the names of Lovecraft's creatures either sound exotically mythological (Azathoth, Nyarlathotep, Cthulhu) or are disturbing precisely due to their generic adjectival blandness (the Old Ones, Those Ones, the Elder Things, the Great Race). By contrast, "Brown Jenkin" sounds repulsively similar to the name a young American girl might choose for a teddy bear, not for a fanged degenerate rat that kills babies and eats the hearts out of sleeping young men. "Jenkin" is apparently an old German name meaning "Little John," which is already sickening enough when referring to such a terrible beast. But to add "brown" to the front of the name is a technique usually employed when referring to such pets as puppies, rabbits, or ducklings. There is the further issue that we are not even sure if Brown Jenkin is the actual name of the witch's familiar. The fact that it is "quaintly known" by this title means that it could have originated wrongly among the populace, and may simply be concealing a far more horrible-sounding name along the lines of Nyarlathotep or Azathoth.

78. An Intuitive Knack for Riemannian Equations

"[Gilman] was getting an intuitive knack for Riemannian Equations, and astonished Professor Upham by his comprehension of fourth-dimensional and other problems which had floored all the rest of the class." (WH 661)

Bernhard Riemann (1826-1866) was a German mathematician regarded as one of the greatest of the nineteenth century. His geometrical ideas about curved space paved the way for Einstein's 1916 general theory of relativity, which in turn completely revolutionized our picture of gravity, acceleration, and mass. Riemann's ideas about spaces of any number of dimensions are foundational for the discipline of topology. As concerns the passage above, it is safe to say that Riemannian equations would be difficult to master. But the fact that many of them extend into dimensions lying beyond normal human experience would apparently make it impossible to gain an "intuitive" grasp of the equations. Yet that is precisely what is being claimed. Up to this point in the story, Gilman has been an indifferent student, often sleeping through classes following his late-night romps with the witch and her familiar through higher dimensions. Gilman's increased intellectual mastery of the fields covered by Riemann stems entirely from these nocturnal visions of Keziah and Brown Jenkin, rather than from any sort of diligent attention to university homework. The class is understandably "floored" by Riemann's challenging forays into dimensions greater than three, yet Gilman strolls with ease amidst this family of problems.

In the very next passage, the story's omniscient narrator gives us an example of Gilman's classroom brilliance on Riemannian themes:

One afternoon there was a discussion of possible freakish curvatures in space, and of theoretical points of approach or even contact between our part of the cosmos and various other regions as distant as the farthest stars or the trans-galactic gulfs themselves– or even as fabulously remote as the tentatively conceivable cosmic units beyond the whole Einsteinian space-time continuum. Gilman's handling of this theme filled everyone with admiration, even though some of his hypothetical illustrations caused an increase in the always plentiful gossip about his nervous and solitary eccentricity. (WH 661)

Here we find a good Lovecraftian allusion to "tentatively conceivable cosmic units" beyond the space-time of Einstein, a space-time which in itself is already far from easy to visualize in commonsense terms. As these "tentatively conceivable" units continue to floor his classmates, Gilman has mastered the subject to the point of offering "hypothetical" illustrations so admirably vivid as to raise suspicions concerning his sanity.

79. Prolately Spheroidal Bubbles

"...a rather large congeries of iridescent, prolately spheroidal bubbles and a very much smaller polyhedron of unknown colours and rapidly shifting surface angles... seemed to take notice of him and follow him about or float ahead as he changed position among the titan prisms, labyrinths, cube-and-plain clusters, and quasi-buildings..." (WH 665)

As always in "The Dreams in the Witch House," the description above is packaged as a scene from a dream. The reader barely believes this caveat, and by story's end there is no longer any reason to think that any of these scenes were dreams rather than reality. We can begin with the final part of the passage, whose architectural roster seems typically Lovecraftian, and which would not be out of place in the Antarctic. "Cube-and-plain clusters" is a daring and vivid coinage, while "quasi-buildings" is as wonderfully suggestive as the previously encountered "semi-entity." While the term "quasi-buildings" might count for Wilson as nothing but an easy pulp trick, we notice that it occurs at the very end of a long list of more plausible geometrical solids, as if it were being effectively smuggled into the club with the assistance of a more socially acceptable group of friends.

That brings us to the more unusual first part of the passage. A prolate spheroid is best described as a sphere that has been vertically stretched, yielding a sort of egg-like shape. A large aggregation of these spheroid bubbles, further described as iridescent, seems to take note of Gilman without any hostile intent. It floats nearby as he wanders through this purported dreamscape. This congeries of iridescent bubbles is surely one of the dangerous *shoggoths* witnessed by Dyer and Danforth in the Antarctic, and according to Old Zadok in Innsmouth, one of them is in preparation for an amphibious assault against the Massachusetts coast. Given the fearsome reputation of these creatures, Gilman seems to be on surprisingly good terms with it. Accompanying the shoggoth is an entity described as a "polyhedron" of "unknown colors" (colors "by analogy," perhaps?) and "rapidly shifting surface angles." (WH 665) We have progressed from zoologically incomprehensible science fiction monsters, to folkloric witches' familiars, to purely geometrical monsters inhabiting a Riemannian poly-dimensional space.

Also of interest is that the congeries of bubbles and the small shifting polyhedron belong to a strange broader class of entities occurring in Gilman's dream: namely, "organic entities whose motions [seem] least fragrantly unmotivated and irrelevant." (WH 665) No one but Lovecraft could ever have invented such a class of beings. He never tells us directly that the other entities in this space are unmotivated and irrelevant in their motions, but the deduction is obviously there for the taking. "Of all the dogs in the show, the least ugly are these three..." While this sort of backhanded compliment is familiar enough from the cattiest circles of human social life, presumably it was never applied before now to the motivation and relevance of the locomotion of living beings.

80. Tall Grass Moving Near Her

"The tall grass near [the old woman] was moving, too, as if some other living thing were crawling close to the ground." (WH 666)

Through the fictitious town of Arkham runs the equally fictious Miskatonic River– an accidental challenge to Hölderlin's Rhein and Ister, as deified by Heidegger. But rather than linking Germans and Greeks in Heidegger's lugubrious fashion, the Miskatonic links the non-Euclidean studies of young Walter Gilman with the folkloric witchery of the "mediocre" Keziah Mason and "quaint" Brown Jenkin, who are anything other than mediocre or quaint. Throughout the day in which the passage above is set, Brown Jenkin is pointing "in a certain direction with a horribly anthropoid fore paw..." (WH 666) Gilman, cutting classes at the university as he so often does, finds himself staring at a slowly moving point on the floor. Leaving home at lunchtime, he finds that he is "turning always to the southeast." (WH 666) Later it turns out that all this human and sub-human attention has been directed towards "a point somewhere between Hydra and Argo Navis," (WH 667) which rotates slowly in the sky according to the usual daily path of the stars.

Gilman crosses the bridge over the Miskatonic and finds himself staring at the "ill-regarded island" in the river (WH 666), whose cause for ill regard is never explained. There he sees the woman who was previously glimpsed only in his supposed dreams; as she turns toward him, he flees. But before doing so, he sees the grass moving near her. The narrator's vagueness as to what living creature might be pushing through the grass is a deliberately pointless hint, since we know exactly what creature it is. In some ways this is merely a homelier version of the similar inference near the close of "The Shadow Over Innsmouth," when an invisible horde emits a perfectly visible suggestion of glistening and undulant motion. Rather than horrific and melancholic signals of this kind, what Gilman now observes is simply motion in the tall grass. In this way, Brown Jenkin's presence is inferred through a miniature ruffling of the plant life. This evidence is paired with a much less physical allusion to the abominable rat's owner: "Distant though the island was, [Gilman] felt that a monstrous and invincible evil could flow from the sardonic stare of that bent, ancient figure in brown." (WH 667) We are led to feel that an equally monstrous and invincible evil can flow from something as typically harmless as the movement of grass on an island.

The equivalence is not quite exact, however. The suggestions made about Keziah point to some evil power withdrawn from all adequate grasp of language. By contrast, the movement of the grass has the "cubist" aspect of just another sensually accessible feature grafted onto a purely earthly entity, belonging to exactly the same order of signs as its sharp teeth, long hair, bearded visage, and oddly hand-like paws. In short, Keziah and Brown Jenkin are the embodiments here of the two main axes of Lovecraft's weird ontography. It makes sense that the two of them need one another, and are never found apart from each other.

81. Some Unearthly Symmetry

"... the tiles were cut in bizarre-angled shapes which struck him as less asymmetrical than based on some unearthly symmetry whose laws he could not comprehend." (WH 669)

In this passage Gilman is lost in yet another "dream," one that takes him into physical terrain already mapped in "At the Mountains of Madness." For what Gilman observes as he looks down is an "endless, Cyclopean city almost two thousand feet below" (WH 669-70). The lack of icy features means little here, since the Antarctic was presumably not frozen during the heyday of its Elder Things many millions of years ago. The more important point is that Gilman is approached by Keziah and Brown Jenkin, along with three "living entities about eight feet high... propelling themselves by a spider-like wriggling of their lower set of starfish arms." (WH 670). The reference to "At the Mountains of Madness" is now perfectly explicit.

The tiles in this place are cut in bizarre-angled shapes, recalling the black stone sent by Akeley to Wilmarth in "The Whisperer in Darkness." In this story just as in that one, and just as with the aquatic tiara seen in Newburyport, the tiles are recognizable neither as belonging to a known human culture, nor as "consciously modernistic defiances" of all human culture. Instead, they point beyond all human culture to laws of symmetry unknown to all human experience so far. Who better than a student of Riemannian manifolds to experience such a thing? The avant garde German geometry of the mid-nineteenth century teaches Gilman to feel at home with such strangely angled cuttings in a way that Akeley, Wilmarth, and the Oberlin narrator of Innsmouth could never possibly be. Even so, Gilman cannot quite comprehend the laws of this symmetry, despite his earlier ability to give strange hypothetical examples in the classroom that seemed to demonstrate a mastery of the topic. Perhaps the best that humans can hope for, when dealing with these unearthly symmetries, is a loose sort of pragmatic know-how. We might assume that the starfish-armed Antarctic creatures must have direct access to these laws, since they are able to construct entire cities that obey them. But even the highly advanced Gilman, tutored in Riemann and guided by a witch and her sickening familiar, is unable to cross the limits imposed on all human access to reality. The surface-effects of this symmetry are visible to Gilman, but their deeper principle remains hidden from him. This might seem like an obviously

Kantian moment in Lovecraft, as if the unearthly symmetry were a "noumenal" feature of reality. But the fact that the symmetry is accessible to the Elder Things as an architectural tool refutes that assumption, given that Kant meant his finitude to hold for all thinking beings, not just for humans. In my 2008 article on Lovecraft and Husserl, I made the anti-Kantian case as follows: "The game of chess is not 'noumenal' for dogs through their inability to grasp it, and neither is Sanskrit grammar for a deranged adult or a three-year-old."[80] We could now add as follows: the unearthly symmetry of the tiles in the Cyclopean city is not "noumemal" for Gilman through his inability to grasp it. He is simply too stupid to do so, despite the assistance of the slightly less stupid Riemann, Planck, Heisenberg, Einstein, and de Sitter, and the perhaps even less stupid Keziah Mason.

82. The Road to Innsmouth

"All around him stretched the bleak emptiness of salt marshes, while the narrow road ahead led to Innsmouth– that ancient, half-deserted town which Arkham people were so curiously unwilling to visit." (WH 670)

The next day, Gilman awakens in a cold sweat and finds his attention drawn to a different spot in the sky than the one between Hydra and Argo Navis. It takes him to a strangely familiar piece of geography. The Oberlin chronicler traveled from Newburyport to Innsmouth via bus, not reaching Arkham that night as planned. The salt marshes shielding Innsmouth from the outer world had been a force for him to reckon with, hindering his preferred movements as he tried to escape the degenerate and doomed seaport ruled by the fish-frog-human hybrids. Gilman now reaches a similar obstacle while coming from a different direction, exiting Arkham on foot. The narrator once more recites the familiar point that Innsmouth is an ancient, half-deserted town too frightening for those of neighboring towns to visit; the residents of Arkham seem to shun the place no less than those of Newburyport. All the threads of Lovecraft's great tales begin to converge, with only "The Colour Out of Space" omitted so far– though not for long, as we will soon see (and in fact the hysterical young Danforth had already alluded to that colour after his trip to Antarctica, at MM 586).

Gilman eats lunch, then passes the time at "at a cheap cinema show, seeing the inane performance over and over again without paying any attention to it." (WH 671) This is all just a prelude to what happens at 9 PM upon returning home. In the previous night's "dream" of the Cyclopean city, Gilman had accidentally broken an ornament from the balustrade protecting him from a two-thousand foot fall. And what he now finds in his room in Arkham is nothing other than this ornament. "Only his tendency toward a dazed stupor prevented him from screaming aloud. This fusion of dream and reality was too much to bear." (WH 671) For the first time, the folkloric world of Elder Things, Nyarlathotep, Keziah and Brown Jenkin has been decisively fused with the scientific world of non-Euclidean geometry and quantum theory studied so haltingly by Gilman at Miskatonic University. The ornamental item from the balustrade suggests the abominable reality of the wriggling-armed creatures of the previous night's dream. "No detail was missing. The ridged, barrel-shaped centre, the thin, radiating arms, the knobs at each end, and the flat, slightly outward-curving starfish-arms spreading from those knobs– all were there." (WH 671) If the usual literary cliché is that what seems real turns out to be only a dream, Lovecraft reverses the gesture and shows us how dreams become real.

83. Nameless Approximations of Form

"He had been taken there by the bubble-congeries and the little polyhedron which always dogged him; but they, like himself, had changed to wisps of milky, barely luminous mist in this farther void of ultimate blackness. Something else had gone on ahead– a larger wisp which now and then condensed into nameless approximations of form..." (WH 674)

Here, the two most formless of all Lovecraftian monsters undergo an additional transformation into something even less tangible. The bubble-congeries (namely, the *shoggoth*) was by definition already the most formless of creatures, shaping itself on command into whatever organs might be needed at any given moment. Gilman's latest "dream" now suggests that even this horrible formlessness was already a deceptive over-formatting of something deeper and even more amorphous. The infinitely mutable bubble-congeries has become nothing but "wisps of milky, barely luminous mist in this farther void of infinite blackness." (WH 674)

Then there is "the little polyhedron" which always "dogged" Gilman, as if we were speaking of a toy poodle rather than a sub-Riemannian topological monstrosity. The polyhedron was already so abstract, with its shifting number and orientation of faces and its "unknown colors," that further abstraction might seem nearly impossible. But here once more, Lovecraft performs the needed operation. The little polyhedron too is dissolved into "wisps of milky, barely luminous mist in this farther void of infinite blackness." Whereas most fictional monsters have definite features and contours, Lovecraft's most abstract creatures have now become something as vague as the cosmic background radiation left over from the Big Bang, or even the barest vacuum fluctuation from a blank field of nothingness.

Yet these newly anointed wisps of milky, barely luminescent mist are still not the highest lords in this realm of near-nothingness. That honor apparently goes to "a larger wisp" in the vicinity, which can at least claim quantitative superiority to the former bubble-congeries and the former polyhedron. No different from the shapeless *apeiron* of the pre-Socratic philosophers, the larger wisp "now and then [condenses] into nameless approximations of form." None of these semi-entities seem to be moving in a straight line, but rather "along the alien curves and spirals of some ethereal vortex," (WH 674) a description containing only the merest hints of content. We seem to be growing ever closer to the blind idiot God, to judge from the sounds that are now heard: "a monstrous, half-acoustic pulsing, and... the thin, monotonous piping of an unseen flute..." (WH 674) It is the ultimate allusion to an utterly imperceptible and incomprehensible landscape.

84. Outside the Periodic Table

"Professor Ellery found platinum, tellurium, and iron in the strange alloy; but mixed with these were at least three other apparent elements of high atomic weight which chemistry was absolutely powerless to classify. Not only did they fail to correspond with any known element, but they did not even fit the vacant places reserved for probable elements in the periodic system." (WH 677)

Earlier it seemed that "The Dreams in the Witch House" was making a point of tying together all the previous great tales of Lovecraft into a single unified mythos. Only "The Colour Out of Space" seemed to be missing from the picture. But the passage above can be read as the bridge between Gilman's Riemannian witch and Nahum Gardner's sadly degenerating farm in the wild hills west of Arkham. We recall that the Miskatonic faculty took away a small sample of the Gardner meteorite, and upon testing it found that "the colour, which resembled some of the bands in the meteor's strange spectrum, was almost impossible to describe; and it was only by analogy that they called it colour at all." (CS 345) In the present case, color *per se* does not seem to be the problem with the object retrieved by Gilman from his "dream," yet there are other serious difficulties with the sample.

Just as Lovecraft likes to lend credibility to fictitious places (Miskatonic University) by placing them in contact with real ones (Harvard), and likes to bolster fictitious authors (von Junzt) by mentioning them in the same breath as real ones (Roger Bacon), he now does the same for chemical objects. The item retrieved by Gilman is not *entirely* unworldly, after all. It does contain platinum, tellurium, and iron of a sort that could presumably be melted down and used to make commcercially available jewelry, solar panels, or vitamin supplements. Yet along with these well-studied elements, the item contains at least three others of high atomic weight that chemistry cannot classify. Assuming that this does not represent the premature discovery of neptunium or plutonium, we are dealing with ultra-exotic elements that ought not to be stable enough to form a solid metallic thing.

Nor is this mystery left hidden for the public good. Instead, the Miskatonic scientists humbly declare their defeat and apparently advertise the mystery in public as a scientific challenge, open to all comers. As Lovecraft describes it with hilarious absurdity: "The mystery remains unsolved to this day, though the image is on exhibition at the museum of Miskatonic University." (WH 677) Whatever star-headed sculptor forged that particular item in the distant past, this is probably not the fate they expected for it. A three-way, three-tale link is hereby forged between Gilman, the Cyclopean Antarctic City, and the unclassifiable element of the Gardner meteorite. Lovecraft errs only in failing to explain why the Miskatonic faculty would not have linked the earlier Gardner meteorite puzzle with the similar challenge to the periodic table in the present story, and why Dyer and the returning Miskatonic survivors from the Antarctic did not notice the peculiarly familiar shape of the item torn from the balustrade in the dream.

85. Cosmic Timbre

"He seemed to know what was coming– the monstrous burst of Walpurgis-rhythm in whose cosmic timbre would be concentrated all the primal, ultimate space-time seethings which lie behind the massed spheres of matter and sometimes break forth in measured reverberations that penetrate faintly to every layer of entity and give hideous significance throughout the worlds to certain dreaded periods." (WH 683)

Gilman now attends the final hideous ceremony of the story, and here all the threads of our degenerate cosmos are tied together once more. A young Polish-American baby has vanished, and is clearly marked for human sacrifice like so many babies before. Luckily, another Pole had given Gilman a crucifix, which seems to work against the witch in ways it would presumably not work against the star-armed Antarcticans or the crab-like Fungi from Yuggoth. Lovecraft's final verbal excrescence is prepared by Gilman's musings while falling asleep: "Unwholesome recollections of things in the *Necronomicon* and the Black Book welled up, and he found himself swaying to infandous[81] rhythms said to pertain to the blackest ceremonies of the Sabbat and to have an origin outside the time and space we comprehend." (WH 682)

But the real gem in these latter pages is the passage at the head of this section. From as early as "The Call of Cthulhu," in the Louisiana swamp, we saw that orgies of bizarre music and dancing frequently accompany the approach to ultimate cosmic depths in Lovecraftian stories. The "cosmic timbre" he hears at this time is immediately reminiscent of the "ghastly, infra-bass timbre" emitted by the monstrous brother of Wilbur Whateley outside Dunwich. But this timbre merely serves as the gateway to what sounds like an evil or amoral version of the neo-Platonic theory of emanation. First, we are told that there are "massed spheres of matter." Behind these is concentrated "all the primal, ultimate space-time seethings" that define the very structure of the cosmos. In turn, these "seethings" do not simply rest there undisturbed, but "sometimes break forth in measured reverberations." They then "penetrate faintly to every layer of entity," much like the One of the neo-Platonists, but lacking all trace of its profound goodness. If Avicenna or Nicholas of Cusa had been seduced by the elder-world beings, they might have produced something not unlike the *Necronomicon* of the mad Arab Abdul al-Hazred.

86. With One Savage Kick

"During her last struggle he felt something bite at his ankle, and saw that Brown Jenkin had come to her aid. With one savage kick he sent the morbidity over the edge of the gulf and heard it whimper on some level far below." (WH 684-5)

Gilman is now sufficiently engaged in what he had mistaken for a dream world that he fights and attempts to kill both Keziah and Brown Jenkin. This violence is justified by the evident preparations for the murder of the young Polish baby. Gilman wrestles with Keziah, frightens her with the crucifix, and eventually wraps it around her neck and begins to strangle her with it. She falls to the floor, whether dead or alive. When Brown Jenkin comes to her aid, Gilman kicks the creature into the abyss as described in the passage above. But the poor baby is not saved, since Brown Jenkin has already done malicious work before being kicked over the railing: "What [Gilman] had prevented the knife from doing to the victim's chest, the yellow fangs of the furry blasphemy had done to a wrist– and the bowl so lately on the floor stood full beside the small lifeless body." (WH 685)

There are surprisingly numerous cases in Lovecraft of normal humans and animals fighting back with physical violence against their otherworldly superiors. The first, graphic example is Johansen's brave reversal of the ship to collide with and temporarily explode Great Cthulhu himself. The posse that visits the Gardner farm commits a sort of violence against the colour out of space by digging up the well where it resides; since the colour seems able to drain people of life only in gradual fashion, they survive the ordeal despite an apparently narrow escape. In "The Dunwich Horror," the Miskatonic Library guard dog kills Wilbur; later, it is Armitage and his fellow academics who perform the more difficult task of destroying Wilbur's monstrous and nameless brother. In "The Whisperer in Darkness" it seems probable that Akeley's random gunfire out the window killed some of the Fungi from Yuggoth, to judge from evidence later found outside. In "At the Mountains of Madness," it is possible that Professor Lake's dissection of an Elder Thing killed a merely hibernating specimen mistaken for a dead one. In Innsmouth there is a general Federal massacre and round-up of the fish-frog-human hybrids. For their part, the elder races score a number of kills as well: through acute angles that behave like obtuse ones, by all-out attacks on Antarctic camps, or in the annual Walpurgis Night sacrifice of an infant. Yet on the whole, it is remarkable how much success Lovecraft's humans and animals achieve in physical combat with these terribly powerful monstrosities.

87. Subconscious Angles

"Confused memories mixed themselves with his mathematics, and he believed his subconscious mind held the *angles* which he needed to guide him back to the normal world– alone and aided for the first time." (WH 685)

In Lovecraft's world, mathematics and physics always mix freely with folklore and occult studies. Depth psychology is now added to the mix as well. Already in "The Shadow Over Innsmouth," the narrator is frequently haunted by "a vague sense of pseudo-memory." Whereas the Freudian unconscious begins largely as a blank slate imprinted by infantile sexual experience, and whereas Jung's merely reaches back into an immemorial mythical past, the Lovecraftian unconscious is already deeply imbued with the angles of Riemannian topology. While Freud seemed daring in his assertion of a human death drive harking back to the emergence of life in protoplasmic puddles,[82] Lovecraft pushes memory back to a point just above the milky wisps of vapor near the monstrous nuclear chaos mercifully cloaked by the *Necronomicon* with the name of Azathoth.

All human knowledge and experience now seems woven together into a single unspeakable tapestry. Bernhard Riemann is just a stone's throw from texts of horrible mystic secrets, and the currently un-unified quantum theory and relativity are unified here in a flopping horde of mindless, amorphous dancers. Gilman is becoming more familiar with this world, but we can hardly blame him for not quite feeling at ease. With Keziah and Brown Jenkin now out of commission, he will need to navigate the strange angles of space by himself, without assistance. "The passage through the vague abysses would be frightful... and at last he would have to hear that hitherto veiled cosmic pulsing which he so mortally dreaded." (WH 685) This pulsing, in the more tangible form of "a low, monstrous shaking" (WH 685) even seems to communicate with the initiates of our Azathoth-saturated cosmos, in which hordes of mindless, amorphous dancers replace Aristotelian prime matter and the neo-Platonic One as the ultimate ingredients of reality.

88. Virtually a Tunnel

"It would be barbarous to do more than suggest what had killed Gilman. There had been virtually a tunnel through his body– something had eaten his heart out." (WH 687-8)

Of all the deaths that occur in Lovecraft, this is surely the worst: even worse than falling into a rock chasm of acute-obtuse angles, or having one's muscles salted and removed by tentacled

Antarctic Elder Things. The passage above is mildly hypocritical, first claiming that it would be "barbarous" to offer more than a suggestion of the cause of Gilman's death, then stating it as bluntly as possible. Although Keziah seems to have died from strangulation via crucifix (as the disappearance of her character-istically violet light suggests at WH 686), Brown Jenkin was not killed by falling over the railing into the depths. It is none other than this "furry blasphemy" who somehow re-emerges into Gilman's room, eating his heart out while he sleeps.

It may seem that having one's heart eaten out at night by a tittering, bearded rat is the very crux of the horror. Once one is dead, after all, it seems to matter little what happens next. Yet there is something deeply disturbing about the fact that Brown Jenkin, having devoured the heart entirely, does not simply turn around and leave Gilman's chest cavity the same way it came in. The fact that Brown Jenkin continues straight on through the body and exits at the other side seems disgustingly gratuitous. Brown Jenkin is apparently moving along a vector aimed straight through the sleeper's physical form, and that vector is not altered by the fact that the apparent mission has been accom-plished. Having once tunneled in and eaten the heart, the furry abomination sees fit to keep on digging in the same direction until exiting the other side. Gilman's body is treated just as moles treat dirt, or as Joe Sargent treats the Innsmouth bus stop when driving from Newburyport to Arkham. Having tunneled out successfully, Brown Jenkin even stays there for awhile as if to gloat over the corpse, and is found by the first party on the scene: "Everybody shrieked when a large, rat-like form suddenly jumped out from beneath the ensanguined bedclothes and scuttled across the floor to a fresh, open hole close by." (WH 687) Later the ultra-Catholic Joe Mazurewicz, who had lent the important crucifix to Gilman, follows "the crimson rat-tracks" (WH 688) leading from Gilman's couch to the rat hole, and finds that the paw prints resemble the shape of tiny human hands. For all the domestic familiarity of rats, Brown Jenkin may be more abominable than an army of Cthulhus or Elder Things, who at least have the excuse of coming from strange and distant homes.

The Shadow Out of Time

This story was completed in February 1935. In my view it is easily the weakest of this group of eight interrelated tales, combining the tedious explorations of alien ruins that marred the second half of "At the Mountains of Madness" with a theme (supposed dreams are actually real) already handled more skillfully in "The Dreams in the Witch House."

In this tale the Miskatonic University faculty extends its remarkable track record of encounters with the weird. This time the protagonist is Nathaniel Wingate Peaslee, Professor of Political Economy. While teaching a class on May 14, 1908 (earlier than the typical 1920's horrors of Lovecraft's great tales) Peaslee gets the strange sense that someone is trying to gain control of his thoughts, and suddenly falls unconscious. He finds himself in a strange room. It turns out that his body has been hijacked by an alien race that gains knowledge by time-traveling and swapping corporeal forms with specimens of numerous other races. Peaslee remains confined for some years in a strange alien city filled with "rugose [i.e., wrinkled], cone-shaped beings." In the meantime, one of the cone-shaped beings occupies Peaslee's body in Arkham, and does a less than perfect job of pretending to be Peaslee. His wife senses that the occupant of his body is someone different from her husband, and files for divorce. His eldest son and young daughter have the same reaction, and refuse to see him ever again, though his second son (a fellow academic named Wingate Peaslee) stays loyal and becomes his father's confidant in later years. In 1913 Peaslee returns to his own body, resuming mid-sentence the lecture he had been giving at the moment of his collapse five years earlier. Peaslee experiences great difficulty re-integrating himself into his former life, though he is still convinced that his time in the city of the cone-shaped beings was merely a dream. These dreams continue, always marked with the same sense of "pseudo-memory" experienced as well by the narrator in Innsmouth. Years later, in 1934, Peaslee receives a letter from a prominent Australian mining engineer named Mackenzie. This Mackenzie had found strange pieces of stone in the Outback desert, and later met a certain Dr. Boyle who marveled at the striking resemblance between Mackenzie's strange stones and the dream-visions described in journal articles by Peaslee. After receiving Mackenzie's letter, Peaslee travels to Australia with four colleagues. One of them is his loyal son Wingate. Another happens to be Professor Dyer, leader of the expedition in "At the Mountains of Madness"! All travel together to the desert site of the black stones. One night Peaslee awakens alone and descends into an underground portion of the site. There he finds vast subterranean facilities, fortunately described with more brevity than the Cyclopean city of the Antarctic. Deep in the ruins he finds a document at least ten million years old, and is shocked to discover writing, in English, in his own hand. His previous confinement in the strange city was not a dream, but reality.

89. Bodily Re-education

"Physical strength returned at once, although I required an odd amount of re-education in the use of my hands, legs, and bodily apparatus in general." (ST 722)

Of all our relations with entities in the world, none is more direct than our relations with our own bodies. Though at times we may trip, stumble, or move more awkwardly than expected, and though the chemical rather than electrical reaction time of the nervous system creates a barely perceptible delay between thought and action, we generally feel a magical power of action at a distance even over our distant fingers and toes. Mastery of basic motor skills is generally achieved at such an early date that we retain no childhood memory of struggling to walk or swallow.

In short, for all practical purposes we seem to have an immediate bond with our own bodies.

In this relatively straightforward passage, the bond between mind and body is briefly torn asunder. Peaslee has lived for a long time in the city of the tall rugose cones, and returns to his human form after a considerable absence. It is said to be five years, but it is unclear whether we are to measure the absence in terms of elapsed twentieth-century time or the elapsed time among the cone creatures. In any case, we are given to understand that the absence has been a long one. All those who have been absent from their home cities for eight months to a year know the strange sensation of forgetting the names of streets, not remembering the cost of simple services, perhaps forgetting the names of several friends, and so forth. How much more bizarre to experience such a discomfort with one's own body. A gap is created between mind and body that is vaguely reminiscent of occasionalist philosophy, though here it is an occasionalism without God.

90. Ugly Reports

"At times there appeared almost ugly reports of my power to influence the thoughts and acts of others, though I seemed to have taken care to minimise displays of this faculty. Other ugly reports concerned my intimacy with leaders of occultist groups, and scholars suspected of connexion with nameless bands of abhorrent elder-world hierophants." (ST 724)

Peaslee pays a heavy price for the involuntary five-year surrender of his body to the rugose cones. He loses his wife and two of his three children, all of them appalled by what happened to his persona in the meantime. Now we learn that he also lost a considerable portion of his reputation outside the family. He is the subject of "almost ugly reports" and flat-out "ugly reports." Peaslee is rather calm in summarizing the actions that were falsely if understandably ascribed to him during his absence. If the previous passage created a split between mind and body by referring to the need for basic bodily retraining on Peaslee's part, the present passage gives us a clever variation on this theme. Here, Peaslee is separated from what *seems* to be his own mind, thanks to the new link between the body of Peaslee and the mind of pseudo-Peaslee (who is in fact one of the rugose cones). Another way of looking at it is that while there is usually an immediate bond between our mind and the outward appearance of our mind, in the present case Peaslee is cruelly deprived of this link, and is thereby blamed for the actions of another.

The "almost ugly" reports concern his ability to influence the thoughts and actions of others. Here we have the reverse phenomenon of all the Lovecraftian splittings. For what is in question in this passage is a *fusion* between the mind of "Peaslee" and the minds and bodies of others, over which he seems to have direct control. The fact that "Peaslee" seems to use this faculty cautiously suggests a furtive manipulation of semblance, or once again, a separation between the intentions of the mind and the appearance of the intentions of the mind. The outright "ugly" reports do not concern influence over unwilling partners, but voluntary association with dubious peers. One report concerns "leaders of occultist groups," which would definitely have surprised Peaslee's family and friends, since he told us earlier that "at no time [prior to 1908] had I the least interest in either occultism or abnormal psychology." (ST 721) By associating with occult leaders, pseudo-Peaslee strikes an alliance with those who hint and probe into the terrible allusive depths of the cosmos, rather than remaining comfortable along its facile surface. The other dubious association is even more remarkable, since it contains an allusiveness that is at least threefold. There are *reports* that Peaslee is associated with certain scholars. These scholars are *suspected* of connection with "nameless bands of abhorrent elder-world hierophants." And this phrase in quotation marks is in turn a classic Lovecraftian allusion resisting immediate comphrensibility in at least three ways: the bands are "nameless"; they are devoted to elder worlds, a perpetually strange concept rendered even more strange by the fact that "elder-world" appears as an adjective for the first time in the great tales; finally, "hierophants" as a concept seems so absurdly archaic that it makes us think of tarot cards more than any known present-day spiritual function.

91. An Unknown Horticultural Tradition

"In a few of the terrace and roof-top gardens were larger and more vivid blossoms of almost offensive contours and seeming to suggest artificial breeding. Fungi of inconceivable size, outlines, and colours speckled the scene in patterns bespeaking some unknown but well-established horticultural tradition." (ST 732)

During the time spent away from his body, Peaslee visits the exotic garden described above. From looking at constellations in the sky he hits the bull's-eye in deducing his position in the universe: "Known outlines were sometimes approximated, but seldom duplicated; and from the position of the few groups I could recognize, I felt I must be in the earth's southern hemisphere, near the Tropic of Capricorn." (ST 732) The deviations from what one would expect to see there are presumably the result of the passage of an inordinately long period, during which the relative positions of the stars has shifted somewhat.

As for the passage at the head of this section, we can begin with a familiar technique found at the end of the passage: "patterns bespeaking some unknown but well-established horticultural tradition." Just as with the tiara kept in Newburyport, and just as with the notion of the townspeople there that bus driver Joe Sargent must be of a foreign race despite not resembling any known type on earth, we now have a strange garden that must nonetheless belong to some unknown tradition of horticulture. All of the garden-content lies beyond comprehension, but certain aspects of its form are vaguely intuitable despite Peaslee's inability to put his finger on just what that tradition might be.

As for the plants themselves, the passage above says only that the blossoms were of "almost offensive contours," without further explanation of how contours might be offensive– a classic Lovecraftian maneuver. But the passage above is truncated for reasons of space, and the omitted preceding sentences give far more detail about the strangeness of the garden plants, which are "almost terrifying in their strangeness" and include "bizarre and unfamiliar forms of vegetation" amidst "curiously carven monoliths." We find "abnormally vast fern-like growths" including some of "a ghastly, fungoid pallor." There are "tufted forms like fabulous cycads," "great spectral things resembling calamites," and "trees of coniferous aspect," which judging from this circumlocution presumably cannot be directly identified as conifers. "Flowers were small, colourless, and unrecognizable, blooming in geometrical beds." It is novel and refreshing to find Lovecraft's descriptive tools at work in a gardening scene, but here as with so much else in the story, the description falls short. It is a mere shadow, for instance, of the momentous assembling of pieces in the architectural descriptions of the Antarctic. The Lovecraft muse seems to be tiring, and there is room for doubt as to whether he could have continued writing in the same vein even if he had not suffered such an unfortunate early death.

92. Curvilinear Hieroglyphs

"One note appended to von Junzt's *Unaussprechlichen Kulten*, however, was alarmingly otherwise. It consisted of certain curvilinear hieroglyphs in the same ink as that of the German corrections, but following no recognized human pattern." (ST 734)

Here again we find a weakened version of one of Lovecraft's earlier stylistic achievements. The stylistic type here is the same as in the previous section: that of the unfamiliar object that belongs to some settled tradition. In a note appended to von Junzt (that fictitious forbidden author) we find "certain curvilinear hieroglyphs." The writing seems to be entirely incomprehensible, and belongs to no known human pattern, but is at least recognizable as curvilinear hieroglyphs.

The real point of the passage, however, seems to be plot-related rather than of stylistic importance. Namely, the key is that the hieroglyphs are written "in the same ink" as the German corrections, which would be possible only if a native German speaker and a scribe of the curvilinear hieroglyphs were present in the room together at the same time. The implication is that either von Junzt himself, or some German-speaking expert on von Junzt, has also been kidnapped by the body-snatching rugose cones and brought to this very place. Peaslee does not seem especially alarmed by this possibility– but then again, up to the very end of the story he thinks that all of these scenes are dreamscapes.

93. Inhuman Root Systems

"Most of these writings were in the language of the hiero-glyphs; which I studied in a queer way with the aid of droning machines, and which was evidently an agglutinative speech with root systems utterly unlike any found in human languages." (ST 744)

Here we have another weakened version of another familiar Lovecraftian tactic. By now we are well accustomed to his colors-by-analogy, ghastly infra-bass timbres, and other such previously unexampled things. But in the present passage we simply have a language that that is "evidently" agglutinative, but whose root system seems to be unparalleled among the known languages of the earth (first allusiveness). The mystery is heightened further by the fact that he cannot understand it directly, but only "in a queer way" (second allusiveness) with the assistance of a "droning machine" (third allusiveness, since no living reader has ever heard of such a device).

The content of these books is even darker than the mysterious root system of the language in which they are written. They include "horrible annals of other worlds and other universes, and of stirrings of formless life outside all other universes." (ST 744) The latter phrase is perfectly fine, if not that it had already been outdone by the crescendo of the earlier stories; the effect is that of a train already passed, and fainter than before. There are also "strange orders of beings which had peopled the world in forgotten pasts, and frightful chronicles of grotesque-bodied intelligences which would people it millions of years after the death of the last human being." (ST 744) But this is merely a recapitulation of the most familiar theme in all Lovecraft stories, softened and diluted. The train passes further away into the night.

94. Major Emotion-Wrenching

"Crime was surprisingly scanty, and was dealt with through highly efficient policing. Punishments ranged from privilege-deprivation and imprisonment to death or major emotion-wrenching..." (ST 750)

The idea of "major emotion-wrenching" as a criminal punishment is mildly amusing. But the real question is why we are given such detail about the civilization of the rugose cones in the first place. In this respect, "The Shadow Out of Time" repeats the weakness that mars the second half of "At the Mountains of Madness." Certain writers might be able to paint alien civilizations in abundant and vivid detail in a manner intriguing as an end in itself. This would require rich atmospheric prose capable of seducing the reader into believing in the details of the alien civilization in question. Lovecraft does not even attempt such a thing in the two stories just mentioned, offering merely a long list of features of these alien worlds, none of it convincing or even especially interesting. Lovecraft is at his most compelling, we have seen, whenever he depicts a severing of the bond between objects and their appearances, or objects and their qualities. Lovecraft works best when *hinting*, not when explicitly declaring or blandly listing.

It follows that it is completely counter-productive for Lovecraft to give us so much detail about his elder-world creatures. They ought to remain basically unknown: just palpable enough to seem physically present, but not grasped down to the minutest details of their lifestyle. What was so regrettable about the second half of "At the Mountains of Madness" was the deadening banality of its lesson that the elder-world creatures are just like us. They too have civilizations that rise and decline, and they too have enemies who seek to harm them (the shoggoths). But however edifying this might seem as potential anti-racist allegory (as if Lovecraft were the one to

provide such a thing), it can only be catastrophic as horror literature. The truly terrifying impact of the first half of the story is
completely undermined by Dyer and Danforth's tediously
detailed, fresco-deciphering stroll through the Antarctic city.
Something similar happens with Peaslee's account of the rugose
cones. It is difficult to find the cones allusive, elusive, or frightening once we know about their jurisprudence and learn that
even their manner of using pen and ink resembles our own.

95. A Monstrous Plasticity

"There were veiled suggestions of a monstrous *plasticity*, and
of temporary *lapses of visibility*, while other fragmentary
whispers referred to their uses of *great winds*." (ST 752)

The passage in question is connected with what we learn of
struggles *between* different species of otherworldly creatures. The
rugose cones (or Great Race) seems to have been vanquished by
the Antarctic monsters (or Elder Things), and this is apparently
what caused the Great Race to embark on their desperate and
massive project of mind-projection into the bodies of all possible
creatures. The struggle between these two species could have been
made truly fascinating in one of two opposite ways. First, some
other science fiction writer of incredible literary aptitude might
have taken us to those battles and managed to get us emotionally
involved with them. This would have been the proper path of a
mainstream writer skilled enough to rise beyond pulp. Second, it
would also be possible to hint vaguely at these struggles in cryptic
and allusive fashion without trying to give impossible direct detail.
This second option would be the proper path of H.P. Lovecraft,
who repeatedly delivers the goods in precisely this fashion on
countless other occasions. But instead of either of these courses of
action, Lovecraft takes an ineffective middle course, simply listing
the details of inter-species culture and combat without making
them vivid or credible. For instance: "The political and economic

system of each unit [of the Great Race] was a sort of fascistic socialism..." (ST 749) *Fascistic socialism?* We also learn that after one alarming battle "greater precautions were taken, and many of the paths were closed for ever– though a few were left with sealed trap-doors for strategic use in fighting the Elder Things if ever they broke forth in unexpected places..." (ST 731) Lovecraft's decline as a stylist becomes almost alarming here, and I'm afraid I may begin to sound like Edmund Wilson at his least generous. Sealed trap-doors used by one alien race against another do seem like the stuff of adolescent pulp fiction, at least when stated as flatly and blandly as this.

All of this is meant to indicate that the passage at the head of this section, although apparently meant as a series of frightening allusions, cannot possibly work as such. To speak of "veiled suggestions of plasticity," "lapses of visibility," and of "fragmentary whispers" that refer to the Elder Things' use of "great winds" is to allude secretly to things already encountered in the flesh by any reader of "At the Mountains of Madness." He might as well have referred to "the unknown Cyclopean city of Chicago, which almost exceeds the descriptive powers of language." It is also somewhat difficult to inspire terror over a race of creatures when sealed trap-doors have already been recommended as a good defensive measure against them.

96. Professor Dyer Was Appalled

"Professor Dyer was appalled at the measureless age of the fragments, and Freeborn found traces of symbols which fitted darkly into certain Papuan and Polynesian legends of infinite antiquity. The condition and scattering of the blocks told mutely of vertiginous cycles of time and geologic upheavals of cosmic savagery." (ST 757)

This passage too is one where critiques of the Wilsonian variety begin to hit the mark. Words such as "appalled," "measureless," "darkly," "infinite," "vertiginous," and "cosmic savagery" are not inherently forbidden to all good prose. We have seen Lovecraft use them skillfully before, when added as spice to work already done elsewhere in a given passage. But here the words in question are called upon for too much heavy labor, and once they are stripped away, too little remains. The fact that Freeborn found "traces of symbols" is not a bad phrase, constituting a good doubly allusive structure. But the attempt to fit them (and fit them "darkly") into Papuan and Polynesian legend is simply a stock trick already exploited more effectively in earlier stories. The same goes, of course, for "vertiginous cycles of time" and "cosmic savagery," which have been evoked in earlier stories by more convincing objects than scattered blocks. Lovecraft almost seems as if he were recovering from an illness, or as if he were short of breath. The most interesting part of the passage is the opening phrase "Professor Dyer was appalled," since it breathes a bit of life into the story by reminding us of the far better executed "At the Mountains of Madness," where Dyer had much better reason to be appalled. Nonetheless, there is cause for retro- spective alarm in Lovecraft's accelerating efforts to tie up all the loose ends from all his stories. We know it is always a bad sign for Hollywood film franchises, for instance, when they feel the need to show us the origin of the Joker from his falling into a vat of chemicals, or the early days of the Corleone Family in the various *Godfather* supplements, or when we are forced to meet the young Owen and his "girlfriend" Beru in one of the miserable *Star Wars* "prequels." Lovecraft does not go quite that far off the rails, but the tying together of all the Miskatonic University faculty stories begins to feel like the last-ditch summation of a series now running dry– a "jumping of the shark," as is it is often put.

97. Each Subtle Shading and Nuance

"What obscure, forgotten iconography could have repro-
duced each subtle shading and nuance which so persistently,
exactly, and unvaryingly besieged my sleeping vision night
after night?" (ST 766)

Stylistically this passage is of little interest, and makes no effort
to be. Referring to a system of iconography as "obscure" and
"forgotten" is a half-hearted effort, far below Lovecraft's usual
high standard of allusiveness, and "subtle shading and nuance"
is even weaker. The point of this passage is not style, but plot–
the table is being set for Peaslee's final realization that the match
between reality and what he remembers of his dreams occurs for
the simple reason that the dreams were never dreams in the first
place. Here as so often in Lovecraft, we the readers guess the
truth long before Peaslee. But rather than leading to the usual
comic effect, as when the Innsmouth narrator dismisses Old
Zadok's horrific Cthulhu chant as "stark raving" even though we
know better, the effect here is merely one of tedious movement
towards a climax foreseen long before it ever arrives.

98. S'gg'ha of Antarctica

"Could I still find the house of the writing-master, and the
tower where S'gg'ha, a captive mind from the star-headed
vegetable carnivores of Antarctica, had chiselled certain
pictures on the blank spaces of the walls?" (ST 767)

The description of the judicial and writing systems of the Great
Race; their use of sealed trap-doors as defenses against the
enemy– all this was bad enough. But in my view, Lovecraft
reaches a new low when he gives us the actual *proper name* of one
of the star-headed creatures of Antarctica: S'gg'ha. The only way
to make things worse would be to give us the birthday of S'gg'ha
(perhaps October 6th), his favorite color (blue?), and perhaps

quote a few passages from his diary. All needed distance from the Elder Things is now lost. They are depicted not only as inhabitants of a history filled with rises and declines too much like our own, but even as potential conversation partners who can be addressed by name. Perhaps S'gg'ha the star-headed vegetable carnivore of Antarctica would even accept a friendly nickname if we got to know him well enough. If not that the authorship of this story were apparently beyond all doubt, moments like this would lead me to suspect a clever forgery. Lovecraft is clearly losing his edge.

99. Poised with Mathematical Genius

"Blocks of stupendous size, poised with mathematical genius and bound with cements of incredible toughness, had combined to form a mass as firm as the planet's rocky core." (ST 771)

In this passage we find a brief return to stylistic form by a truly great writer. The notion of blocks "poised with mathematical genius" is a good one. It is effective at creating the sense of an insuperable barrier. It is nicely allusive, not telling us exactly how genius found a way to "poise" blocks in such a fashion as to make their arrangement effective in reaching the desired aim. "Cements of incredible toughness" nicely combines the world of allusion with that of engineering. And finally, the passage continues the eminently Lovecraftian theme of linking advanced mathematics and science with the same otherworldly beings who are revealed by the occult and by madmen roaming the Arabian desert wastes.

100. Dormant, Rudimentary Senses

"Dormant, rudimentary senses seemed to start into vitality within me, telling of pits and voids peopled by floating horrors and leading to sunless crags and oceans and teeming cities of windowless basalt towers upon which no light ever shone." (ST 781)

After finding so much fault with "The Shadow Out of Time," it is refreshing to be able to close on a stronger note. This passage, which occurs just two pages from the rather anti-climactic ending of the story, is skillfully executed. The notion that we possess dormant, rudimentary senses not usually accessible in everyday life is a strong Lovecraftian theme, reflected in his ascribing of special intuitive power to such animals as dogs, horses, and wolves. But whereas many of the usual Lovecraftian tricks in this eighth great tale seem like pale replays of earlier examples, this brief reference to the dormant and rudimentary is nearly as good as those in the earlier stories.

These dormant cryptic senses come to life inside Peaslee. They "tell him" of the existence of "pits and voids"– a conjunction showing a nice mix of concrete horror (dangerous physical pits) with a more abstract sense of threat (voids that may be metaphysical, cosmological, or spiritual rather than physical). Moreover, these pits and voids lead to "sunless crags and oceans and teeming cities of windowless basalt towers upon which no light ever shone." This beautifully concrete fantasy gives us a nice final taste of Lovecraft's essentially romantic imagination.

Part Three:

Weird Realism

Gathering the Threads

The mission of this final part of the book is to tie together the various threads of the first two. Part One raised a number of general philosophical themes that become visible in Lovecraft's fiction, while Part Two provided a bulk experience of those themes by considering one hundred individual passages displaying the strengths (and sometimes weaknesses) of Lovecraft as a stylist. As far as I am aware, such extensive attention has never been paid to Lovecraft's style. He has been treated instead on the level of *content*, as a horror writer whose plots might be summarized and sifted for insights into his general world-view. The problem with all such efforts is their excessive literalization of the author, which reduces him to someone who happens to express certain views about the cosmos in the form of short stories in the mixed genre of horror/science fiction. This leaves him open to the dismissive charge of writing adolescent pulp, as lodged by Edmund Wilson among others, while also leaving him vulnerable to admirable but half-correct praise from those who happen to love such fiction rather than hate it. Above all, it gives us a Lovecraft who could have written tritely and unconvincingly that the Cthulhu idol was "an octopus, a dragon, and a human all rolled into one." In this way he becomes *Lovecraft Made Easy*, the equivalent of Žižek's mocking paraphrase of Hölderlin's *Wo aber Gefahr ist, wächst das Rettende auch* as: "When you're in deep trouble, don't despair too quickly, look around carefully, the solution may be just around the corner."[83] Such rewritings are empty for the same reasons given by Žižek in his brilliant reflection on the inherent stupidity of all proverbs. Among other difficulties, this version of *Hölderlin Made Easy* can easily be countered by the opposite proverb: "When you're in deep trouble, it is absurd to look for simple solutions. Think carefully, because only a fool believes that difficult problems are solved in a snap." Here we are left with nothing but dueling platitudes.

Nor is this problem faced only by literature, since it is equally disastrous to literalize *philosophy* to an excessive degree, turning it into a question of correct and incorrect dogmatic theses. After all, we might imagine the following passage from the preface to a book called *Nietzsche Made Easy*:

> Nietzsche believed that everything in the universe was characterized by will to power, through which everything tries to impose its own perspective on everything else. He also believed in the eternal recurrence of everything that has ever happened, an infinite number of times without cease; he viewed this thought as so horrible that anyone who could endure it would have the status of a rare superman able to give birth to a new type of human who would be as far above us as we are above the apes. From this we can see the roots of Nietzsche's strongly anti-democratic politics.[84]

While not strictly incorrect, this relatively bland summary resembles Nietzsche *much less* than would a thinker defending precisely the opposite doctrines but in a more Nietzschean style. It is quite possible to imagine an alternate Nietzsche who would attack the will to power, while ridiculing the eternal return in favor of the transient singularity of each event, and also defending the turbulent democratic masses against ennervated aristocrats as the only soil from which true greatness can emerge. This counter-Nietzsche would have more in common with the real Nietzsche than the literalized *Nietzsche Made Easy* ever could. On this basis, all summarizing scholarship might seem to be imperiled for the same reason that Wilson's version of Lovecraft comes up short. I take this to be one clear implication of Kant's subversion of all dogmatic statement by the unknowable thing-in-itself. The opposing proverbs generated by

Žižek show us how the Kantian antinomies apply to *any* pair of counterposed statements, not just to those cosmological theories that happen to be placed side-by-side in the *opus magnum* of Kant. Yet even if content is stupid, it cannot be *worthless*: for in another sense it is neither inaccurate nor pointless to call Nietzsche the philosopher of the will to power and the eternal recurrence. This forms a genuine problem for our dispute with literalization. For it obviously does make a difference, for instance, whether you believe that there is some smallest material particle or that the division must continue without limit. The reversibility of these two dogmas according to Kant is simply an equivalence in terms of their equal non-verifiability, and obviously does not make them intellectually equivalent in all senses.

The most important themes that emerged from our discussion of Lovecraft were as follows. We saw that Lovecraft is not simply a pulp writer, but one who keeps pulp at a distance through two separate fissures that obstruct the power of literal language. First, there are the numerous moments when Lovecraft merely *alludes* to realities that are impossible to describe, as we saw in countless cases in Part Two. Second, there are those additional moments that we described as forms of *literary cubism* (close in spirit to the philosophy of Husserl), in which no allusion is made to a thing exceeding the powers of language. Instead, in these cases numerous bizarre or troubling features of a palpable thing are piled up in such excessive number that it becomes difficult to combine all these facets neatly into a single object, thereby giving us the sense of a purely immanent object that is nonetheless distinct from any bundle of features. Third, there were a small number of additional cases in which both the object *and* its features resist all description, as when we were colorfully informed of "the blind idiot god Azathoth, Lord of All Things, encircled by his flopping horde of mindless and amorphous dancers, and lulled by the thin monotonous piping of a daemoniac flute held in nameless paws." (WH 664) Admittedly, this could be read as the literal claim that a god named Azathoth is actually encircled by flopping dancers amidst the music of flutes. But given the numerous strictures that work against a literal reading of the passage (such as Lovecraft's statement at WD 464 that the name Azathoth is merely a "merciful cloaking" of "monstrous nuclear chaos"), I take the ostensibly more tangible features of this bizarre scene to be no less allusive than the chaos that lurks behind the name of Azathoth. Fourth, there are cases in Lovecraft (normally associated with failed scientific testing) in which a known and perfectly accessible object such as a meteorite or metallic ornament is found to have unintelligible but real features. These four basic tensions in Lovecraft's writings are the same four that belong to the philosophical discipline of "ontography."[85] In this respect, Lovecraft is a writer tailor-made for object-oriented philosophy, much like Hölderlin for Heidegger or Mallarmé for Derrida or Meillassoux.

But while this fourfold ontography is certainly the key aspect of Lovecraft for the purposes of object-oriented philosophy, it is far from the whole story. We also need to consider both the difference and the close relation between tragedy and comedy. In part two we saw repeatedly that Lovecraft's narrators often become comical even in the midst of the most horrific perils. We recalled further that this important theme was raised briefly by Socrates at the end of Plato's *Symposium*, and we might also wonder about the relation of this theme to the others discussed in this book. Furthermore, many of the passages cited in Part Two as fine examples of Lovecraftian style are neither allusive nor cubistic in structure, and for this reason we need to look closely at what they accomplish and see if they relate to the "ontographical" Lovecraft in any way. It should also be added that, even though Lovecraft's suggestive power increases his effectiveness as a horror writer, such suggestion can be employed in numerous contexts that are not the least bit horrifying. For this reason, we also need to ask about the significance of Lovecraft's being a writer of horror rather than of some other genre. Finally, there is the fact that even in those cases where rifts between objects and qualities are clearly in play in Lovecraft's writing, he is obviously a writer of short stories, not of metaphysical treatises. If Lovecraft is more important for philosophy than many readers suspect, it would still be excessive to call him primarily a philosopher, and obviously absurd to call him one of the greatest twentieth century philosophers, though I am happy to risk calling him one of that century's greatest writers of fiction. In this closing portion of the book, we need to tie all these themes together as neatly as the situation allows.

Fusion

Our first step is to look a bit more closely at Lovecraft's "ontography," or the way in which he deals with the interaction between objects and their qualities. This is a central element of Lovecraft's literary style no less than of object-oriented philosophy itself. We have repeatedly encountered the classic Lovecraftian gesture in which an entity is described as having certain properties while also being said to resist description by those very properties, as if such details were able to give us nothing more than a hopelessly vague approximation. The clearest example of this species of allusion is probably the description of the Cthulhu idol: "If I say that my somewhat extravagant imagination yielded simultaneous pictures of an octopus, a dragon, and a human caricature, I shall not be unfaithful to the spirit of the thing... but it was the *general outline* of the whole which made it most shockingly frightful..." (CC 169) The "spirit of the thing" and even "the general outline of the whole" may be taken to allude to a *real object*, since it is one that never quite crystallizes for the reader into a palpable sensual object, as would be the case if Cthulhu were simply a giant octopus and nothing more. The matter is complicated by the fact that a physical Cthulhu also exists within the story who is merely represented by the idol. To simplify the issue, we can forget the physical entity Cthulhu that chases the ship in the South Pacific. When we say "real object" here, all we mean is the "spirit" or "general outline" of the idol itself, quite apart from its reference to a genuine monster. An artwork or religious artifact is a "real" object in the sense that it cannot be exhausted by any sum total of specific experiences or linguistic propositions, but to some extent resists all perception and all analysis, which forever fail to exhaust it. In this respect the Cthulhu idol is no different from a hammer, a chair, an atom, or a human.

237

In all such cases, no *direct* contact with the real object is possible. In Heidegger's tool-analysis, for example, the hammer that breaks does not suddenly emerge from dark visibility into directly accessible form. The broken or explicit hammer lying before our eyes still harbors unfathomed depths, and the same is even more obviously true for Lovecraft's narrator when confronting the Cthulhu idol. The real object never becomes directly present under any circumstances. To this extent we would even agree with the idealist argument that the thought of things-in-themselves is still a thought, and is therefore completely circumscribed by the laws of thought. We simply disagree that no *indirect* access to the things-in-themselves is possible. For this is precisely what *allusion* does, by pointing towards a thing without making it present.

This indirect access is achieved by allowing the hidden object to deform the sensual world, just as the existence of a black hole might be inferred from the swirl of light and gases orbiting its core. Notice that the narrator *does not* merely give us a vagueness of the following sort: "Any attempt to give a description would be unfaithful to the spirit of the thing, for it was the general outline of the whole which made it most shockingly frightful." Here the failed attempt at description is altogether missing. The result is too empty to sink one's teeth into, and fails through *excessive* allusiveness. Instead of this, Lovecraft offers the known physical qualities of dragon, octopus, and humanoid as rough indicators. But by invoking the "spirit" and "general outline" of the idol, he also points to an inaccessible deeper unit that is somehow capable of ruling this grotesque assortment of features. Stated differently, the Cthulhu description is like a metaphor with one of the terms deleted. In *Guerrilla Metaphysics*,[86] I analyzed Max Black's tepid but useful metaphor: "man is a wolf." (Gender-neutral language was not yet the norm in Black's early 1960's.) The point of this metaphor is *not* that we literally claim that humans are vicious, carnivorous pack animals overly influenced by phases of the moon. Instead, we are never quite sure *just what* the relation is here between human and wolves. A human being is the subject of the metaphor, but not the accessible human we encounter every day in numerous contexts. Instead, it is a human deeper than all access, now orbited strangely by inscrutable wolf-qualities. If the metaphor were reversed into "a wolf is a man," the opposite would hold. In this case a real wolf-object would lie in the depths, orbited indistinctly by numerous hazy human-qualities. But in both cases the underlying object is not entirely unfamiliar, since we are loosely acquainted with the basic ontological style of both humans and wolves. The Cthulhu idol is a somewhat different case, since the monster Cthulhu was in no way the subject of everyday stock platitudes in our society before Lovecraft wrote about him. This means that the description of the Cthulhu idol is the rough equivalent of saying: "X is a wolf." Or rather: "X is an octopus-dragon-humanoid." We know that this structure is common in Lovecraft. His use of metaphor in the normal sense is somewhat infrequent compared with most writers. Instead, he prefers metaphors in which one of the terms is completely and deliberately unknown, defined not at all by any of the social preconceptions linked with it (unlike "man is a wolf"), but solely by its gravitational work of bending the qualities that form the only testimony to its existence. In this respect, "black hole" would be a good technical term for the sort of allusive, withdrawn object that Lovecraft so often loves to establish. In terms of ontography, this is the tension that I have called "space."[87] For it embodies the fact that objects spatially removed from us are both *absolutely* distant (since they are not directly melted together with us), but also near to us insofar as they *inscribe* their distance in directly accessible fashion.

But there is also the tension called "essence,"[88] in which neither the object nor its qualities are directly accessible. Depictions of this structure are as rare in Lovecraft as anywhere else, precisely because it is so difficult to pull off two vaguenesses simultaneously. But I have claimed that one such example is the aforementioned case of the blind idiot god Azathoth, surrounded by flopping hordes of mindless dancers. Unless we want to read this passage literally as the description of an actual scene in which a tangible entity called Azathoth is actually surrounded by dancers and flute music, then *both* sides of this description need to be read as allusions. We already know that the name Azathoth in the *Necronomicon* is nothing but the "merciful cloaking" of a deeper monstrous nuclear chaos lying behind that name. And given that nuclear chaos would be difficult to ornament with actual flute music and actual dancers (however amorphous), these too should be read as allusions to certain deeper and less tangible qualities.

As the title of this section indicates, what space and essence have in common is that both are cases of *fusion*. In "man is a wolf" and in all other metaphors, qualities are fused with an object that we do not normally associate with them (for example, human-object fused with wolf-qualities). This results in an object that *feels* real, simply because it is too difficult to register vividly as a normal sensual object. Something analogous happens in the case of essence, since it gives the imagination an excellent workout to try to envision Azathoth and the dancers and flutes coming together as one. But of course, this fusion requires a prior fission, since these qualities were not there beforehand just floating in the ether. Wolf-qualities were attached to wolves, and octopus-qualities to octopi, before they were fused with a foreign body.

Fission

We now turn to "fission," the obvious terminological opposite of fusion. Rather than bringing qualities together in uneasy relationship with some inaccessible real object, fission splits the usual relation between an accessible sensual thing and its accessible sensual qualities. I have referred to it as a "cubist" rift between objects and qualities, because here just as in cubist painting, a guitar or mountain or postman is broken into such a multitude of surfaces that it can no longer be identified with any mere summation of them. We saw a classic example of this in Professor Dyer's description of the Antarctic city: "There were truncated cones, sometimes terraced or fluted, surmounted by tall cylindrical shafts here and there bulbously enlarged and often capped with tiers of thinnish scalloped discs; and strange, beetling, table-like constructions suggesting piles of multitudinous rectangular slabs or circular plates or five-pointed stars with each one overlapping the one beneath." (MM 508-9) To damage the cubistic effect of this passage, we need only simplify it as follows: "The city was made up mostly of truncated cones, sometimes terraced or fluted." Reduce a cubist portrait of a city to just one or two angles and you no longer have a cubist painting, but something resembling a traditional academic portrait. The same holds for Lovecraft's style. Usually an object does not seem very different from the sum of qualities it presents to us; this is the grain of truth in Hume's "bundle" theory. In order to produce the sort of strain that causes the bond between objects and qualities to crack, one obvious technique is to multiply the qualities to such an extreme that whatever unifies them begins to seem like an overstressed independent force lying at their basis, like a sturdy bridge that creaks and groans under the weight of ten thousand passing carnival floats. We find the same technique in Husserl's philosophy no less than in the paintings of Picasso and Braque; indeed, some of Braque's paintings of buildings are the best visual approximations we have of Lovecraft's own disturbing architectural descriptions. Husserl asks us to multiply the adumbrations of an object in thought so as to strip away the vast majority of inessential features and thereby gain insight into the object itself.

It is important to notice that however strange the Antarctic city may be, it does not have the same literary structure as the Cthulhu idol (this is a change from my view of several years ago). Lovecraft never tells us that his architectural description is merely "not untrue to the spirit of the city," or that "the general urban outline" is something more terrible than any of the individual buildings. Instead, the Antarctic city is perfectly deployed right in front of us; it simply strikes us as rather bizarre, due to its unification of a vast list of strange architectural features. We are dealing here only with the sensual version of the city, fully accessible to us and not withdrawn in the least, locked in dubious relation with the mass of strange qualities that are so difficult to unify. Instead of the "spirit of the thing," we are dealing with something more like the *body* of the thing, although that body is riddled with fractures. In fission, the qualities of the thing break off from the thing as a whole and seem partially distinct from it for the first time. This structure is also common in Lovecraft. I often call it "time,"[89] since this is precisely what our experience of time involves– the fluctuation of numerous qualities around somewhat enduring (but not permanent) objects that remain the same throughout those fluctuations.

Along with this fission between sensual objects and their sensual qualities, Lovecraft also gives us several cases of sensual objects in tension with their subterranean *real* qualities. As far as I am aware, this happens solely in cases when scientific testing fails to unlock the true nature of an unusual object. We have already discussed the following passage, for instance: "Professor Ellery found platinum, tellurium, and iron in the strange alloy;

but mixed with these were at least three other apparent elements of high atomic weight which chemistry was absolutely powerless to classify. Not only did they fail to correspond with any known element, but they did not even fit the vacant places reserved for probable elements in the periodic system." (WH 677) In Husserl's philosophy, not *all* qualities are transient accidents floating along the surface of things and shifting with the flow of time. Some qualities are the essential ones, without which the thing would not be what it is for us, and these are the ones to be found through the so-called "eidetic reduction." That is why I often use the name *eidos*[90] for this tension between accessible sensual objects and the inaccessible qualities that are of structural importance for them. In Lovecraft this always happens as a result of scientific *failure*, with the unstated implication that scientific *success* would have given us the real qualities. And Husserl generally seems to agree, holding that complete knowledge of the qualities is possible. Yet he also admits that they can never be *sensual*, but can be known only through the mind, and in this way he at least concedes that they are not of the same order as sensual qualities.

Both of these tensions, which I have called "time" and "eidos," are forms of *fission*. Unlike the two varieties of fusion described in the previous section, they do not melt together objects and qualities that are not normally linked. Instead, they break apart pre-existent everyday bonds between objects and their qualities. But we saw above that all fusion requires a prior fission, and we find here by analogy that all fission leads to a new form of fusion. When stripped from their underlying object, the qualities thus liberated seem to form new objects: the truncated cones cease to be part of the general Antarctic ambience and instead become freestanding objects in their own right, no longer enslaved as atmospheric coloring for a larger urban object.

The Taxonomic Fallacy

This book has opposed any attempt to paraphrase Lovecraft's stories in the form of literal content. In some respects such claims are not new. At least one familiar twentieth-century critic makes a similar point in connection with English poetry. I speak of Cleanth Brooks (1906-1994). Brooks was a prominent figure among the now unfashionable American "New Critics," mostly well-bred Southern gentlemen who favored close readings of literary texts and downplayed any reading of works according to their historical context. A poem was to be treated as an autonomous entity, working like a machine to create certain effects. After dominating American criticism during the 1940's and 1950's, the New Critics gave way to trends such as New Historicism, which refused to acknowledge literary works as special cultural productions distinct in kind from their non-literary environments. In this respect, the New Critics in literature endured a fate similar to that of the art critic Clement Greenberg, who was cited favorably in Part One above. At times object-oriented philosophy has been criticized for similar reasons, and thus it is important to show briefly where I agree and disagree with Brooks's assault on paraphrase.

Roughly speaking, the New Critics (and Clement Greenberg) are attacked for two basic reasons. One is their supposed ivory tower aestheticism and elitism, with its refusal to sufficiently acknowledge the historical, material, and political conditions under which literary works are produced. From this objection arise various attempts to counter their position by placing art on the same level as every other cultural production. Here I would agree with the critique, though for the opposite reason. Namely, if we are to oppose the special status of artworks, this should not be by denying their autonomous reality and putting them back into a gigantic historico-sociologico-economic context. Instead, we should allow the various elements of that context to enjoy the same autonomous life that the New Critics grant to literature alone. For while it is palpably true that most things are heavily dependent on a certain number of other things, it is by no means the case that the world is a massive holistic contexture in which everything affects everything else. Such wild holism is one of the insidious intellectual dogmas of our time, and I will soon show how it even infects the position of Brooks himself. For while it is certainly true that an artwork is better understood when we learn about its historical and material background conditions, the application of such learning can never be rampant and promiscuous. It takes a careful historical judge to weigh which environmental aspects of a given thing are assimilated by it, and which can be excluded as irrelevant. The philosophy of Spinoza, for instance, is no doubt heavily influenced by the position of the Jews in seventeenth-century Amsterdam,[91] but some aspects of that situation have more influence on his philosophy than others, and some perhaps no impact in the least. Certain aspects of Jewish culture in Amsterdam will obviously prove to be so trivial or peripheral to the topic at hand that no Spinoza scholar would dream of mentioning them. More generally, any object absorbs certain forces and influences from its environment while remaining completely insensitive to others. Contextuality is never total; the dogma of "system" must be opposed here as everywhere else. There is also the more basic point that Spinoza's philosophy has spread across the globe and across the centuries into historical places that have nothing at all to do with the Jews of seventeenth century Amsterdam. In short, Spinoza's philosophy is an *object*, and though that object has a history, it is no more reducible to that history than a child is to its parents. Objects resemble escape pods that jettison clear of their original environments, even if those environments have left certain traces (but not others) on the objects. This is true not only of poems, philosophies, and children, but of legal documents, *lettres de cachet*, jail cells and manacles, medical clinics, insane asylums, human subjects, pianos, worms, notebooks, and pieces of butter-scotch candy. An object is only an object when it partially closes off from the world and is able to shift into other contexts, releasing its energies into neighborhoods foreign to those of its birth. Instead of opposing aesthetic elitism by putting artworks back in their context, we should do so by breaking up all contexts into trillions of autonomous artworks, some more important than others.

A second charge against the New Critics is that by shifting our attention from historical context and literal meaning towards recurring structures of irony and paradox, they are guilty of a "formalism" (like Greenberg, once again) that turns criticism into an empty intellectual game without social or political ramifica-tions– or indeed, a game that serves the reigning ideology of the day. Brooks addresses the "formalism" charge by denying that the only alternative is between true literal statement and external aesthetic ornament.[92] Though he is right to do this, he fails to acknowledge the size of the problem that results from downplaying the content of literature so severely in favor of structural irony and paradox. For it is not strictly true that John Donne's "The Canonization" is simply an unreadable paradox, since it also happens to be concerned with a very *specific* paradox; likewise, Lovecraft does not break the bond between objects and their qualities in the context or romance or detective fiction, but only in the service of horror. And pushing into territory that Brooks specifically excludes, the inadequate literal form of *philo-sophical* and *scientific* statements is also paradoxical, but in each case is a paradox with a specific content. In other words, despite Žižek's brilliant point about the stupidity of all proverbs, it really does make a difference whether you follow the principle of *carpe diem* or choose instead to focus ascetically on the afterworld. There are obvious limits to the inherent stupidity of all content, and these limits must be accounted for; paraphrase is a heresy, but only a half-heresy. While Brooks occasionally assures us that he knows this, these assurances lack the fire and enthusiasm with which he discusses the other side of the issue.[93]

It will be helpful to give a brief summary of what is right and wrong in the attitude of Brooks, which by analogy can be applied to other "formalisms" as well. Above all, we can only agree with the general spirit of his attack on paraphrase. The main dogma to be combated is "that the poem constitutes a 'statement' of some sort, the statement being true or false, and expressed more or less clearly or eloquently or beautifully; for it is from this formula that most of the heresies about poetry derive."[94] This insight holds far beyond the sphere of poetry, but for now we continue to follow Brooks in his chosen profession of poetry critic. As he sees it, any attempt to summarize the meaning of a poem will fall short, and in attempting to make the summary more adequate, the critic will need to add so many qualifications, hesitations, and even metaphors that the result will be nothing like a literal statement at all.[95] A paraphrase is no better than an "abstraction,"[96] just as any form of presence-at-hand for Heidegger is a mere abstraction from the deeper subterranean life of tool-being. Thus, a poem is not a set of ornamented literal statements, but "a pattern of resolved stresses,"[97] much like architecture, painting, ballet, music, or drama. Brooks's primary tool in showing the insufficiency of literal content is the detection in poems of irony and paradox, or the "recognition of incongruities"[98] more generally. In some of the English poetry that Brooks considers, we find for example that: "it is the child who is the best philosopher; it is from a kind of darkness... that light proceeds; growth into manhood is viewed, not as an extrication from, but as an incarceration within, a prison."[99] As he puts it, in a helpful image, statements in a poem are bent like sticks in water.[100] Many of the greatest poems in world literature, he plausibly asserts, are built around such paradoxes.[101]

So far, there is little cause to disagree with this warning against looking for true and false content in poems. Yet Brooks makes two additional claims that must be rejected. The first is his assertion that the impossibility of paraphrase makes literature unique: "one can never measure the poem against the scientific or philosophical yardstick for the reason that the poem, when laid along the yardstick, is never the 'full poem' but an abstraction from the poem..."[102] But this is a case of what I have elsewhere called the Taxonomic Fallacy.[103] For while it is correct to identify a difference between literal content and the unparaphrasable, there is no justification for allotting these two structures to two different *types* of human intellectual pursuits– a division of labor in which philosophy and science would be responsible for literal truths, while literature would handle all the irony and paradox. For on the one hand, poems contain all manner of literal claims: if Dante is not reducible to a political treatise on the limits of Papal power, we also cannot remove his political claims arbitrarily. And on the other, philosophy and science display as much irony and paradox as literature: Aristotle already noted that a substance is that which can have contrary qualities at different times, while the wave/particle duality of light in physics is at least as paradoxical as anything written by John Donne. Irony and paradox cannot be local peculiarities of literature, then, but are an ontological structure permeating the cosmos.

Another more serious objection concerns the reason why Brooks holds that paraphrase is impossible. And here we have an irony as great as those in the poems he discusses. For while Brooks is viewed as a mortal foe of historical-social context who treats poems as encapsulated or autonomous objects, this is true only as concerns the social context lying *outside* the poem. Once we are inside the work, Brooks becomes an ardent champion of context. As he puts it, an ironic and paradoxical statement such as the famous line of John Keats that beauty is truth and truth is beauty, "is given its precise meaning and significance by its relation to the *total context* of the poem."[104] I emphasize the words "total context" to note that Brooks is guilty here of the same exaggeration as his opponents, as already described above. Just as a poem absorbs and consolidates discrete influences from its context, without being holistically penetrated by the whole of that context, the same partial autonomy must hold for discrete elements *within* the poem. To consider the example from Keats, it cannot be the *total* context of the poem that unlocks the penultimate line. For imagine that we were to change lines 11-12 of "Ode on a Grecian Urn." Instead of the current "Heard melodies are sweet, but those unheard / are sweeter...," we would change just one key word: "Heard melodies are *sour*, but those unheard / are sweeter..." This certainly changes the poem and our sense of the speaker, but has little effect on how we interpret "Beauty is truth, truth beauty" in distant line 49. And this change from "sweet" to "sour" is already a fairly significant one. Peppering the poem with trivial alternate spellings and punctuation, or replacing any number of less important words, would be even less likely to affect how the famous next-to-last line does its work. We might even imagine that the existing poem might turn out one day to have been merely one of Keats's discarded drafts, and that the author's true version is suddenly discovered hidden in some dusty library. We might further imagine that all the lines of this newly discovered version are different except for the last two, and yet these final two lines might still have the same effect as before. All of this is to say that, just as Brooks is right to split off the poem from its total socio-historical context and treat it as a partially autonomous unit, he is wrong to deny the same liberty to individual elements *within* the poem.

And he is even more wrong to combine his two mistakes as follows: "A scientific proposition can stand alone. If it is true, it is true. But the expression of an attitude, apart from the occasion which generates it and the situation which it encompasses, is meaningless."[105] Yet it is wrong to hold that poetry is any more or less holistic than science, and equally wrong to hold that holism is the right way to escape paraphrase. This is the same error as when Heidegger's tool-analysis is interpreted as telling us that the relationality of the tool-system is what frees us from the independence of present-at-hand entities in consciousness. For whether tools relate to human consciousness or to each other, in both cases they are reduced to their relation to something else. And whether the elements of a poem are paraphrased as what they literally mean to us, or are mutually defined by belonging to a shared context, each element is falsely held to be exhausted by its interrelations. In other words, Brooks falls into the Taxonomic Fallacy twice: the first time by distinguishing falsely between the rhetorical status of literature and other disciplines, and the second time by saying that holism is bad when it reduces the poem to its historical context, but good when it reduces it to an internal context of interrelated meanings.

Weird Content

The similarities and differences between object-oriented philosophy and the "formalism" of Brooks's New Criticism can be summed up as follows. We agree with the point that nothing can be paraphrased. More generally we should say that nothing in this world, whether it be a poem, hammer, atom, lizard, or flower, can be converted into anything else without distortion. To reduce any of these objects to the circumstances in which it was formed is to ignore the fact that nothing is merely the additive product of its surroundings– Shakespeare does things that his Elizabethan environment is incapable of doing, and the same holds for a puppy in connection with its parents, and nuts or berries with respect to the initial trees and bushes from which they emerge. We should also not ignore the fact that nothing is reducible to the effects it has on its surroundings once it is finally born: Shakespeare, puppies, and nuts and berries are objects rather than events. The literary revolutions, romps in the park, and feasts to which these entities give rise are undoubtedly events. Yet these events are composed of objects that might easily have participated instead in different events, or perhaps in none at all. Instead of being immediately consumed, berries' can be cartoned and shipped to Malaysia, or they can rot without being eaten at all, and all these diverse events are incidents in which *these particular berries* participate. They are not different berries each time they have a different environmental effect. And furthermore, the events in which berries participate can be objects in their own right, since a breakfast or a wedding is a discrete reality inexhaustible by any sum total of interpretations and irreducible to any effects it might have in the world.

This is precisely why we must disagree that "context" is what saves a poem or anything else from being paraphrased. To paraphrase something by redescribing it in literal terms, or any other kinds of terms, is to place that something in context–namely, its context *with respect to us*. I have said that Brooks's appeal to context is no different from the same appeal when made by most readers of Heidegger's *Being and Time*. Heidegger denies that the hammer is reducible to an appearance in consciousness, as Husserl implicitly claims when turning philosophy into a description of phenomena. And true enough, Heidegger seems to combat the phenomenality of beings precisely by saying that the hammer cannot be taken in isolation, but must be considered in its assignment to a total system of equipment. But as I have often argued in print,[106] the hammer that appears in consciousness ("the broken hammer") is no less immersed in a relational context than is the hammer in its inter-actions with boards, nails, and supply wagons. The hammer in consciousness is a false paraphrase of the real hammer, not because it is context-free, but because it is *utterly determined* by its context, reduced to a caricature that exists only in the context of my own experience of it. This is why the hammer can surprise us with sudden breakdowns: because the hammer is not the effects it has on us, but something more. Likewise, the hammer that strikes iron nails and makes dents in copper and aluminum sheets is *utterly determined* by its context as a vengeful force inflicting blows on these poor metals, and is thereby reduced to a caricature thanks to the minimal range of interactions they have with it. This is why the hammer can effectively surprise the metals (even if they are not conscious of it) by suddenly inflicting a greater or weaker force on them than was the case previously: because the hammer is not the effects it has on the metals, but something more. If we wish to avoid easy paraphrase and let things be what they really are, the only way to do this is to recognize that all objects are inherently context-free. Brooks grasps this point when he tries to protect poems from being dissolved into a series of social influences or literal meanings, but misses the very same point when he tries to turn the *interior* of a poem into a holistic wonderland of mutual influence between terms. In the same fashion, Heidegger is right to insist that tools have existence outside their contextual relation with our phenomenal consciousness, but wrong not to see the same withdrawal from context in the case of interrelations between *inanimate* beings. Indeed, I have frequently argued that this is Heidegger's chief philosophical mistake, the one that leaves so much work for his successors.

We cannot support formalism, which holds that the specific content of any experience is relatively unimportant. But neither can we support materialism, which grants privilege to the original soil from which anything grows, and thereby denies the autonomy or relative independence of that reality itself. Instead, we can only support *objects*. The reason objects are not formalizable is because they cannot be reduced to their conditions of knowability, whether mathematical or otherwise. But objects are also not "materializable," because the neighborhood conditions of their genesis are relevant only within strict limits. Nor are objects a hylemorphic combination of *both* form and matter, since objects are precisely what lies *between* these two extremes, engaging with them only occasionally and indirectly. Instead, objects are what the classical tradition called *substantial forms*, inhabiting a mezzanine level of the cosmos, and can be paraphrased neither as a meaning for some observer nor as the dangling product of some genetic-environmental backstory.

Formalism obviously belittles content, since it treats content as mere fodder for larger structural relations– for gestures of irony and paradox in which the exact content embedded in these structures is either reversible, or else is simply whatever random content happens to be on hand. For example, any social theory that views everything as a result of "the system," with no significant role to be played by individual leadership or the personal quirks of those who attain power, can be viewed as a formalist theory of society. Every brand of structuralism clearlys fall into this category. But materialism belittles content as well, since it treats all content as derivative of a prior or deeper history. One example of this would be those cultural historians who evacuate Heidegger's writings of autonomous philosophical content, reducing him either to the typical product of an anti-Weimar current of reactionary irrationalism, or to an outright Nazi propagandist.[107] But to dodge both formalism and materialism by focusing solely on the content of a poem or perception or experience *also* belittles content, since we have seen that it thereby becomes a literal meaning that can be repeated in a transmissible form that effectively *replaces* the poem, perception, or experience itself. A good example of this would be the *Shakespeare Made Easy* series mocked by Žižek. I am not in a position to pass judgment on the pedagogical effectiveness of this series. But it hardly seems risky to assert that the books contained in the series cannot *replace* the works of Shakespeare himself; nor is it likely that series editor John Durband would be happy if this were the result of his labors.

What we are here calling "content" can be identified with what we have also called the sensual realm. While real objects and qualities always withdraw from access, and are incommensurable with any form of presence, we are always pressed up against sensual objects and qualities just as the faces of children are pressed against the windows of toy stores and pet shops. This is the world of content, and content is a world of *sincerity*. If we happen to be jaded hipsters or dissolute libertines who sneer at the very word "sincerity," even in this case we are sincerely involved in disdain or corruption rather than in more wholesome pastimes such as enjoying fresh juice or assisting the poor. At every moment we are doing certain things rather than others: listening to a joke rather than a symphony, believing that the world had a beginning in time rather than not believing this, or reading H.P. Lovecraft rather than John Donne, Emily Brontë, or Plutarch. And it is this sincerity, rather than Brooks's "total context" of an experience, that makes content unparaphrasable. It does this by welding content together with the real. This can easily be seen if we add a single additional twist to what we have already learned about ontography and the strife it describes between objects and their qualities.

We have spoken of the withdrawal of real objects (RO) and real qualities (RQ), and the full accessibility of sensual objects (SO) and sensual qualities (SQ). This led us to reflect on the four differing permutations in which objects exist in tension with their qualities. The names given to these four were time (SO-SQ), space (RO-SQ), essence (RO-RQ), and eidos (SO-RQ). In Lovecraft we find many passages that capitalize on the first two tensions (in his "cubist" and "allusive" moments, respectively) but also a few examples in which the other two tensions are at stake. Normal sensual experience does not feel haunted by any sort of withdrawn real background; it is Heidegger who shows us that this occurs in relatively rare cases of broken equipment, profound boredom, or *Angst*. And furthermore, in normal sensual experience we also detect no explicit strife between an apple as a unit and its collection of sensual or real traits; it takes a Husserl to draw our attention to this point explicitly. But in the cases that were described as fusion or fission, the strife becomes impossible to ignore, since we are now forcibly confronted with a marriage between objects and qualities that do not seem to fit easily together. An Antarctic city is amassed from dozens of strange and incongruous qualities, or the outlines of octopus, dragon, and human are locked in orbit around some deeper "spirit of the thing" or "general outline of the whole." In both fusion and fission, the thing and its qualities do not fit neatly together as one. The qualities acquire a jarring independence that remains only partial, since we feel ourselves making the effort to compress octopus, dragon, and human together with some unseen general spirit. The object is there, and its qualities-become-objects are there, but we do not yet know what links them.

Along with the four *tensions* between objects and their qualities, ontography looks at two other types of link. One is the quality-quality partnership, in which numerous real and sensual qualities belong together in the same object; these links are called *radiations*, but they are not especially relevant for the moment. The other is the object-object link, or lack thereof, which are called *junctions*.[108] This type of link is far more pertinent to the present discussion. We know that the link between real objects (RO-RO) can never be direct, since real objects withdraw from one another; at best, their link can only be indirect or vicarious.[109] We also know that the link between real and sensual objects (RO-SO) *is* direct, since we experience it constantly. My life does not consist solely of black holes withdrawing from access and inaccessible to every view. Instead, I am directly concerned with tables, computers, subway trains, and farm implements, though in the form of sensual objects rather than withdrawn real ones. This contact between a real object (the observer) and sensual objects (the observed) is the only form of *direct* contact that exists in the cosmos. As a real object I do not even have direct contact with sensual *qualities*, since they are always mediated for me by the objects to which they belong: the green of a leaf is never the same as the green of cars or spray paint even if the wavelengths of light prove to be identical in all three cases. And finally, two sensual objects (SO-SO) have a link only in the sense that both co-exist in my experience. I never confront a monolithic world-block or holistic world-contexture; instead, my experience is broken into pieces from the start. In this respect, it is I (or any observer, whether human or inhuman) who am the mediator for any relation between sensual objects, which obviously can have no direct contact with one another, since they are merely images and make contact only in my experience.

Every link described by ontography, other than direct contact between real and sensual objects, needs a mediator. And though we need not account for all ten of these mediations in a book on

H.P Lovecraft, one point is especially striking: the observing entity (which is a real object, RO) is the mediator for all four of the links known as *tensions*, all of which we found embedded in the heart of Lovecraft's style. Or at least this is true of the *break-downs* in these tensions that we called "fission" and "fusion," since in such cases the qualities acquire partial independence from their master-objects and become objects in their own right. Here it is a question of two sensual objects, and we already know that two sensual objects can be mediated by the real object that experiences both of them simultaneously. Given that sensual reality only exists in the experience of an observer, it is clear that such an observer (which, to repeat, is a real object and need not be human) must always be on the scene in the case of the three tensions that we called time, space, and eidos. And while in principle that is not the case for the tension between real objects and their real qualities, it should be recalled that in Lovecraft's essence-like example of Azathoth surrounded by flopping hordes of mindless dancers, we are not dealing with this tension itself, but only with a literary *allusion* to it. And obviously, we the observers (real objects that we are) are on hand to experience this allusion.

The problem with paraphrase is that it claims to be able to convert a real thing into an accessible meaning without energy loss. A literary text is turned into a communicable lesson, while a genuine withdrawn hammer is turned into a hammer-for-us or hammer-for-wood without awareness of the distortions that thereby occur. In this way, things can be picked up and trans-ported for efficient use elsewhere, yet they can also be turned into caricatures and clichés. The ostensible stupidity of content came from the fact that content seemed to be a free-floating immediate fact, not grounded in anything real. Yet what we now find is that *there is* a strong dose of reality in all content, and it comes from the observing agent (always a real object, whether human or otherwise) which truly invests its energy at any given moment in being involved with certain things rather than others. Real objects exist in themselves, regardless of whether anything else registers their existence. But content is always content *for* some entity. Normally we do not notice this in our own lives, since we take ourselves for granted and assume that merely by opening our eyes we see everything exactly as it is. We are normally unaware of the contortions imposed on the things by our own limitations and even our own gifts. For this reason, we do not usually experience the tension between ourselves and our experiences, any more than we usually notice the tension between an apple and its real or sensual qualities. For this to happen, we need to endure a breakdown of the usual situation in which perceptions and meanings simply lie before us as obvious facts, or in which we stalk through life in quasi-robotic union with the empty words we utter and the learned habitual gestures that have come to seem like natural extensions of ourselves.

One way a breakdown can occur in this situation is through the allusive or cubistic techniques found in such lucid form in Lovecraft's style. In the case of both techniques, new objects are created in which two poles are locked in unresolved tension, and the strain and novelty of taking these objects seriously empha- sizes our separateness from them. It is not just that the hidden Cthulhu-object is in tension with the octopus-, dragon-, and human-qualities ascribed to it, but also that we ourselves invest energy in paying attention to this object. Our lack of ease in doing so produces fission between us as observers and the newly created object. This experience is most definitely the experience of a *content*; after all, experience is never directly of real objects or qualities, and hence there is nothing to experience besides content. Even in everyday life, an experience is always an object in its own right, since it can be analyzed endlessly without ever being exhausted, and without being replaced with any number of analyses whatsoever. Normally we do not realize this, any more than we are aware that the tension between an apple and its qualities is actually a tension. But when new and difficult experience is produced by breakdowns along the fault-lines of things, it becomes evident that our experience of the new object is unparaphrasable, and that it is thus is a reality in its own right. It may not be real in the sense that it lies in the depths at a distance from us, yet it remains real in the sense that we ourselves are sincerely invested in it.

But along with these results of fission, the same result can be achieved by what was termed fusion. This cannot happen directly through our own experience, since we always feel ourselves vaguely fused with our experiences in the first place. Instead, it requires the fusion of some *surrogate* observer with the content observed. Rather than simply encountering the Sphinx, the Trojan War, the clown costume, or the banana peel in their own right, we encounter some *other* observer encountering it. Our sincerity is outsourced to an external agent. We have already seen how it is possible to create a new object by fusing together sensual hammer-qualities with an absent real hammer, or sensual Cthulhu-qualities with a real "spirit of the thing" or "general outline of the whole." But now we see that it is equally possible to create a new object by fusing a sensual experience with a real object that is an observing agent other than ourselves. Here we are not fascinated directly by the events, but rather by the involvement of another observer of those events. And we have seen that this can take only two basic forms: comedy or tragedy. We cannot say that comedy must always have a happy ending, since there are many laughs to be had from books whose literal content is appalling by any standard: Voltaire's *Candide*, Céline's *Journey to the End of Night*, and especially Sade's *120 Days of Sodom* all come to mind. Nor can we define tragedy as always having a sad ending. Though examples are harder to come by here, there may be numerous books in which nothing measurably negative occurs, but which are marked nonetheless by a vaguely tragic air of melancholy: numerous illustrated children's books have this effect, at least on me. Instead, the only definition of these terms that makes sense is Aristotle's initially simple-sounding effort: "Comedy aims at representing men as worse, Tragedy as better than in actual life."[110] And we have already seen that "better" and "worse" cannot indicate superiority or inferiority in terms of rank, class, education, wealth, or beauty, but only superiority or inferiority in terms of what objects an observer is currently taking seriously. In both of these ways –the comic and the tragic– a new real object is produced that contains a full dose of reality despite being generated directly in our midst, by fusing together a real object (the observing agent) with sensual experience. We can take literature to be the systematic production of sincerities, even if they be the ill-reputed enchantments of Sadean debauchery. In this respect it differs from philosophy, which aims at the real outside experience rather than attempting to produce new realities on the interior of that experience.

This is also the way in which we avoid the Taxonomic Fallacy in our own position. For admittedly, the object-oriented standpoint initially runs the risk of holding that unparaphrasable reality lies only in the absent depths of the world while experienced content is always literal and transferrable. Yet what we now find is the explicit production of unparaphrasable real objects (Antarctic cities, Cthulhu idols) in the very midst of the sensual realm. Deprived of access to the real objects that lurk beneath perception and all other contexts, we produce our own real objects in the midst of them– as if countless black holes were suddenly and deliberately generated in banks, hospitals, and malls, or in Florence, Stratford, and Providence.

Footnotes

1. Michel Houellebecq, *H.P. Lovecraft: Against the World, Against Life*, trans. D. Khazeni. (San Francisco: Believer Books, 2005.) Page 41.

2. The other main authors working in the OOO current are Ian Bogost, Levi Bryant, and Timothy Morton. While all of them endorse the withdrawal of real objects from their transient sensual qualities, none are likely to endorse in full the fourfold structure I defend, in which real and sensual objects are paired with both real and sensual qualities. See Graham Harman, *The Quadruple Object*. (Winchester, UK: Zero Books, 2011.)

3. Graham Harman, "On the Horror of Phenomenology: Lovecraft and Husserl," *Collapse* IV (2008), pp. 333-364.

4. Edmund Wilson, *Literary Essays and Reviews of the 1930's and 1940's*. (New York: Library of America, 2007.) Page 700.

5. Wilson, *Literary Essays and Reviews of the 1930's and 1940's* pp. 701-2.

6. Wilson would be no happier about the inclusion of "pulp" detective writers Raymond Chandler and Dashiell Hammett, whose writing he also disdains. See Wilson's contemptuous 1945 essay on detective fiction, "Who Cares Who Killed Roger Ackroyd?" In Wilson, *Literary Essays and Reviews of the 1930's and 1940's*, pp. 677-683.

7. Clement Greenberg, *The Collected Essays and Criticism, Volume 4: Modernism with a Vengeance, 1957-1969*. (Chicago: Univ. of Chicago Press, 1993). Page 118.

8. Wilson, *Literary Essays and Reviews of the 1930's and 1940's*, p. 702.

9. Cleanth Brooks, *The Well Wrought Urn*. (New York: Harcourt, Brace, & World, 1947.) See especially Chapter 11, "The Heresy of Paraphrase."

10. Wilson, *Literary Essays and Reviews of the 1930's and 1940's*, p. 701.

11. Slavoj Žižek, *The Parallax View.* (Cambridge, MA: MIT Press, 2006). Page 11.

12. Žižek, *The Parallax View*, p. 12.

13. Slavoj Žižek/F.W.J. Schelling, *The Abyss of Freedom/Ages of the World*, with the Schelling portion trans. J. Norman. (Ann Arbor, MI: Univ. of Michigan Press, 1997.) Pages 71-72.

14. Žižek, in Žižek/Schelling, *The Abyss of Freedom/Ages of the World*, p. 72.

15. It is useful to compare ostensibly similar examples of dispute in books by Bruno Latour and Quentin Meillassoux. On pages 64-67 of Latour's *Science in Action* (Cambridge, MA: Harvard Univ. Press, 1987) we have a potentially endless argument between a scientist and a dissenter. On pages 55-59 of Meillassoux's *After Finitude*, trans. R. Brassier (London: Continuum, 2008) the argument is between a dogmatic theist and an equally dogmatic atheist. In Latour's pragmatic approach, the quarrel terminates only when someone gives up. In Meillasoux's speculative approach, it ends when the speculative philosopher comes along and provides the correct answer that transcends both of the dogmatic ones. My own approach lies midway between those of Latour and Meillassoux: one of the two proverbs may turn out to be more true than the other (unlike for Latour), but the matter is not to be decided by directly accessible literal proof (unlike for Meillassoux). There are many truths and there is one reality, but their relationship must remain oblique rather than direct. The whole of the present book is based on this notion of a purely oblique access to a genuine reality, which Lovecraft grasps better than any other writer of fiction.

16. Martin Heidegger, *Towards the Definition of Philosophy*, trans. T. Sadler. (London: Continuum, 2008.) Pages 56-58.

17. Martin Heidegger, *Being and Time*, trans. J. Macquarrie & E. Robinson. (New York: Harper, 2008.)

18. For the most elaborate version, see Graham Harman, *Tool-Being: Heidegger and the Metaphysics of Objects*. (Chicago: Open Court, 2002.)

19. Alfred North Whitehead, *Process and Reality*. (New York: The Free Press, 1978.) Page 11.

20. For a discussion of this point, see Graham Harman, *Guerrilla Metaphysics: Phenomenology and the Carpentry of Things*. (Chicago: Open Court, 2005.) Pages 110-116.

21. From "The Playboy Interview: Marshall McLuhan," *Playboy*, March 1969. Available online at http://www.mcluhanmedia.com/m_mcl_inter_pb_01.html

22. Published posthumously as Marshall & Eric McLuhan, *Laws of Media: The New Science*. (Toronto: Univ. of Toronto Press, 1992.)

23. Clement Greenberg, "Modern and Postmodern," in *Late Writings*, ed. R. Morgan. (Minneapolis: University of Minnesota Press, 2003.) Page 28.

24. Greenberg, "Avant-Garde and Kitsch." In *The Collected Essays and Criticism, Volume 1: Perceptions and Judgments, 1939-1944*. Pages 5-22.

25. Wilson, *Literary Essays and Reviews of the 1930's and 1940's*, pp. 701-2.

26. H.P. Lovecraft, *Collected Essays. Volume 2: Literary Criticism*, ed. S.T. Joshi. (New York: Hippocampus Press, 2004.) Pages 82-135.

27. Wilson, *Literary Essays and Reviews of the 1930's and 1940's*, p. 702.

28. Lovecraft, *Collected Essays. Volume 2: Literary Criticism*, pp. 178-182.

29. Lovecraft, *Collected Essays. Volume 2: Literary Criticism*, p. 178.

30. Lovecraft, *Collected Essays. Volume 2: Literary Criticism*, p. 179.

31. Lovecraft, *Collected Essays. Volume 2: Literary Criticism*, p. 180.

32. Lovecraft, *Collected Essays. Volume 2: Literary Criticism*, p. 181.

33. Lovecraft, *Collected Essays. Volume 2: Literary Criticism*, p. 178.

34. Lovecraft, *Collected Essays. Volume 2: Literary Criticism*, p. 178.

35. Lovecraft, *Collected Essays. Volume 2: Literary Criticism*, p. 179.

36. Lovecraft, *Collected Essays. Volume 2: Literary Criticism*, p. 179.

37. Michel Houellebecq, *H.P. Lovecraft: Against the World, Against Life*, p. 32.

38. The 2008 article is the aforementioned "On the Horror of Phenomenology: Lovecraft and Husserl," pp. 333-364. The theme of the gap between sensual objects and sensual qualities in Husserl is addressed in detail in Chapter 2 of my book *The Quadruple Object*.

39. For one of numerous examples of misreadings of what Brentano means by "intentionality," see Thomas Metzinger's *Being No One: The Self-Model Theory of Subjectivity* (Cambridge, MA: MIT Press), p. 16. See also my article "The Problem with Metzinger," *Cosmos and History*, vol. 7, no. 1 (2011), pp. 7-36.

40. G.W. Leibniz, "Monadology." In *Philosophical Essays*, trans. R. Ariew & D. Garber. (Indianapolis: Hackett, 1989.)

41. Xavier Zubíri, *On Essence*, trans. A.R. Caponigri (Washington: Catholic University Press, 1980.)

42. Harman, *The Quadruple Object*, Chapter 9.

43. Martin Heidegger, *Elucidations of Hölderlin's Poetry*, trans. K. Hoeller. (Amherst, NY: Humanity Books, 2000). Page 52.

44. Harman, "On the Horror of Phenomenology: Lovecraft and Husserl," p. 338.

45. Friedrich Nietzsche, *Ecce Homo & The Antichrist*, trans. T. Wayne. (New York: Algora Publishing, 2004.) Page 30.

46. Harman, *Guerrilla Metaphysics*. Pages 101-124.

47. Greenberg, *The Collected Essays and Criticism, Vol. 1: Perceptions and Judgments, 1939-1944*, p. 66.

48. Franz Brentano, *Psychology from an Empirical Standpoint*, trans. A.C. Rancurello et al. (London: Routledge, 1995.) A more literal translation of the title would be *Psychology from the Empirical Standpoint*.

49. The already classic discussion of how intentionality does not escape the human-world correlate is Meillassoux, *After Finitude*. See especially pp. 5 ff.

50. Henri Bergson, *Laughter: An Essay on the Meaning of the Comic*. (Rockville, MD: Wildside Press, 2008.)

51. Of the eight stories serving as the focus of Part Two below, only "The Dunwich Horror" and "The Dreams in the Witch House" use an omniscient third-person narrator. In the other six, the narrator is more or less personally involved in the events being described, as is generally the case in Poe as well. "The Colour Out of Space" presents the special situation of a first-person narrator relating events from decades ago, of which he himself was told by an aged eyewitness of the time.

52. Wilson, *Literary Essays and Reviews of the 1930's and 1940's*, pp. 701-2.

53. Aristotle, *Poetics*, trans. S.H. Butcher. (CreateSpace, 2011.) Page 14.

54. Plato, *Symposium*, trans. A. Nehamas. (Indianapolis: Hackett, 1987.) Page 77.

55. David Hume, *An Enquiry Concerning Human Understanding*. (Cambridge, UK: Cambridge Univ. Press, 2007.) Page 16.

56. Heidegger, *Towards the Definition of Philosophy*. See pages 57 ff.

57. Houellebecq, *H.P. Lovecraft: Against the World, Against Life*, p. 106.

58. Cited in Houellebecq, *H.P. Lovecraft: Against the World, Against Life*, pp. 106-7.

59. Houellebecq, *H.P. Lovecraft: Against the World, Against Life*, p. 107.

60. Edgar Allan Poe, "The Black Cat." In *Poetry and Tales*. (New York: Library of America, 1984.) Page 602.

61. Poe, "Arthur Gordon Pym," in *Poetry and Tales*, p. 1007.

62. Poe, "The Cask of Amontillado," in *Poetry and Tales*, p. 848.

63. Houellebecq, *H.P. Lovecraft: Against the World, Against Life*, p. 55.

64. See Greenberg, *The Collected Essays and Criticism, Vol. 3: Affirmations and Refusals, 1950-1956*, p. 239.

65. Giorgio Vasari, *The Lives of the Artists*, trans. J.C. Bondanella & P. Bondanella. (Oxford: Oxford Univ. Press, 1998.)

66. S.T. Joshi, *H.P. Lovecraft: A Life*. (West Warwick, RI: Necronomicon Press, 2006.) Pages 448-451.

67. Houellebecq, *H.P. Lovecraft: Against the World, Against Life*, p. 70.

68. Poe, *Poetry and Tales*, p. 600.

69. Aristotle, *Poetics*. In *The Basic Works of Aristotle*. (New York: Random House, 1941.) Page 1478.

70. Bill James, *The New Baseball James Historical Abstract*. (New York: The Free Press, 2001.) Page 433.

71. James, *The New Bill James Historical Abstract*, p. 434.

72. Poe, "The Fall of the House of Usher," in *Poetry and Tales*, p. 325.

73. L. Ron Hubbard, *Battlefield Earth*. (Los Angeles: Bridge Publications, 1999.) Page 1.

74. See especially Latour, *Science in Action*.

75. Latour, *Science in Action*, p. 43.

76. Latour, *Science in Action*, pp. 146-50.

77. Thomas Kuhn, *The Structure of Scientific Revolutions*. (Chicago: Univ. of Chicago Press, 1970.)

78. Bram Stoker, *Dracula*. (London: Penguin, 1994.)

79. S.T. Joshi, *H.P. Lovecraft: A Life*, p. 500.

80. Harman, "On the Horror of Phenomenology: Lovecraft and Husserl," p. 340.

81. "Infandous" means roughly "too odious even to be mentioned."

82. Sigmund Freud, *Beyond the Pleasure Principle*, trans. G. Richter. (Peterborough, Canada: Broadview Press, 2011.)

83. Žižek, *The Parallax View*, p. 12.

84. This fictional passage is not meant as a satire on beginner's guides to philosophers, of which I have proudly authored one myself (*Heidegger Explained: From Phenomenon to Thing*. Chicago: Open Court, 2007). Instead, it is a challenge to the assumption that beginner's guides ought to consist of lists of propositionally expressed doctrine that count as the essential content of a philosophy, while paying no attention to the half-expressed undertones and basic stylistic atmosphere of that philosophy.

85. Harman, *The Quadruple Object*, Chapter 9.

86. Harman, *Guerrilla Metaphysics*, pp. 116 ff.

87. See Harman, *The Quadruple Object*, pp. 99-102.

88. See Harman, *The Quadruple Object*, pp. 99-102.

89. See Harman, *The Quadruple Object*, pp. 99-102.

90. See Harman, *The Quadruple Object*, pp. 99-102.

91. For one illuminating account, see Steven Nadler, *Spinoza: A Life*. (Cambridge, UK: Cambridge Univ. Press, 2001.)

92. Brooks, *The Well Wrought Urn*, p. 196.

93. See for example page 200 of *The Well Wrought Urn*: "The relation between all the elements must be an organic one– there can be no question about that. There is, however, a very serious question as to whether the paraphrasable elements have primacy."

94. Brooks, *The Well Wrought Urn*, p. 196.

95. Brooks, *The Well Wrought Urn*, p. 198.

96. Brooks, *The Well Wrought Urn*, p. 205.

97. Brooks, *The Well Wrought Urn*, p. 203.

98. Brooks, *The Well Wrought Urn*, p. 209.

99. Brooks, *The Well Wrought Urn*, p. 210.

100. Brooks, *The Well Wrought Urn*, p. 211.

101. Brooks, *The Well Wrought Urn*, p. 212.

102. Brooks, *The Well Wrought Urn*, p. 202.

103. Harman, *The Quadruple Object*, p. 116.

104. Brooks, *The Well-Wrought Urn*, p. 205. Emphasis added.

105. Brooks, *The Well Wrought Urn*, p. 207.

106. See for example Harman, *Tool-Being: Heidegger and the Metaphysics of Objects*.

107. For an especially dismal example of the latter tendency, see Emmanuel Faye's own work of propaganda, *Heidegger: The Introduction of Nazism into Philosophy in Light of the Unpublished Seminars of 1933-1935*. Translated by Michael B. Smith. (New Haven, CT: Yale Univ. Press, 2011.)

108. See Harman, *The Quadruple Object*, pp. 129-135.

109. See Harman, "On Vicarious Causation," *Collapse* II (2007), pp. 171-205.

110. Aristotle, *Poetics*, page 14.

Contemporary culture has eliminated both the concept of the public and the figure of the intellectual. Former public spaces – both physical and cultural – are now either derelict or colonized by advertising. A cretinous anti-intellectualism presides, cheerled by expensively educated hacks in the pay of multinational corporations who reassure their bored readers that there is no need to rouse themselves from their interpassive stupor. The informal censorship internalized and propagated by the cultural workers of late capitalism generates a banal conformity that the propaganda chiefs of Stalinism could only ever have dreamt of imposing. Zer0 Books knows that another kind of discourse – intellectual without being academic, popular without being populist – is not only possible: it is already flourishing, in the regions beyond the striplit malls of so-called mass media and the neurotically bureaucratic halls of the academy. Zer0 is committed to the idea of publishing as a making public of the intellectual. It is convinced that in the unthinking, blandly consensual culture in which we live, critical and engaged theoretical reflection is more important than ever before.